Prompting Go for Systems Development

Build High-Performance APIs, Microservices, Concurrent Systems, and Cloud Backends Faster with AI-Powered Prompt Engineering

Drishti Jain

www.orangeava.com

First Published: April 2026

Published By: Orange Education Pvt Ltd, AVA®

Address: 9, Daryaganj, Delhi, 110002, India

275 New North Road Islington Suite 1314 London,

N1 7AA, United Kingdom

ISBN (PBK): 978-93-49887-27-5

ISBN (E-BOOK): 978-93-49887-21-3

Scan the QR code to explore our entire catalogue

www.orangeava.com

Get a Free eBook

We hope you're enjoying your recent book purchase! Your feedback is incredibly valuable to us and helps other readers discover books that truly make a difference.

If you found this book useful or enjoyable, we'd greatly appreciate it if you could leave a short review with a 5-star rating on Amazon. Your review supports our work and allows us to reach more learners worldwide.

As a thank-you, we're happy to offer you a **free digital copy of this book** plus a **30% discount code** for your next purchase on our official websites:

www.orangeava.com

www.orangeava.in (For the Indian Subcontinent).

☑ **How it works:**

Leave your review on Amazon, take a screenshot of the confirmation or use the following link to submit the claim and email it to **info@orangeava.com.** Once received the required detail, we will send your rewards within 24 hours, **along with one month free subcription to the book on AVA SkillShelf!**

Claim Form
https://rebrand.ly/4d2477

Thank you for your support–it truly means a lot to us.

Enjoy 1 Month of Free Access to AVA SkillShelf!

The future belongs to lifelong learners. With AVA SkillShelf, you go beyond reading books and start building real, job-ready skills curated by industry experts.

Your membership unlocks **200+ learning products** covering AI, Cloud, Python, Cybersecurity, Data Science, DevOps, and more—all in one platform. Our bestselling technical books are transformed into structured courses designed for practical, real-world application.

Learn directly from experienced professionals and published authors, with no filler—just actionable insights. Earn **verified digital certifications** to strengthen your CV, LinkedIn profile, and professional credibility.

Learn anytime, anywhere, on any device, at your own pace. Ideal for students, professionals, career switchers, and tech leaders.

For full access to all current and future courses, choose our **Annual Membership**. Simply scan the QR to get started!

For 1 month Free access, simply refer to the steps on the previous page titled: Get a Free ebook!

https://www.avaskillshelf.com/

Downloading the code bundles and colored images

Please follow the links or scan the QR codes to download the ***Code Bundles and Images*** of the book:

https://github.com/ava-orange-education/Prompting-Go-for-Systems-Development

The code bundles and images of the book are also hosted on ***https://rebrand.ly/927e69***

In case there's an update to the code, it will be updated on the existing GitHub repository.

Errata

We take immense pride in our work at **Orange Education Pvt Ltd,** and follow the best practices to ensure the accuracy of our content to provide an indulging reading experience to our subscribers. Our readers are our mirrors, and we use their inputs to reflect and improve upon human errors, if any, that may have occurred during the publishing processes involved. To let us maintain the quality and help us reach out to any readers who might be having difficulties due to any unforeseen errors, please write to us at:

errata@orangeava.com

Your support, suggestions, and feedback are highly appreciated.

Dedicated To

My Beloved Mom:

Barkha Jain,

My Strength and Support System.

About the Author

Drishti Jain is a technology professional, researcher, and global tech speaker with a strong focus on artificial intelligence and machine learning. She holds a Master of Science in Computer Science from the Georgia Institute of Technology, USA, specializing in Machine Learning, and a Bachelor of Engineering in Computers from Cummins College of Engineering, Pune, India.

Drishti has contributed to building AI systems in the fields of education and healthcare in the United States. She has worked with leading product-based companies and FinTech organizations, gaining experience in developing scalable technology solutions. Alongside her professional work, she is committed to expanding access to knowledge and opportunities through her initiative *SkillUp with Drishti* and her non-profit organization, the *Samyak Drishti Foundation*, which focus on empowering individuals through technology education and mentorship.

An internationally recognized technology speaker, Drishti has delivered talks at more than 100 conferences across the globe, including events in the United States (US), the United Kingdom, Europe, Singapore, Colombia, Thailand, Brazil, and India. She is active in the Go and Artificial Intelligence communities, and has been invited to speak at renowned conferences such as *GopherCon EU*, *AI in Production* USA, *PyCon EU*, *PyCon Asia*, and *PyCascades* USA. She is also a published technical book author, an invited panellist at international technology forums, and a judge at hackathons, startup competitions, and technical contests in the US.

Beyond her technical achievements, Drishti is passionate about environmental conservation. She has been honored three times by the Government of Maharashtra, India, with the title of "Eco-Warrior", and leads a volunteer network of over 400 individuals across India.

About the Technical Reviewer

Noopur Tanwar is a Senior Backend Developer specializing in high-scale distributed systems and cloud-native infrastructure. With a career spanning the automobile, telecommunications, retail, and transport sectors, she brings a robust, multi-industry perspective to technical architecture. Currently, Noopur focuses on building scalable APIs and backend services for AI-driven hosting platforms, ensuring high availability and performance.

An engineer proficient in Golang, Noopur is a strong advocate of idiomatic coding and Microservices. She expertly integrates AI-driven workflows into her development lifecycle to enhance productivity and code quality. Her work is dedicated to making complex codebases more readable, maintainable, and resilient, bridging the gap between sophisticated engineering and clear technical documentation.

Acknowledgments

Writing this book has been an incredibly rewarding experience. Exploring how Go's performance and simplicity can be combined with modern AI techniques opened the door to many practical ideas for building intelligent and scalable systems. Combining Go's efficiency with the rapidly evolving AI ecosystem made this project both technically engaging and deeply rewarding.

I would like to acknowledge the Go community and the team behind the Go programming language for creating a powerful and elegant tool for building scalable systems. I am also grateful to the broader open-source and AI communities whose research, tools, and shared knowledge continue to push the boundaries of what developers can build today. The official Go documentation and open-source resources were invaluable references throughout the process of writing this book.

To all those at the publication house, Orange Education Pvt. Ltd. who contributed in various capacities, their collective efforts greatly enriched this endeavor. I appreciate the collaborative spirit that has fueled the creation of the book.

On a personal note, I would like to extend my deepest appreciation to my mother, Barkha Jain, whose encouragement and constant support have always been a source of motivation as I work toward my goals. Her belief in my work has made this journey possible.

Finally, to the readers—thank you for choosing this book. I hope it helps you explore the intersection of Go and AI, and inspires you to build intelligent, scalable systems of your own.

Preface

This book covers many important aspects of the Go programming language and its role in building modern, scalable software systems. It introduces readers to the significance of Go in today's technology landscape, especially in areas such as cloud computing, distributed systems, microservices, and high-performance backend development. The book explains how Go helps developers build reliable and efficient applications with simplicity and strong concurrency support. It also emphasizes how Go is widely used in real-world industry environments where performance, maintainability, and scalability are critical.

This book also highlights how Go can be used for building practical applications such as web servers, APIs, data processing systems, and concurrent pipelines. The goal is to provide readers with a strong understanding of Go programming concepts, while demonstrating how those concepts are applied in real-time software systems. Along the way, the book refreshes fundamental programming concepts such as functions, packages, modular design, and error handling, while introducing Go-specific ideas like goroutines, channels, and context management.

The book takes a practical and hands-on approach to learning Go. It focuses not only on explaining concepts but also on demonstrating them through realistic examples that resemble real industry use cases. Readers will learn how Go can be used to design efficient backend systems, build REST APIs, manage databases, and deploy scalable microservices. The book also introduces the use of modern development practices such as containerization, CI/CD pipelines, and monitoring. In addition, it highlights how AI tools can assist developers in writing, debugging, and optimizing Go applications.

This book is divided into ten chapters. Each chapter focuses on a specific area of Go development, gradually building from fundamental programming concepts to advanced topics such as concurrency pipelines and production deployment. The chapters also explore how modern AI-assisted development tools can improve productivity and code quality when working with Go.

Chapter 1: This introduces the Go programming language. It explains what Go is, why it was created, and why it has become popular for building scalable systems. This chapter covers the key features of Go, including its simplicity, compiled nature, strong standard library, and support for concurrent programming. It also explains how Go differs from other programming languages, and how to install and configure the Go development environment.

Chapter 2: This focuses on the fundamental building blocks of Go programs. It explains the structure of a Go program, variables, data types, control structures, and basic syntax. Readers learn how Go programs are organized, and how to write simple but effective programs using Go's straightforward language constructs.

Chapter 3: This introduces functions, packages, and modular code organization. The chapter explains how functions are defined and used, including concepts such as recursion, varied functions, and anonymous functions. It also discusses how Go uses packages to organize codes, and promote modular software design. Readers will understand how to structure applications using custom packages, and maintain clean code architecture.

Chapter 4: It focuses on error handling and debugging in Go. Unlike many programming languages that use exceptions, Go follows a unique approach to error handling using the error interface. This chapter explains idiomatic error handling techniques, panic and recovery mechanisms, and how to debug applications using Go's standard libraries and logging tools.

Chapter 5: It introduces concurrency in Go, which is one of the language's most powerful features. This chapter explains how goroutines and channels enable efficient concurrent execution. It also covers synchronization patterns, race conditions, and strategies for building reliable concurrent systems. Readers will learn how to design scalable programs that handle multiple tasks efficiently.

Chapter 6: It discusses how Go applications interact with databases and manage application context. It also explains how to connect to relational databases such as PostgreSQL and MySQL using the database/sql package and ORM libraries like GORM. The chapter also introduces context management for controlling timeouts, request cancellation, and long-running operations.

Chapter 7: This focuses on building web servers and REST APIs using Go. Readers learn how to use the net/http package to create web servers, route requests, and handle JSON data. The chapter also introduces middleware patterns and techniques for designing reliable API services.

Chapter 8: It explains concurrent data processing pipelines in Go. It covers patterns such as fan-out and fan-in, worker pools, and channel-based communication strategies. These concepts help developers design efficient systems that process large volumes of data concurrently.

Chapter 9: This explores how AI tools can assist developers when working with Go. It explains how modern AI assistants can help generate codes, debug programs, and optimize performance. The chapter also discusses the importance of writing effective prompts and the limitations as well as ethical considerations of AI-generated codes.

Chapter 10: This focuses on deploying production-grade Go microservices. It explains how Go applications can be containerized using Docker, and deployed using CI/CD pipelines. The chapter also covers monitoring, logging, performance optimization, and future trends in Go development and AI-assisted software engineering.

Overall, this book aims to provide readers with a practical understanding of Go programming and its role in building modern software systems. Thus, by the end of the book, readers will be well-equipped with the knowledge and skills required to develop efficient, scalable, and production-ready Go applications.

DID YOU KNOW

Did you know that Orange Education Pvt Ltd offers eBook versions of every book published, with PDF and ePub files available? You can upgrade to the eBook version at **www.orangeava.com** and as a print book customer, you are entitled to a discount on the eBook copy. Get in touch with us at: **info@orangeava.com** for more details.

At **www.orangeava.com**, you can also read a collection of free technical articles, sign up for a range of free newsletters, and receive exclusive discounts and offers on Print Books and eBooks.

PIRACY

If you come across any illegal copies of our works in any form on the internet, we would be grateful if you would provide us with the location address or website name. Please contact us at **info@orangeava.com** with a link to the material.

ARE YOU INTERESTED IN AUTHORING WITH US?

If there is a topic that you have expertise in, and you are interested in either writing or contributing to a book, please write to us at **business@orangeava.com**. We are on a journey to help developers and tech professionals to gain insights on the present technological advancements and innovations happening across the globe and build a community that believes Knowledge is best acquired by sharing and learning with others. Please reach out to us to learn what our audience demands and how you can be part of this educational reform. We also welcome ideas from tech experts and help them build learning and development content for their domains.

REVIEWS

Please leave a review. Once you have read and used this book, why not leave a review on the site that you purchased it from? Potential readers can then see and use your unbiased opinion to make purchase decisions. We at Orange Education would love to know what you think about our products, and our authors can learn from your feedback. Thank you!

For more information about Orange Education, please visit **www.orangeava.com**.

Table of Contents

CHAPTER 1
Introduction to Go and AI-Assisted Development

Introduction

This chapter provides an overview of Go (Golang) and its significance in modern software development. It discusses the core features and advantages of using Go for building backend systems, cloud-native services, and high-performance applications. The chapter explains the key strengths of Go–concurrency, memory efficiency, and scalability–and how these features make it ideal for developing distributed and resource-optimized solutions. It also covers the setup of the Go development environment and introduces AI-assisted coding tools such as ChatGPT, GitHub Copilot, and AWS CodeWhisperer, along with their installation and configuration for streamlined development workflows.

Structure

In this chapter, we will cover the following topics:

- Overview of the Go Programming Language and Its Applications
- Features of Go
    - Concurrency
    - Memory Management
    - Scalability
- Setting up Go Development Environment
- Introduction to AI-Assisted Coding Tools
    - ChatGPT

    - GitHub Copilot
    - CodeWhisperer (Now Amazon Q Developer)
- Installing and Configuring AI Coding Assistants
- Benefits of AI-Assisted Go Development

Overview of the Go Programming Language and Its Applications

Every few years, a new programming language emerges that reshapes how software is built. Golang, or Go, is one of these languages. Developed at Google by Robert Griesemer, Rob Pike, and Ken Thompson in 2007, Go was designed to solve the challenges of modern software engineering–building scalable, maintainable, and high-performance systems–without the complexity found in traditional languages. Go combines the speed and efficiency of low-level languages such asC with the simplicity and readability of higher-level scripting languages, providing developers with a language that is both powerful and approachable.

Go's design emphasizes simplicity, clarity, and reliability. Its static typing and memory safety features reduce common programming errors, while its built-in garbage collector ensures efficient memory management. One of the standout features of Go is its concurrency model, which allows developers to run multiple tasks simultaneously using goroutines and communicate between them via channels. This makes Go particularly suitable for building cloud-native applications, microservices, networked systems, and real-time backend services.

The language also includes a rich standard library, offering packages for file I/O, networking, cryptography, and formatting, allowing developers to build robust applications without relying heavily on third-party tools. Furthermore, the toolingin Go–such as the built-in compiler, formatter, linter, and testing framework–supports a smooth developer workflow, enabling fast compilation, efficient debugging, and maintainable codebases. The widespread adoption of Go in industry-leading projects such as Docker, Kubernetes, Terraform, and Prometheus demonstrates its practicality and reliability in production environments. The official documentation is found at **`https://go.dev`**.

Software development practices are evolving alongside programming languages, with Artificial Intelligence (AI) now playing an increasingly significant role. AI-assisted tools, including ChatGPT, GitHub Copilot, and CodeWhisperer (now part of Amazon Q Developer), complement human developers by suggesting code, explaining errors, and even assisting in designing modules. These tools accelerate routine tasks and improve productivity, allowing developers to focus on problem-solving, architecture, and innovation while maintaining high-quality Go code.

Features of Go

Go is intended to streamline the development of software that is both high-performance and dependable. It is an ideal language for developing modern backend systems and distributed systems due to its emphasis on maintainability, simplicity, and speed. Concurrency, memory management, and scalability are three of the numerous capabilities that differentiate it in terms of their influence on the development of scalable and efficient applications.

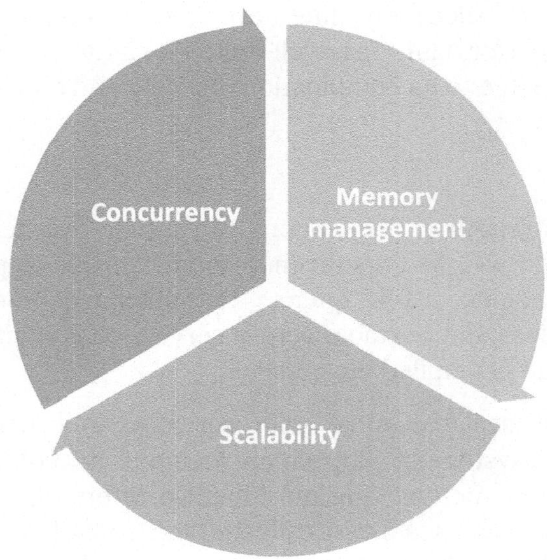

Figure 1.1: *Features of Go*

Concurrency

Built-in concurrency support is one of the most distinctive characteristics of Go. Concurrency lets more than one activity operate at the same time. This is important for apps that handle a lot of network requests, perform background processing, or manage operations in real time. Go introduces goroutines, which are lightweight threads that are managed by the Go runtime. These threads can be created with minimal latency using the go keyword. Channels facilitate communication and synchronization among goroutines, offering a secure and organized method of data sharing without the need for explicit locking mechanisms.

Go's concurrency approach allows developers to write highly concurrent applications efficiently while keeping the code clean and maintainable. The simplicity of goroutines and channels removes much of the complexity associated with traditional multithreading, making concurrent programming accessible even to developers new to parallelism.

Memory Management

Go provides automatic memory management through a built-in Garbage Collector (GC). The GC automatically allocates and frees memory, reducing the risk of memory leaks and simplifying the development process. Static typing and a transparent ownership model in Go facilitate the ability of developers to rationalize memory usage, while the garbage collector guarantees minimal latency in high-load scenarios.

Furthermore, Go promotes the efficient utilization of memory by means of value semantics, pointers, and slices, enabling developers to create applications that are both predictable and performant. Go is well-suited for large-scale systems that require resource optimization due to its combination of safety and efficiency.

Scalability

Scalability is a core strength of Go. Its minimal runtime overhead, efficient memory management, and lightweight concurrency model enable applications to expand seamlessly from managing a few queries to millions of concurrent operations. Deployment is effortless and portable across servers or containers due to the self-contained nature of Go's compiled binaries.

The development of scalable APIs, microservices, and networked systems is facilitated by the ecosystem of Go, which includes its comprehensive standard library and frameworks such as Gin and Fiber.Go offers developers the ability to create applications that can scale vertically and horizontally in a manner optimized for modern cloud-native architectures, in conjunction with goroutines and channels.

Setting up Go Development Environment

The Go development environment can be setup based on the Operating System (OS) you are using. Follow the steps based on your operating system.

Linux

For Linux machines, installing Go is as follows:

1. Download the latest Go package file from:

   https://go.dev/doc/install

2. Delete the **`/usr/local/go`** directory to remove any previous Go installations:

```
        rm -rf /usr/local/go && tar -C /usr/local -xzf go1.25.4.
linux-amd64.tar.gz.
```

3. Extract the archive that was downloaded to create a fresh Go tree in **`/usr/local/go`**.
4. Put the package path in your **`PATH`** environment variable. You can add the following to your **`$HOME/.profile`** or the **`/etc/profile`** file:

   ```
   export PATH=$PATH:/usr/local/go/bin.
   ```
5. Verify the installation by running the following command in the command prompt:

   ```
   go version
   ```

   This should return the installed version of Go.

Mac

The following are the steps for installation on macOS machines:

1. Download the latest Go package file from:

   https://go.dev/doc/install.
2. Open the package file and follow the installation instructions.
3. Put the package path in your **`PATH`** environment variable. (The package is installed in **`/usr/local/go`**, and **`/usr/local/go/bin`** should be in the **`PATH`** variable.)
4. Verify the installation by running the following command in the terminal:

   ```
   go version
   ```

   This should return the installed version of Go.

Windows

The following are the steps for installation on Windows machines:

1. Download the latest Go package MSI file from:

   https://go.dev/doc/install
2. Open the MSI file and follow the installation instructions.
3. Verify the installation by running the following command in Command Prompt:

   ```
   go version
   ```

   This should return the installed version of Go.

Introduction to AI-Assisted Coding Tools

AI-powered coding tools have changed the way developers write, evaluate, and improve code in the last several years. To detect code patterns, infer intent, and make intelligent recommendations, these technologies employ Large Language Models (LLMs) and machine learning algorithms trained on massive volumes of programming data. Rather than depending exclusively on static documentation, developers now make use of AI systems that produce contextually appropriate code, explain errors, and offer prompt solutions to intricate issues.

AI-driven development is not intended to supplant programmers—it rather aims to enhance their capabilities. By automating repetitive tasks and accelerating the coding process, these tools allow developers to focus on architecture, design, and problem-solving. They serve as real-time collaborators, improving productivity, reducing cognitive load, and supporting continuous learning within the development workflow.

In the context of Go development, AI-assisted tools such as ChatGPT, GitHub Copilot, and AWS CodeWhisperer have become valuable companions. Each brings a unique approach—ChatGPT offers conversational guidance, Copilot provides in-editor code completions, and CodeWhisperer integrates with cloud-native ecosystems.

ChatGPT

ChatGPT, developed by OpenAI, is a conversational AI model that helps developers understand, generate, and debug code through natural language interaction. Developers can describe a problem, ask conceptual questions, or request code snippets in plain English, and ChatGPT can respond with detailed explanations and functional Go examples.

ChatGPT can be used to:

- Generate Go functions, packages, and test cases.
- Explain errors or unexpected behavior.
- Refactor the existing Go code for clarity and performance.
- Offer guidance on concurrency and memory optimization patterns.

By bridging the gap between language and code, ChatGPT provides developers with an interactive learning and development partner capable of accelerating both understanding and implementation.

GitHub Copilot

GitHub Copilot, powered by OpenAI's Codex model, functions as an **AI pair**

programmer within popular IDEs such as Visual Studio Code and GoLand. As the developer types, Copilot analyzes the context and offers intelligent code suggestions ranging from line completions to entire functions.

In Go projects, Copilot assists by:

- Auto-completing repetitive structures such as loops, structs, and function templates.
- Suggesting idiomatic Go syntax and best practices.
- Generating tests and documentation inline.
- Helping developers learn through example-driven coding.

The seamless integration of Copilot makes it especially valuable for maintaining speed and consistency in large Go codebases, thus allowing developers to focus on solving problems instead of writing boilerplate code. Copilot also offers flexibility in selecting the model from which to receive responses. This gives the user control over the model being used in AI-assisted development.

CodeWhisperer (New Amazon Q Developer)

AWS CodeWhisperer is an AI-powered coding assistant by Amazon, designed to help developers build applications faster and more securely within the AWS ecosystem. Initially launched as a standalone tool, CodeWhisperer has now been integrated into **Amazon Q Developer**, which unifies AI-assisted development and AWS productivity features. It provides context-aware code suggestions, detects potential security vulnerabilities, and offers code snippets optimized for AWS services such as Lambda, S3, and DynamoDB. This integration into Amazon Q Developer enhances the experience by combining coding assistance, cloud automation, and natural language querying, allowing developers to seamlessly transition between coding, configuring, and deploying applications—all within one environment.

CodeWhisperer supports developers by:

- Suggesting Go implementations for AWS SDK usage.
- Generating infrastructure code snippets for AWS services such asS3, Lambda, and DynamoDB.
- Identifying potential security vulnerabilities or inefficiencies.
- Offering optimized code tailored for scalability and cloud readiness.

By combining Go's lightweight concurrency model with the intelligent insights of CodeWhisperer, developers can build secure, performant, and resource-efficient applications aligned with AWS best practices.

Installing and Configuring AI Coding Assistants

AI-assisted coding tools are designed to integrate smoothly with widely used Integrated Development Environments (IDEs) such as Visual Studio Code, JetBrains IDEs, and cloud-based editors such as AWS Cloud9. A proper setup enables these tools to deliver accurate and context-aware code suggestions that align with the development environment.

Installation involves adding the appropriate plugin or extension to the IDE. GitHub Copilot can be installed directly from the Visual Studio Code marketplace, while Amazon Q Developer, which now includes all CodeWhisperer features, is distributed through the AWS Toolkit extension. Amazon Q Developer can also be used in IDEs as an extension for JetBrains, VS Code, and the command line. Following installation, authentication through platforms such as GitHub, AWS, or OpenAI is required to enable the AI models to function within the environment.

The following figure shows the GitHub Copilot extension, which can be searched in the extensions marketplace in VS Code. Install the first one distributed by the official GitHub account.

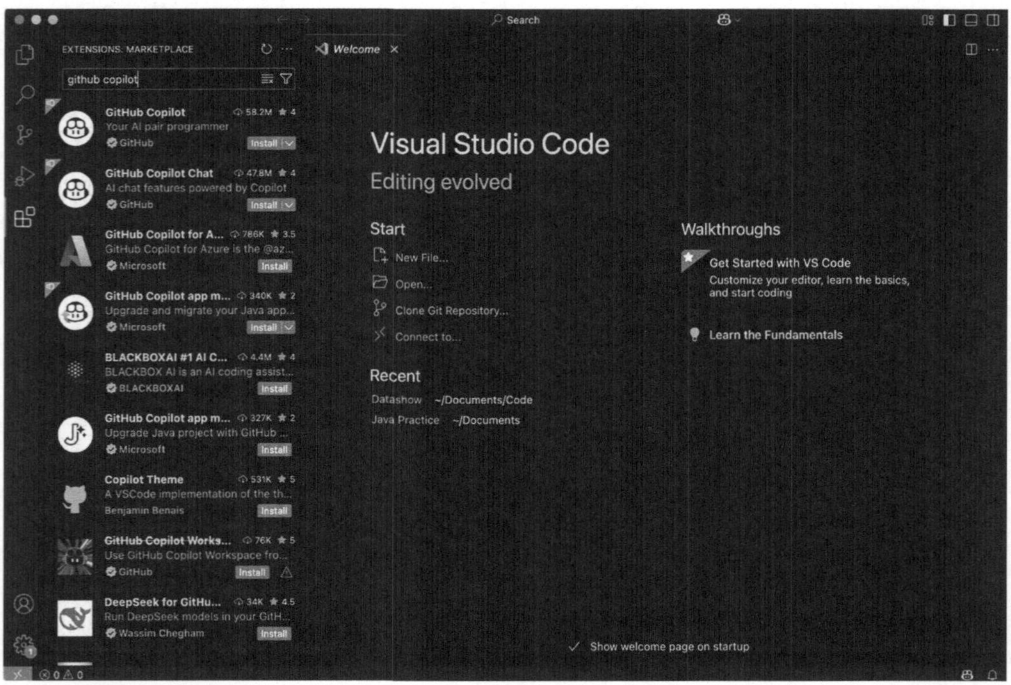

Figure 1.2: *GitHub Copilot Extension in VS Code*

Similarly, Amazon Q can be installed as an extension in the VS Code IDE.

For Amazon Q Developer, there is a command-line installation via Homebrew, which is useful for developers accustomed to developing on the command line rather than IDEs. Run the following command to install Amazon Q Developer CLI with Homebrew:

```
brew install --cask amazon-q
```

Configuration settings allow for fine-tuning the behavior of these tools. Most AI assistant tools give the user control to modify the suggestion frequency, specify programming language preferences, and adjust privacy or data usage parameters. Enterprise environments may enable team or organization-level configurations for shared policies, version control integration, and compliance management.

In the case of ChatGPT, configuration typically involves API integration using credentials from OpenAI or the setup through third-party IDE extensions that connect to the ChatGPT API. Model parameters such as temperature, context length, and response format can be adjusted (via the API) to suit specific development tasks such as documentation generation, debugging, or automated testing.

Overall, installing and configuring AI coding assistants involves establishing a connection between the development environment and the AI service, performing authentication, and refining settings for optimal performance. Once configured, these assistants operate seamlessly in the background, offering intelligent guidance that improves productivity and code quality.

Benefits of AI-Assisted Go Development

Developing a Go application by integrating AI tools into the workflow of a developer provides a number of benefits. The following are the key benefits:

- **Enhanced Productivity**

  AI-assisted technologies markedly enhance productivity by automating monotonous and labor-intensive coding tasks. In Go development, this includes:

  - Generating boilerplate code for functions
  - `struct` definitions
  - API endpoints
  - Test files and
  - Scaffolding project structures and modules

  Developers can spend more time creating scalable systems, streamlining concurrent operations, and addressing complex challenges by automating these repetitive tasks.

  Beyond simple automation, AI tools can anticipate the intent of the developer based on the existing project context, suggesting entire code blocks or implementations that follow idiomatic Go practices.

For example, when building a concurrent processing pipeline, AI assistants can propose efficient goroutine and *channel setups*, eliminating much of the trial-and-error typically involved. This reduces development friction and ensures consistency across packages and modules. It accelerates project timelines, especially in large-scale backend systems and cloud-native applications.

- **Improved Code Quality and Readability**

  AI coding assistants enhance code quality by offering immediate assistance on grammar, style, and best practices for Go. They suggest idiomatic improvements, enforce linting rules, and highlight potential anti-patterns. These improvements act as enhancements, ensuring that code is not only functional but also maintainable. Refactoring suggestions help developers restructure existing code for clarity and efficiency, fostering clean and modular design throughout the project.

  Additionally, AI tools assist in writing documentation and comments that accurately describe the purpose and functionality of code segments. This is particularly valuable for team collaboration, where readable, well-structured code improves comprehension across developers and accelerates onboarding. Over time, these practices cultivate a culture of clean coding and adherence to Go's philosophy of simplicity and clarity. This reduces technical debt and makes long-term maintenance more efficient.

- **Faster Debugging and Error Resolution**

  Debugging Go applications can be challenging, especially when dealing with concurrency issues, memory management, or complex data structures. AI-assisted tools can analyze the code context and identify patterns of common runtime errors such as nil pointer dereferences, unhandled panics, goroutine leaks, or race conditions. They provide targeted recommendations that guide developers toward correct implementations, often explaining both the cause and the solution in plain language.

  Integration with debugging environments allows AI tools to highlight suspicious code lines, suggest breakpoints, and even propose test cases that reproduce errors. This predictive capability reduces the time spent on trial-and-error debugging and minimizes the likelihood of subtle bugs reaching production. By complementing human reasoning with AI insights, developers can maintain robust, error-resistant Go applications, especially in high-performance, concurrent, or cloud-native systems.

- **Accelerated Learning for Developers**

  As developers write code, AI tools give them immediate, context-based advice, like having a mentor available at any time. For learners or early-career engineers, the ability to ask natural language questions, such as:

`"Why is my goroutine not synchronizing?"`

Or,

`"How do I optimize this channel pattern?"`

This turns the coding environment into an interactive classroom. Instead of searching through forums or documentation, developers receive direct, relevant explanations and examples that apply to their current project.

In addition to providing answers, these assistants also promote best practices. For example, when a developer writes inefficient code for concurrent data access, AI tools can highlight potential race conditions and explain the correct use of **`sync.Mutex`** or **`sync.WaitGroup`**. Over time, this creates a feedback loop where the developer learns *not just what to fix, but why* – leading to stronger mental models of Go's design principles.

AI-assisted environments adapt to the developer's skill level. Novices may obtain more comprehensive step-by-step guidance, whereas seasoned developers can gain from concise suggestions and performance evaluations. This personalization transforms the development process into a guided learning experience, where each coding session contributes to skill improvement.

AI also supports learning beyond syntax and logic—it can generate small practice problems, suggest Go idioms to refactor existing code, and even provide explanations for standard library functions such as:

- **`fmt`**,
- **`time`**, and
- **`os`**.

The result is a continuous learning ecosystem, where knowledge acquisition happens naturally as developers build, debug, and optimize their applications.

- **Smarter Concurrency and Performance Optimization**

  The powerful concurrency model of Go is one of its distinguishing features, and AI-assisted tools help developers leverage it effectively. By analyzing goroutines, channels, and memory usage patterns, AI can suggest optimizations that reduce resource contention, prevent deadlocks, and improve execution speed.

  AI tools can also propose changes to data structures or algorithm design to achieve better scalability. For example, when processing large datasets concurrently, AI might suggest:

  - Buffered channels,

- Worker pools, and
- Optimized scheduling strategies.

These insights allow developers to write high-performance Go applications without spending excessive time on manual profiling and benchmarking. By combining Go's lightweight concurrency with AI-guided recommendations, developers can achieve both correctness and efficiency in production-grade systems.

- **Streamlined Collaboration and Code Reviews**

  The integration of AI in development further optimizes team workflows by facilitating collaboration and automating code review procedures. Tools such as GitHub Copilot Chat and Amazon Q Developer can analyze pull requests, summarize changes, and highlight potential issues before human reviewers examine the code.

  This minimizes the duration developers allocate to mechanical evaluations, allowing teams to concentrate on architecture, logic, and product design. AI can also enforce coding standards, suggest consistent styling, and detect potential security or concurrency issues across a shared codebase. In distributed or remote teams, AI-assisted code review becomes a force multiplier, improving overall project quality and ensuring that Go applications adhere to organizational best practices.

- **Integration across the Development Lifecycle**

  AI-assisted tools support developers throughout the Go application lifecycle–from initial design and prototyping to deployment and monitoring.

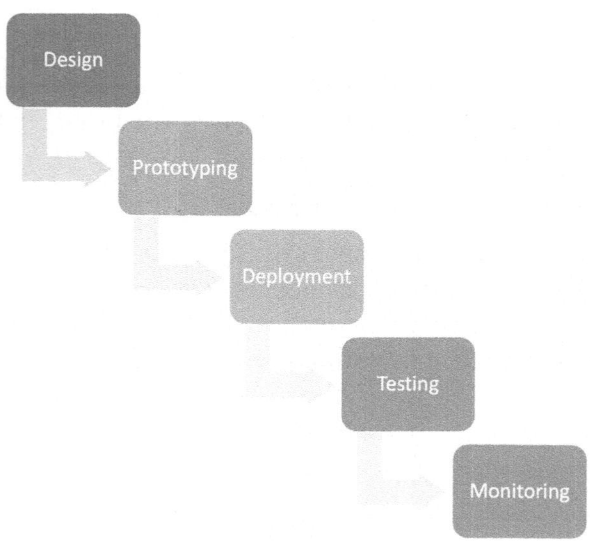

Figure 1.3: *Go Development Lifecycle*

During the design phase, AI can suggest API structures, module layouts, or standard library utilities. It also offers syntax recommendations, code creation, and documentation support during coding.

During testing, AI can generate unit tests, detect edge cases, and even propose performance benchmarks.

For deployment, especially in cloud-native environments, AI can suggest optimal resource configurations, integrate with CI/CD pipelines, and provide infrastructure-as-code recommendations for services like AWS Lambda, S3, or DynamoDB.

By operating seamlessly across all stages, AI ensures that Go development is not only faster and more efficient, but also more robust, reliable, and maintainable. The continuous support across the workflow enables developers to build production-grade systems with confidence, while maintaining high standards for performance, scalability, and code quality.

Conclusion

In this chapter, we explored the fundamentals of Go (Golang) and the growing influence of AI-assisted development tools in shaping modern programming practices. The discussion centered on how the clean design, efficiency, and scalability of Go make it an exceptional choice for building high-performance applications, whereas AI-powered assistants only enhance the speed, quality, and creativity of the development process.

We began with an overview of Go's origins and design goals. Created by engineers at Google, Go was designed to simplify the process of building fast and reliable software systems. It blends the performance of compiled languages with the readability of modern programming languages, resulting in code that is both efficient and easy to maintain. Go's strengths–such as static typing, memory safety, and built-in concurrency–allow developers to build scalable software systems. Its lightweight goroutines and channels make concurrent programming approachable and effective, especially for backend services, APIs, and distributed systems.

In the subsequent sections, the chapter continued to outline how to set up the Go development environment on different operating systems. Whether working on Linux, macOS, or Windows, developers can quickly install Go from the official website, configure their environment variables, and verify the setup using a simple command-line check. These steps prepare the system for writing and running Go programs smoothly, forming the base for further exploration in later chapters.

Next, we explored AI-assisted coding tools in modern programming. The chapter introduced three assistants that are changing the developer experience: ChatGPT, GitHub Copilot, and Amazon Q Developer. ChatGPT uses natural language to explain code, generate examples, and help debug. GitHub Copilot is available as an extension in code editors to expedite development with real-time code suggestions, function templates, and best practices. Amazon Q Developer (formerly CodeWhisperer) recommends optimized and secure Go code snippets for AWS services using AI. These technologies collaborate with developers to reduce routine tasks and let them focus on problem-solving and design.

The chapter also elucidated on how to install and configure these AI assistants within popular IDEs such as Visual Studio Code, GoLand, and AWS Cloud9. Once installed, users authenticate through their respective platforms and can customize preferences such as suggestion frequency, privacy settings, and supported languages. This setup ensures that the tools integrate seamlessly into the existing workflow, offering relevant and context-aware assistance during development.

In the latter part, we explored the key benefits of using AI-assisted tools in Go development. AI enhances productivity by generating repetitive code, scaffolding projects, and automating routine tasks like writing unit tests or refactoring. It contributes to higher code quality through real-time suggestions that align with Go's idiomatic style, promoting cleaner and more maintainable projects. AI assistants also accelerate debugging and troubleshooting, helping developers quickly identify and resolve issues related to concurrency, memory, or syntax.

Another major advantage we discussed was continuous learning. As developers code, these tools provide instant feedback, explanations, and examples—creating an environment where every project becomes a learning opportunity. Over time, this results in stronger coding habits and a deeper understanding of Go's core principles. The chapter also highlighted how AI can improve collaboration by automating code reviews, summarizing pull requests, and maintaining consistency across team projects.

To conclude, this chapter established a foundation for building modern applications using Go, combined with AI-powered development support. Go provides the efficiency, concurrency, and reliability needed for large-scale systems, while AI tools bring intelligent automation and insight to every stage of the workflow—from design to deployment. Together, they enable developers to write cleaner, faster, and more maintainable code, setting the stage for smarter and more productive software engineering in the chapters ahead.

In the next chapter, we will dive deeper into Go syntax, variables, and data types. It subsequently examines Go's extensive array of data types, beginning with primitive kinds and advancing to composite and sophisticated types, including structs, maps, interfaces, and channels.

CHAPTER 2
Go Syntax, Variables, and Data Types

Introduction

This chapter provides a thorough introduction to the core building blocks of Go programming. It begins by examining the syntax and structural conventions of Go, which emphasize clarity, consistency, and predictability–traits that make Go particularly effective for building maintainable software systems. The chapter additionally, explores Go's rich set of data types, starting from primitive types and progressing to composite and advanced types such as structs, maps, interfaces, and channels. Readers will also learn how Go handles variables, constants, type inference, zero values, and memory references through pointers. Alongside foundational concepts, the chapter aims to introduce essential I/O operations using the **`fmt`** and **`bufio`** packages. AI-assisted coding tools are integrated throughout, demonstrating how ChatGPT, GitHub Copilot, and Amazon Q Developer can accelerate type selection, variable generation, and code scaffolding. By establishing a strong understanding of Go's type system and structural principles, this chapter lays the groundwork for more advanced programming patterns in subsequent chapters.

Structure

In this chapter, we will cover the following topics:

- Go's Syntax and Structure
  - Code Structure and Entry Point
  - Packages and Imports
  - The Formatting Philosophy of Go
- Variables and Constants
- Primitive Data Types
  - Boolean Types

    - Numeric Types
    - String Types
- Composite Data Types
    - Array Types
    - Slice Types
    - Struct Types
    - Map Types
    - Pointer Types
    - Function Types
    - Interface Types
        - Basic Interface
        - Embedded Interface
        - General Interface
    - Channel Types
- Type Inference, Zero Values, and Type Conversion
- Basic Input/Output with `fmt` and `bufio`
- AI-Assisted Code Generation for Data Types and Variables

Go's Syntax and Structure

The syntax of Go is intentionally crafted to be simple, consistent, and highly readable. The language avoids unnecessary symbols, ambiguous constructs, and overly complex abstractions, making it approachable for newcomers while still powerful enough for large-scale systems. Its design enforces clarity through strong conventions, predictable patterns, and a tooling ecosystem that emphasizes uniformity. This section introduces the core structural elements that define how Go programs are written and organized.

Code Structure and Entry Point

Every Go application begins with a clear and predictable structure. An executable program must declare the **`main`** package, which serves as the root of the application. Within this package, the **`main()`** function acts as the entry point—similar to **`int main()`** in C but with Go's streamlined syntax.

At a high level, a minimal Go program contains:

```
package main

import "fmt"

func main() {
    fmt.Println("Hello, Readers!")
}
```

This simple program demonstrates the three essential components of any Go executable:

- Package declaration
- Import statements
- Function definitions

Go programs are organized into packages to support modularity, code reuse, and clean separation of concerns.

Packages and Imports

In Go, packages are one of the essential building units. Each Go file is a part of a package, which aids in organizing similar features. Numerous built-in packages for I/O, networking, concurrency, text processing, encryption, and other areas are available in the standard library.

The **`import`** keyword is used to include these packages:

```
import "net/http"
```

Go allows importing multiple packages in a grouped, readable form:

```
import (
    "fmt"
    "strings"
    "time"
)
```

These imports make functionality available without clutter or verbosity. The package system in Go encourages clear modularization and fosters large, maintainable codebases.

The Formatting Philosophy of Go

One of the defining traits of Go is its strict opinion on formatting. The language tool, **`gofmt`** (and its editor integrations), automatically formats code according to the industry-standard rules. This eliminates style debates and ensures that every Go codebase looks consistent, regardless of the author.

Key formatting principles include:

- Mandatory curly braces on the same line as control structures.
- Tabs over spaces (enforced by **gofmt**).
- Automatic semicolon insertion, making semicolons practically invisible to developers.
- Consistent whitespace and indentation.

This uniform formatting reduces cognitive load and helps developers quickly understand the unfamiliar code.

Control Structures and Flow

Go provides familiar control structures but trims away unnecessary complexity. The language uses variations of three primary constructs:

- **if** statements without parentheses.
- **for** loops as the only looping mechanism.
- Flexible switch statements without fall through (unless explicitly enabled).

Examples:

```
if value > 10 {
    fmt.Println("Large value")
}

for i := 0; i < 5; i++ {
    fmt.Println(i)
}

switch day {
case "Monday":
    fmt.Println("Start of week")
default:
    fmt.Println("Midweek or weekend")
}
```

The simplicity of these constructs reflects the philosophy of Go: expressive enough for real-world tasks, yet decently minimal to avoid confusion.

Variables and Constants

Variables and constants form the foundation of Go's data model. Go emphasizes clarity and explicitness, encouraging developers to declare values in a way that is both predictable and easy to maintain. Variables can be declared with the var keyword or using shorthand syntax (`:=`) when the type can be inferred. Constants, defined with const, must represent compile-time values and are commonly used for configuration, fixed limits, and symbolic identifiers.

Go supports two primary forms of variable declaration:

- **Explicit Declaration:**

  ```
  var count int
  var name string = "Go"
  ```

  This style is preferred when clarity of type is important.

- **Shorthand Declaration:**

  ```
  count := 10
  ```

  When used inside functions, this form reduces verbosity while still preserving type safety.

Typed and Untyped Constants

Go distinguishes between typed and untyped constants:

- *Typed constants* have a fixed type and participate in type-checked operations.
- *Untyped constants* provide flexibility without compromising security by adapting to the situation in which they are used.

This duality allows constants to behave predictably while remaining convenient in expressions and function calls.

Common Pitfalls

- Shorthand declarations cannot be used at the package level, which sometimes surprises newcomers.
- Values generated at runtime, and such function calls or dynamic expressions, cannot be assigned to constants.
- Declaring a variable without using it will result in a compile-time error, reinforcing Go's emphasis on clean code.

Primitive Data Types

The primitive data types consist of a number of data types. In the following sub-sections, we will look into the main primitive data types in Go.

Boolean Types

A *boolean* type is the collection of Boolean truth values represented by the predefined constants **`true`** and **`false`**. The predefined boolean type is **`bool`**, which is a defined type.

Numeric Types

Numeric types consist of integer value, floating-point and complex values. An integer, floating-point, or complex type represents the set of integer, floating-point, or complex values, respectively.

The predeclared architecture-independent numeric types are:

Numeric Types	Description
`uint8`	the set of all unsigned 8-bit integers (0 to 255)
`uint16`	the set of all unsigned 16-bit integers (0 to 65535)
`uint32`	the set of all unsigned 32-bit integers (0 to 4294967295)
`uint64`	the set of all unsigned 64-bit integers (0 to 18446744073709551615)
int8	the set of all signed 8-bit integers (-128 to 127)
`int16`	the set of all signed 16-bit integers (-32768 to 32767)
`int32`	the set of all signed 32-bit integers (-2147483648 to 2147483647)
`int64`	the set of all signed 64-bit integers (-9223372036854775808 to 9223372036854775807)
`float32`	the set of all IEEE 754 32-bit floating-point numbers
`float64`	the set of all IEEE 754 64-bit floating-point numbers
`complex64`	the set of all complex numbers with float32 real and imaginary parts
`complex128`	the set of all complex numbers with float64 real and imaginary parts
`byte`	alias for uint8
`rune`	alias for int32

Table 2.1: *Numeric Types*

The set of pre-declared integer types with implementation-specific sizes:

Numeric Types	Description
`uint`	either 32 or 64 bits
`int`	same size as uint
`uintptr`	an unsigned integer large enough to store the uninterpreted bits of a pointer value

Table 2.2: *Pre-declared Integer Types*

String Types

The collection of string values is represented by a string type. A string value is a series of bytes that could be empty. The length of the string is its byte count, which is always positive. Strings are immutable, meaning that once they are generated, their contents cannot be altered. String is a defined type that has been predeclared.

The built-in function **`len`** can be used to find the length of a string. If the string is a constant, then the length is a compile-time constant. The integer indices **`0`** through **`len(s)-1`** can be used to access the bytes of a string. Taking the address of such an element is prohibited; if **`s[i]`** is a string's **`i`**'th byte, then **`&s[i]`** is invalid.

Composite Data Types

Composite data types are data types that provide advanced functionality in programming in Go.

Array Types

A sequence of numbered elements of a single type—referred to as the element type—is called an array. The length of an array, which is the total number of elements, is always positive.

```
ArrayType   = "[" ArrayLength "]" ElementType .
ArrayLength = Expression .
ElementType = Type .
```

The array's length is a component of its type; it must be evaluated to a non-negative constant that may be represented by an int value. The built-in function len can be used to find the length of array a. The integer indices 0 through len(a)-1 can be used to address the elements. Although array types can be combined to create multi-dimensional types, they are always one-dimensional.

```
[32]byte
[2*N] struct { x, y int32 }
[1000]*float64
```

```
[3][5]int
[2][2][2]float64  // same as [2]([2]([2]float64))
```

If those enclosing types are solely array or struct types, then an array type T may not directly or indirectly contain an element of type T or of a type containing T as a component.

Invalid Array Types:

```
type (
        T1 [10]T1                   // element type of T1 is T1
        T2 [10]struct{ f T2 }       // T2 contains T2 as component
                                       of a struct
        T3 [10]T4                   // T3 contains T3 as component
                                       of a struct in T4
        T4 struct{ f T3 }           // T4 contains T4 as component
                                       of array T3 in a struct
)
```

Valid Array Types:

```
type (
        T5 [10]*T5                  // T5 contains T5 as component
                                       of a pointer
        T6 [10]func() T6            // T6 contains T6 as component
                                       of a function type
        T7 [10]struct{ f []T7 }     // T7 contains T7 as component
                                       of a slice in a struct
)
```

Source: go.dev/ref/spec

Slice Types

A slice gives access to a numbered sequence of elements from an underlying array and serves as a descriptor for a contiguous segment of that array. The collection of all array slices of a certain element type is indicated by a slice type.

Key points for slices:

- The length of the slice (number of elements) is always positive.
- An uninitialized slice has no value (value = nil).
- After initialization of a slice, it is associated with the underlying array that holds its value.
- A slice shares storage with its array and with other slices of the same array; by contrast, distinct arrays always represent distinct storage.

The built-in function **make**, which takes a slice type and parameters indicating the length and possibly the capacity. It can be used to create a new, initialized slice value for a given element type T. Every time a slice is made using make, a new, hidden array is allocated, to which the slice value that is returned points. In other words, upon executing the following command generates an identical slice as allocating an array and slicing it.

```
make([]T, length, capacity)
```

Thus, these two expressions are equivalent:

```
make([]int, 50, 100)
new([100]int)[0:50]
```

Slices are always one-dimensional, just like arrays, but they can be combined to create higher-dimensional objects. While the inner arrays of arrays of arrays are always the same length by design, the inner lengths of slices of slices (or arrays of slices) might change dynamically. Additionally, each inner slice needs to be started separately.

Struct Types

A sequence of named items, or fields, with names and types is termed a struct. Both explicit (**IdentifierList**) and implicit (**EmbeddedField**) field names are possible. Non-blank field names must be distinct within a struct.

```
StructType    = "struct" "{" { FieldDecl ";" } "}" .
FieldDecl     = (IdentifierList Type | EmbeddedField) [ Tag ] .
EmbeddedField = [ "*" ] TypeName [ TypeArgs ] .
Tag           = string_lit .
```

The following is an empty struct:

```
struct {}
```

A struct with 5 fields:

```
struct {
        x int
        u float32
        _ float32
        A *[]int
        F func()
}
```

An embedded field is the one, which is specified with a type, but does not have an explicit field name. `T` or `*T`, where T is not a pointer type or type parameter, is required to specify an embedded field; `T` must not be an interface type. Field names are defined by the unqualified type name.

A struct with four embedded fields of types **T1**, ***T2**, **P.T3** and ***P.T4**:

```
struct {
        T1          // field name is T1
        *T2         // field name is T2
        P.T3        // field name is T3
        *P.T4       // field name is T4
        x, y int    // field names are x and y
}
```

A field or method **f** of an embedded field in a struct **x** is called promoted if **x.f** is a legal selector that denotes that field or method **f**.

A struct type **T** shall not include a field of type **T** itself, neither a field of a type that contains **T** as a component, whether directly or indirectly, provided that the containing types are solely array or struct types.

Invalid struct types:

```
type (
        T1 struct{ T1 }              // T1 contains a field of T1
        T2 struct{ f [10]T2 }        // T2 contains T2 as component
                                        of an array
        T3 struct{ T4 }              // T3 contains T3 as component
                                        of an array in struct T4
        T4 struct{ f [10]T3 }        // T4 contains T4 as component
                                        of struct T3 in an array
)
```

Valid struct types:

```
type (
        T5 struct{ f *T5 }           // T5 contains T5 as component
                                        of a pointer
        T6 struct{ f func() T6 }     // T6 contains T6 as component
                                        of a function type
        T7 struct{ f [10][]T7 }      // T7 contains T7 as component
                                        of a slice in an array
)
```

Map Types

A map is an unordered collection of elements of a single type, known as the element type. It is indexed by a set of unique keys of a different type, referred to as the key type. The value of a map that has not been initialized is **nil**.

```
MapType = "map" "[" KeyType "]" ElementType .
KeyType = Type .
```

The comparison operators `==` and `!=` must be comprehensively implemented for operands of the key type; consequently, the key type must not be a function, map, or slice. If the key type is an interface type, these comparison operators must be explicitly defined for the dynamic key values. A failure to do so will result in a run-time alarm.

```
map[string]int
map[*T]struct{ x, y float64 }
map[string]interface{}
```

The number of map elements is referred to as its length. For a map `m`, its length may be determined using the built-in function **`len`** and may vary throughout execution. Elements can be incorporated during execution by assignments and accessed via index expressions; they can be eliminated using the **`delete`** and **`clear`** built-in functions.

A new, vacant map value is created with the built-in function **`make`**, which accepts the map type and an optional capacity hint as parameters:

```
make(map[string]int)
make(map[string]int, 10)
```

The initial capacity does not limit its size: maps expand to meet the quantity of items stored, except for **`nil`** maps. A **`nil`** map is analogous to an empty map, with the exception that none of the elements can be appended.

Pointer Types

A pointer type signifies the collection of all pointers to variables of a certain type, referred to as the base type of the pointer. An uninitialized pointer holds a value of null.

```
PointerType = "*" BaseType .
BaseType    = Type .
```

Function Types

A function type represents the collection of all functions that share identical parameter and return types. An uninitialized variable of function type holds a value of nil.

```
FunctionType  = "func" Signature .
Signature     = Parameters [ Result ] .
Result        = Parameters | Type .
Parameters    = "(" [ ParameterList [ "," ] ] ")" .
ParameterList = ParameterDecl { "," ParameterDecl } .
ParameterDecl = [ IdentifierList ] [ "..." ] Type .
```

In a set of parameters or results, the names (**IdentifierList**) must be either entirely present or entirely absent. Each name, if present, represents a singular object (parameter or result) of the designated type, and all non-blank names in the signature must be distinct. In the absence of a specific item, each category represents a singular item of that sort. Parameter and result lists are consistently enclosed in parentheses, except when there is precisely one unnamed result, which may be expressed as an unparenthesized type.

The last parameter in a function signature may have a type beginning with `...`. A function having this parameter is termed variadic and can be invoked with zero or more arguments for that parameter.

```
func()
func(x int) int
func(a, _ int, z float32) bool
func(a, b int, z float32) (bool)
func(prefix string, values ...int)
func(a, b int, z float64, opt ...interface{}) (success bool)
func(int, int, float64) (float64, *[]int)
func(n int) func(p *T)
```

Interface Types

An interface type delineates a group of types. An interface-type variable can hold a value of any type included in the interface's type set. A type is described as implementing the interface. An uninitialized variable of interface type holds a value of **nil**.

```
InterfaceType  = "interface" "{" { InterfaceElem ";" } "}" .
InterfaceElem  = MethodElem | TypeElem .
MethodElem     = MethodName Signature .
MethodName     = identifier .
TypeElem       = TypeTerm { "|" TypeTerm } .
TypeTerm       = Type | UnderlyingType .
UnderlyingType = "~" Type .
```

An interface type is defined by a compilation of interface elements. An interface element comprises of either a method or a type element, with a type element defined as a union of one or more type terms. A type word is either a singular type or a singular underlying type.

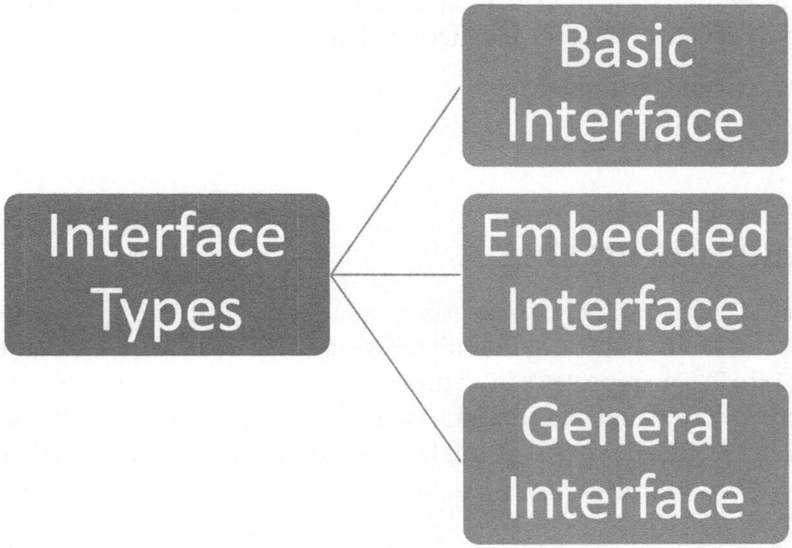

Figure 2.1: *Interface Types*

Basic Interfaces

An interface, in its simplest form, delineates a (potentially empty) enumeration of methods. The type defined by this interface comprises all types that implement its methods, and the accompanying method set includes precisely the methods outlined by the interface. Interfaces that can be completely characterized by a compilation of methods are referred to as the basic interfaces.

```
interface {
        Read([]byte) (int, error)
        Write([]byte) (int, error)
        Close() error
}
```

The name of each explicitly specified method must be unique, and not blank.

```
interface {
        String() string
        String() string  // illegal: String not unique
        _(x int)         // illegal: method must have non-blank name
}
```

All types within the type set of an interface adhere to its implementation. Any specific type may implement multiple distinct interfaces. All kinds, for example, implement the empty interface, representing the collection of all non-interface types:

```
interface{}
```

Similarly, consider this interface specification, which appears within a type declaration to define an interface called Locker:

```
type Locker interface {
        Lock()
        Unlock()
}
```

Embedded Interfaces

An interface T may utilize a (potentially qualified) interface type name E as an interface element in a more generalized form. This is referred to as embedding interface E into T. The type set of T is the intersection of the type sets established by T's expressly declared methods and the type sets of T's included interfaces. The type set of T comprises of all types that implement every expressly declared method of T, as well as all the methods of E.

```
type Reader interface {
        Read(p []byte) (n int, err error)
        Close() error
}

type Writer interface {
        Write(p []byte) (n int, err error)
        Close() error
}
```

ReadWriter's methods are Read, Write, and Close:

```
type ReadWriter interface {
        Reader  // includes methods of Reader in ReadWriter's
        method set
        Writer  // includes methods of Writer in ReadWriter's
        method set
}
```

Source: go.dev/ref/spec

When embedding interfaces, methods with the same names must have identical signatures.

```
type ReadCloser interface {
        Reader   // includes methods of Reader in ReadCloser's
        method set
        Close()  // illegal: signatures of Reader.Close and Close
        are different
}
```

General Interfaces

An interface element can be represented as a generic type term T, a term of the form ~T denoting the underlying type T, or a union of terms t1|t2|...|tn. Alongside method specifications, these components facilitate the exact delineation of an interface's type, which is set as follows:

- The type set of the empty interface comprises all non-interface types.
- The type set of a non-empty interface is the intersection of the type sets of its constituent parts.
- The type set of a method specification comprises all non-interface types whose method sets contain that method.
- The type set of a non-interface type word comprises solely that type.
- The type set of a term of the form ~T comprises all types whose underlying type is T.
- The type set of a union of terms t1|t2|...|tn is the amalgamation of the type sets of the individual terms.

By construction, the type set of an interface never contains an interface type.

```
// An interface representing only the type int.
interface {
	int
}

// An interface representing all types with underlying type int.
interface {
	~int
}

// An interface representing all types with underlying type int
that implement the String method.
interface {
	~int
	String() string
}

// An interface representing an empty type set: there is no type
that is both an int and a string.
interface {
	int
	string
}
```

The type T in an expression of the form T or ~T cannot serve as a type parameter, and the type sets of all non-interface terms must be mutually exclusive (the pairwise intersection of the type sets must be null). Considering a type parameter P:

```
interface {
      P                 // illegal: P is a type parameter
      int | ~P          // illegal: P is a type parameter
      ~int | MyInt      // illegal: the type sets for ~int and
MyInt are not disjoint (~int includes MyInt)
      float32 | Float  // overlapping type sets but Float is an
interface
}
```

Source: go.dev/ref/spec

Implementation Restriction: A union (comprising of many terms) cannot include the predeclared identifier 'comparable' or interfaces that define methods, nor can it incorporate 'comparable' or interfaces that delineate methods.

Implementing an Interface

A type **T** fulfills an interface **I** if

- **T** is not an interface and belongs to the type set of **I**; or
- **T** is an interface and the type set of **T** is a subset of the type set of **I**.

A type **T** fulfills an interface if **T** adheres to the specifications of the interface.

In Go, any is an alias for **`interface{}`** introduced in Go 1.18 to improve readability and express intent. It allows a variable or type parameter to accept values of any type while preserving Go's static type safety through explicit type handling.

Channel Types

A channel facilitates the concurrent execution of functions by enabling the transmission and reception of values of a designated element type. An uninitialized channel holds a nil value.

```
ChannelType = ( "chan" | "chan" "<-" | "<-" "chan" ) ElementType .
```

The optional `<-` operator designates the channel direction, either send or receive. If a direction is specified, the channel is directional; if not, it is bidirectional. A channel may be restricted to either transmission or reception by assignment or explicit conversion.

```
chan T          // can be used to send and receive values of type T
chan<- float64  // can only be used to send float64s
<-chan int      // can only be used to receive ints
```

The <- operator associates with the leftmost channel available:

```
chan<- chan int    // same as chan<- (chan int)
chan<- <-chan int  // same as chan<- (<-chan int)
<-chan <-chan int  // same as <-chan (<-chan int)
chan (<-chan int)
```

A new initialized channel value can be created using the built-in function make, which accepts the channel type, and an optional capacity as parameters:

```
make(chan int, 10)
```

The channel buffer size depends on capacity, in elements. Without capacity, the channel is unbuffered and communication only works when both the sender and the receiver are ready. If the channel buffer is not full (sends) or empty (receives), communication continues without blocking. Non-communication channels are never ready.

Channels can be closed with the built-in function **`close`**. The receive operator's multi-valued assignment form indicates whether a received value was sent before channel closure.

Any number of goroutines can use a single channel for send, receive, and **`cap`** and **`len`** calls without synchronization. Channels are first-in-first-out queues. If one goroutine sends values on a channel and a second receives them, they are received in order.

Type Inference, Zero Values, and Type Conversion

Go promotes a balance between explicitness and convenience, and this balance is reflected in its approach to type inference, default initialization (zero values), and controlled type conversion. Writing idiomatic and predictable Go code requires an understanding of these ideas.

Type Inference

The compiler of Go is capable of inferring types in many situations, most notably when using the shorthand declaration operator (`:=`). In these cases, the type is derived from the value on the right-hand side:

```
total := 42          // inferred as int
message := "hello"   // inferred as string
ratio := 3.14        // inferred as float64
```

Type inference reduces verbosity without compromising type safety. However, Go does not perform implicit type coercion; the inferred type is fixed at the moment of declaration.

Zero Values

If no explicit value is supplied, all specified variables in Go are automatically initialized to zero. This behavior guarantees consistent program behavior, and gets rid of uninitialized memory errors. Zero values vary according on the type:

```
Numeric types → 0
Boolean → false
String → "" (empty string)
```

Pointers, interfaces, slices, maps, channels, and functions → nil.

```
var count int     // zero value: 0
var active bool   // zero value: false
var data []int    // zero value: nil
```

Understanding zero values is particularly important when working with composite and reference types, as checks against nil are common in Go.

Type Conversion

Go requires explicit type conversion, reinforcing clarity and preventing unintended data loss. A conversion uses the target type as a function:

```
var x int = 10
var y float64 = float64(x)
```

Conversions must be explicitly described, even when they occur between compatible numeric types. Additionally, conversions between byte slices and strings are explicit:

```
s := "go"
b := []byte(s)     // string → []byte
```

Attempting to use a value of one type where another is required without conversion results in a compile-time error. This strictness helps maintain strong typing and ensures that code behavior is always explicit and predictable.

Basic Input/Output with `fmt` and `bufio`

Input and Output operations form the backbone of many Go programs, whether they involve printing information to the console, reading user input, or processing large amounts of text. Go provides two primary packages—**`fmt`** and **`bufio`**—that together deliver both simplicity and efficiency for handling I/O tasks. While **`fmt`** offers convenient, high-level functions suitable for everyday output, **`bufio`** introduces buffered I/O mechanisms designed for performance-critical operations such as reading files, streaming data, or handling user input interactively.

Formatted Output with the `fmt` Package

The **`fmt`** package is the most commonly used tool for producing textual output. It offers functions that resemble those found in languages like C or Python, but with Go's characteristic emphasis on clarity and type safety.

Printing Values

Functions such as **`fmt.Print`**, **`fmt.Println`**, and **`fmt.Printf`** enable straightforward printing:

- **`Print`** writes values without adding spaces or newlines.
- **`Println`** adds spaces between arguments and a trailing newline.
- **`Printf`** supports format specifiers for structured output.

```
fmt.Println("Welcome to Go")
fmt.Printf("Counter: %d\n", 42)
```

For developers formatting time, numerical output, or structured logs, **`Printf`** provides fine-grained control using verbs like **`%s`** for strings, **`%v`** for generic values, **`%f`** for floating-point numbers, and **`%t`** for booleans.

Input Using `fmt`

`fmt` also supports interactive input via functions such as **`Scan`**, **`Scanln`**, and **`Scanf`**, which reads whitespace-separated values from standard input:

```
var name string
fmt.Print("Enter your name: ")
fmt.Scanln(&name)
```

These functions work well for basic user input but are less suited for large datasets or controlled parsing, where buffering and scanning methods become preferred.

Efficient Input with the bufio Package

While **`fmt`** prioritizes convenience, **bufio** is designed for efficiency. It wraps an underlying reader or writer–such as a file, network connection, or standard input–and improves performance not only by minimizing the number of system calls, but also through enabling controlled, buffered processing of data.

Buffered Reading

`bufio.NewReader` allows reading input one line, rune, or arbitrary byte sequence at a time:

```
reader := bufio.NewReader(os.Stdin)
text, _ := reader.ReadString('\n')
```

ReadString reads input until a delimiter (often newline) is encountered. For even more control, developers may use:

- **ReadBytes** for byte slices,
- **ReadRune** for Unicode-aware character processing,
- **ReadLine** for manual line handling without allocation guarantees.

This level of granularity is especially useful when processing logs, streaming content, or large files where performance matters.

Buffered Writing

bufio.Writer provides an efficient mechanism for output, accumulating data in buffer memory before writing it in bulk:

```
writer := bufio.NewWriter(os.Stdout)
writer.WriteString("Buffered output example\n")
writer.Flush()
```

Explicitly calling **Flush** ensures that all buffered content is written, which is essential for applications producing incremental output or interacting with external systems.

Using `bufio.Scanner` for Tokenized Input

For line-by-line text processing, **bufio.Scanner** offers a clean, high-level interface:

```
scanner := bufio.NewScanner(os.Stdin)
for scanner.Scan() {
    line := scanner.Text()
    fmt.Println("Received:", line)
}
```

By default, **Scanner** splits input by lines, but it can be customized to split by words, or custom patterns using **scanner.Split(bufio.ScanWords)** or custom split functions. This makes it ideal for parsing configuration files, processing CLI input, or building REPL-style applications.

Choosing between `fmt` and bufio

Developers often use both packages depending on the task:

Requirement	Recommended Package
Quick printing or debugging	Fmt
Structured or formatted output	fmt.Printf
Basic user input	fmt.Scan*

High-performance reading or writing	bufio.Reader / bufio.Writer
Line-by-line text processing	bufio.Scanner

Table 2.3: *Recommended Packages for a Given Requirement*

By understanding the strengths of each package, Go developers can write programs that are both simple and efficient, balancing readability with performance.

AI-Assisted Code Generation for Data Types and Variables

Modern Go development increasingly leverages artificial intelligence to accelerate coding workflows, reduce errors, and enforce best practices. AI-assisted coding tools, such as ChatGPT, GitHub Copilot, and Amazon Q Developer (formerly CodeWhisperer), can assist developers in generating, validating, and refining variable declarations and data types. This section explores how AI can be seamlessly integrated into the Go development process, particularly for tasks involving variables, constants, and type assignments.

Generating Variable Declarations

One of the most immediate benefits of AI-assisted development is the automatic generation of variable declarations. Developers can write natural language prompts such as:

"Create a variable to store the user's age as an integer and initialize it with 18."

AI models interpret these prompts and generate idiomatic Go code:

```
age := 18
```

This reduces the friction of remembering syntax details, especially for newer developers or when switching between languages with different type systems. AI can produce numerous related variables in a consistent manner for large projects, making the code easier to comprehend and manage.

Type Suggestions and Inference Assistance

AI tools are also capable of recommending the most appropriate data type for a variable, based on the context. For example, given a dataset representing financial transactions, AI might suggest:

```
var balance float64
```

or, for structured records:

```
type Transaction struct {
    ID     int
    Amount float64
    Date   string
}
```

Such suggestions help developers follow Go's idiomatic conventions, and avoid subtle bugs caused by inappropriate type choices, such as using int instead of float64 for fractional numbers.

Automatic Initialization and Zero-Value Awareness

AI coding assistants are aware of the zero-value system of Go and can generate code that leverages default initialization safely. For instance, instead of requiring developers to explicitly assign initial values, AI can produce:

```
var isActive bool       // defaults to false
var scores []int        // defaults to nil
```

This ensures safe defaults while maintaining concise and idiomatic code.

Refactoring and Consistency

In addition to generation, AI can suggest refactoring existing variable declarations for better clarity, maintainability, and adherence to Go conventions. For example:

- Converting multiple single-line declarations into grouped form:

  ```
  var x, y, z int = 1, 2, 3
  ```

- Recommending short declaration syntax (:=) where appropriate for function-scoped variables.
- Identifying unused variables and suggesting removal to comply with Go compiler rules.

These capabilities reduce human error, enforce consistency across the codebase, and accelerate development velocity.

Integration with Development Workflow

AI-assisted variable and type generation seamlessly integrates with command-line interfaces and IDEs like VS Code and GoLand. Developers are able to:

- Create brief bits of code while keeping in mind the surrounding code.

- Get on-demand data type recommendations based on struct definitions or function signatures.
- Quickly prototype intricate data structures and mappings with AI.

By leveraging AI in this way, you can spend less time on repetitive boilerplate tasks and more on solving high-level logic, designing algorithms, and optimizing performance.

AI can generate idiomatic variable declarations and type assignments directly from natural language prompts. It can recommend types based on context, improving correctness and code clarity. AI-assisted refactoring follows Go best practices, minimizes unused code, and guarantees consistency.

Integration with IDEs and editors makes AI a seamless development partner, accelerating the workflow from prototype to production-ready code.

Conclusion

This chapter has provided a comprehensive introduction to Go programming, laying the groundwork for writing clear, maintainable, and efficient code. It began with Go's syntax and structure, covering packages, imports, code formatting conventions, control structures, and module-based dependency management. Furthermore, we have examined variables and constants, highlighting both explicit and shorthand declarations, as well as the role of typed and untyped constants.

Primitive and composite data types were explored in detail, including booleans, numeric types, strings, arrays, slices, structs, maps, pointers, functions, interfaces, and channels. Key concepts such as type inference, zero values, and explicit type conversion were discussed to ensure predictable and idiomatic code. The chapter also explained input and output using the **`fmt`** and **`bufio`** packages, emphasizing how developers can balance simplicity with performance.

The chapter finally concludes with using AI-assisted coding tools, demonstrating how ChatGPT, GitHub Copilot, and Amazon Q Developer may help with refactoring, enforce idiomatic techniques, recommend suitable data types, and expedite variable generation. Developers can focus on higher-level design and logic, decrease repetitious effort, and enhance code quality by combining these technologies.

The next chapter shall focus on the functions, packages, and modules. These are the building blocks of programming in Go and using AI assistance to speed up development in Go.

CHAPTER 3
Functions, Packages, and Modular Code

Introduction

Functions, packages, and modules form the foundation of well-structured Go applications. This chapter introduces how Go organizes code into reusable components, beginning with its functions—the primary building blocks of the language—and extending into packages and modules that enable clean separation of concerns. It further examines how Go encourages clarity, maintainability, and scalability through its modular design principles. The chapter also demonstrates how modern AI-assisted tools can support developers in refactoring, optimizing, and structuring Go code more effectively, ensuring that projects remain robust as they grow in size and complexity.

Structure

In this chapter, we will cover the following topics:

- Functions in Go
  - Function Parameters
  - Return Values
  - Recursion
- Variadic and Anonymous Functions
  - Variadic Functions
  - Anonymous Functions
  - Combining Variadic and Anonymous Functions
- Packages, Modules, and Imports
  - Package Clause
  - Import Declarations

- Package Naming Conventions
- Exported versus Unexported Identifiers
- Directory Structure and Package Layout
- Import Declarations
- Package Initialization
- Importing Dependencies Recursively
- Evaluating Package-Level Variables
- Executing init() Functions
- How Modules Work
- Managing Dependencies
- Nested Modules and Multi-Module Repos

- Custom Packages
  - Creating a Custom Package
  - Organizing Packages Effectively
    - Package Focus
    - Package Names
    - Avoid Circular Dependencies
  - Building, Installing, Testing, Versioning, and Publishing Custom Packages
- File Handling Using os, io, and bufio
- Logging and Formatting with `fmt` and `log`
  - The `fmt` Package: Human-Readable Formatting
  - The `log` Package: Structured Logging for Applications
  - Choosing between `fmt` and `log`
  - Integrating Logging with Other Go Components
- Dependency Management with Go Modules
- AI-Assisted Refactoring and Code Suggestions

Functions in Go

Functions are one of the core building blocks of Go programs, enabling developers to organize logic into modular, reusable units. Go encourages a clean, minimalistic design philosophy, and its function syntax reflects this focus on clarity and predictability. Writing idiomatic Go code requires knowing how to define and use functions, whether the objective is to organize the behavior of a large-scale service or compose a simple utility.

Function Parameters

Go functions can have zero or more parameters, each explicitly typed to maintain strong compile-time safety. Unlike some languages where types precede variable names, Go places the type after the identifier, contributing to its clean, regular syntax. The language also supports grouping multiple parameters of the same type—for example,

```
func add(a, b int)
```

which improves readability.

The function receives a duplicate of each argument, since go parameters are supplied by value. Developers use pointers to pass references when modification is necessary. This distinct division promotes intentional design and helps avoid unintended side effects. Variadic parameters, declared with ellipsis syntax (similar to **`func sum(nums ...int)`**), allow flexible argument lists, and are commonly used in formatting, logging, and aggregation functions.

Return Values

Go functions may return a single value or multiple values, a feature that distinguishes Go from many traditional languages. Multiple return values are widely used for error handling, where a function returns both a result and an error object:

```
result, err := compute()
```

This pattern allows error propagation without relying on exceptions, keeping control flow explicit and predictable.

Named return values, in which the return variables are specified in the function signature, are likewise supported by Go. When combined with the **`return`** statement without explicit arguments, named returns can make code more descriptive. However, Go developers use them judiciously to preserve readability. Hence, whether returning a simple integer or a complex struct, Go emphasizes clarity and explicitness in function outcomes.

Recursion

The capacity of a function to call itself in order to solve an issue by decomposing it into smaller, easier-to-manage subproblems is known as recursion in Go. Although Go is often associated with iterative, loop-based solutions—thanks to its emphasis on simplicity and performance—recursion, however, remains an essential tool for problems that naturally follow a hierarchical or divide-and-conquer structure.

At its core, a recursive function in Go consists of two key elements:

- A base case, which specifies the circumstance in which the recursion comes to an end.
- A recursive case, which occurs when the function invokes itself with a simplified or a reduced version of the initial problem.

This pattern ensures that the recursion progresses toward termination and avoids infinite loops or excessive stack consumption. Developers must structure recursive logic carefully, as Go does not provide tail-call optimization, which means deeply recursive operations may increase stack usage. For this reason, many Go developers choose iterative solutions when performance or memory constraints are vital, but recursion remains invaluable for specific domains.

The following Go function demonstrates this pattern:

```
package main

import "fmt"

func factorial(n int) int {
	// Base case
	if n == 0 || n == 1 {
		return 1
	}

	// Recursive case
	return n * factorial(n-1)
}

func main() {
	result := factorial(5)
	fmt.Println("Factorial of 5:", result)
}
```

In this example, each call to factorial reduces the problem size by one, moving closer to the base case. When the base case is reached, the recursive calls begin to resolve in reverse order, ultimately producing the final result. This stepwise decomposition illustrates how recursion simplifies complex problems by breaking them into smaller, logically identical subproblems.

Common scenarios where recursion shines include:

- Tree and graph traversal (which includes walking a filesystem, exploring JSON structures, processing ASTs).
- Divide-and-conquer algorithms (such as quicksort, mergesort, binary search).

- Mathematical operations (including factorial, Fibonacci, combinatorics).
- Parsing nested structures such as XML, directories, or configuration files.

The explicit error-handling model of Go also integrates well with recursive design. For instance, recursive directory walkers often return errors up the call stack, making it easy to handle failure conditions at any point in the recursion chain.

To support more complex recursive logic, Go allows developers to define helper functions or closures inside outer functions. This pattern reduces global namespace pollution and keeps recursive logic encapsulated. Additionally, the strong typing of Go ensures that the compiler catches mismatched return types or incorrect parameters early, creating a safer environment for recursive programming, which can otherwise be error-prone in dynamically typed languages.

While Go does not encourage overly clever or deeply nested recursion, it provides all the tools needed to implement concise and expressive recursive algorithms when appropriate. A balanced understanding of recursion enables developers to select the right approach–recursive or iterative–based on the problem at hand, the expected input size, and the performance characteristics of the system they are building.

Variadic and Anonymous Functions

Go provides two powerful function capabilities–**Variadic functions** and **Anonymous functions**–that enhance flexibility, modularity, and expressiveness in code. Variadic functions allow developers to pass an arbitrary number of arguments, making them ideal for operations such as aggregation, logging, or formatting. Anonymous functions allow the creation of functions without names, which can be stored in variables, passed around as arguments, or executed right away. Together, these features support more functional programming patterns while retaining the emphasis of Go on simplicity and readability.

Variadic Functions

A Variadic function accepts zero or more arguments of the same type. This is achieved by using the **...** operator before the parameter type. Internally, Go converts all the passed values into a slice of that type.

Variadic functions are frequently used in scenarios where the number of inputs is variable. The **fmt.Println** and **append** functions are classic examples from the standard library.

```
func Sum(nums ...int) int {
    total := 0
    for _, n := range nums {
        total += n
```

```
    }
    return total
}
```

This allows calls such as:

```
Sum(10, 20)
Sum(5, 15, 20)
Sum() // valid; nums becomes an empty slice
```

In writing Go code, you can also combine variadic parameters with fixed parameters. However, the variadic parameter must always appear last.

```
func PrintWithPrefix(prefix string, values ...string) {
    for _, v := range values {
        fmt.Println(prefix, v)
    }
}
```

Variadic functions provide a clean way to express flexible APIs. They help avoid unnecessary overloads, and reduce boilerplate. This is essential while working with logs, middleware pipelines, aggregation functions, and configuration loaders.

Anonymous Functions

Anonymous functions in Go are functions, which do not have a function name specified. The anonymous functions have flexibility in such a way, that they can be assigned to variables, be stored in data structures, as well as, be passed as arguments to other functions. Anonymous functions allow developers to define small units of behavior exactly where they are needed, thus, improving readability, and reducing the need for separate named functions.

```
greet := func(name string) string {
    return "Hello, " + name
}

fmt.Println(greet("Go Developer"))
```

Since the function is assigned to a variable, it can be reused just like a named function.

```
func ProcessValues(values []int, callback func(int)) {
    for _, v := range values {
        callback(v)
    }
}

ProcessValues([]int{1, 2, 3}, func(n int) {
```

```
        fmt.Println("Processing:", n)
    })
```

This pattern is useful for event handlers, middleware, filtering, transformations, and concurrency operations involving goroutines.

Go also supports immediately invoked anonymous functions, which is often used for scoping or performing setup logic.

```
result := func(a, b int) int {
    return a + b
}(35, 5)

fmt.Println(result) // Output: 40
```

This technique is particularly helpful for initializing variables that require complex logic while keeping the code tidy and encapsulated.

Combining Variadic and Anonymous Functions

Go even allows anonymous functions to be variadic, enabling highly flexible inline behavior.

```
func main() {
    concat := func(parts ...string) string {
        return strings.Join(parts, " ")
    }

    fmt.Println(concat("Go", "is", "exciting"))
}
```

This demonstrates how Go's function model supports expressive patterns while maintaining strict type safety.

Packages, Modules, and Imports

Go programs are assembled through the integration of multiple packages. A package is composed of one or more source files that collectively declare constants, types, variables, and functions associated with the package, and which are accessible across all files within the same package. These elements may be exported and utilized in a different bundle.

Each source file comprises a package clause that specifies its associated package, succeeded by an optional series of import declarations that identify the packages whose contents it intends to utilize, and concluded by an optional set of declarations for functions, types, variables, and constants.

```
SourceFile = PackageClause ";" { ImportDecl ";" }
{ TopLevelDecl ";" } .
```

Package Clause

A package clause initiates each source file, and specifies the package to which the file is assigned.

```
PackageClause = "package" PackageName .
PackageName   = identifier .
```

The **PackageName** must not be the blank identifier.

```
package math
```

A collection of files with the identical **PackageName** constitutes the implementation of a package. An implementation may necessitate that all source files for a package reside within the same directory.

Import Declarations

An import declaration indicates that the source file relies on the functionality of the imported package and facilitates access to the package's exported identifiers. The import designates an identifier (**PackageName**) for access and an **ImportPath** that delineates the package to be imported.

```
ImportDecl = "import" ( ImportSpec | "(" { ImportSpec ";" } ")" ) .
ImportSpec = [ "." | PackageName ] ImportPath .
ImportPath = string_lit .
```

The **PackageName** is utilized in qualified identifiers to access the exported identifiers of the package within the importing source file. It is specified in the file block. In the absence of the **PackageName**, it defaults to the identifier designated in the package clause of the imported package. If a period (**.**) is used instead of a name, all exported identifiers from the package's package block will be declared in the importing source file's file block, and must be accessed unqualified. Imports are arranged idiomatically.

Package Naming Conventions

Go enforces and encourages readable, concise naming:

- Package names should be short and lowercase (**fmt**, **io**, **http**).
- Avoid underscores and camelCase.

- The best package name naturally matches its folder name.
- The name should describe the primary purpose of the package.

The two broad types of Packages:

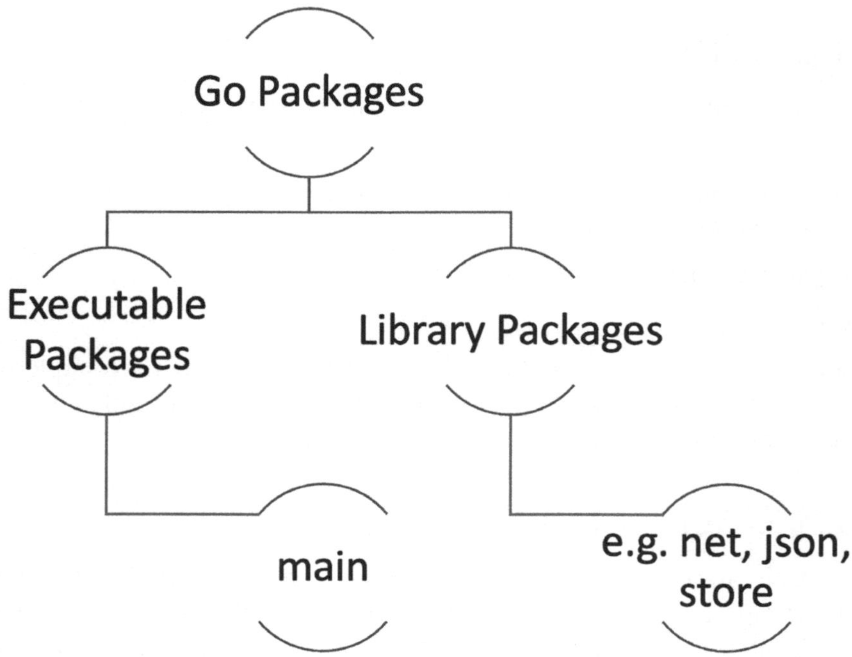

Figure 3.1: *Go Packages*

Exported versus Unexported Identifiers

A vital aspect of packages is controlling visibility. One needs to consider that:

- Identifiers beginning with an **uppercase letter** are *exported* and accessible outside the package.
- Identifiers with a **lowercase letter** are *unexported*, visible only within the package.

In Go, there are no keywords like **`public`** or **`private`**.

```
package mathutils

var Pi = 3.14         // exported
var internalPi = 3.14 // unexported

func Add(a, b int) int { // exported
    return a + b
```

```
}

func subtract(a, b int) int { // unexported
    return a - b
}
```

Directory Structure and Package Layout

In Go:

- **One directory = one package**, with rare exceptions.
- The directory name usually becomes the package name.

A sample project layout:

```
project/
    main.go             → package main
    utils/
        strings.go      → package utils
        numbers.go      → package utils
    handlers/
        auth.go         → package handlers
        users.go        → package handlers
```

Import Declarations

Imports allow one package to use functionality from another.

In Go programming, you can import one package per line, like:

```
import "fmt"
```

One can also import multiple packages together:

```
import (
    "fmt"
    "os"
    "strings"
)
```

While importing packages, you can use a shorter alias for an ease of programming in larger applications. In order to have a custom name for the package, use the following format:

```
import m "math"
```

In the above scenario, you can use "m" in your code. So instead of:

```
val := math.Sin(0.5)
```

By renaming the package, you can use:

```
val := m.Sin(0.5)
```

And, if you want to import all exported identifiers into the local namespace, use the dot as follows:

```
import . "fmt"
```

As a coding practice, even though the dot operator can be used to import all exported identifiers, it is not recommended as it reduces clarity on the actual functionalities used in the code. This will subsequently weaken the readability for fellow developers, who have contributed to the project. Therefore, as a coding practice, it is better to import only the packages that you plan to use.

In Go, there is an import using the _ identifier. It runs the packages' initialization, but does not import any names.

```
import _ <package-name>
```

This though does not import any names but is useful for plugin-style packages and database drivers.

Package Initialization

In Go, the initialization of the packages follows the following process:

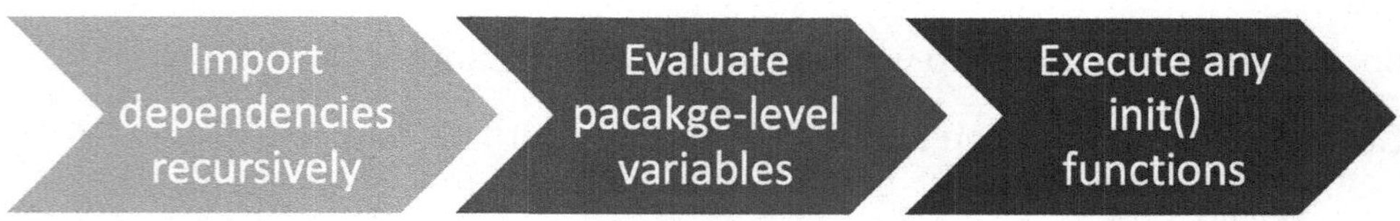

Figure 3.2: *Package Initialization Workflow*

Go follows a well-defined, and deterministic initialization sequence to ensure that packages are set up correctly before program execution begins. Understanding this initialization flow is essential for writing predictable and maintainable code, especially in larger applications where multiple packages interact with one another. The initialization process ensures that dependencies are loaded in a consistent manner, global state is prepared, and any required setup logic runs exactly at once.

Importing Dependencies Recursively

Initialization begins by resolving and loading the dependencies of a package. When a package is imported, Go recursively imports all of its dependencies first. Only after all upstream packages are fully initialized does Go initializes the importing package. This topological ordering prevents undefined behavior, and guarantees that every package has the entire of its dependencies ready before its own initialization runs.

For example, if **package p1** imports **package p2** the initialization order is:

```
package p2
package p1
```

This ensures that packages are always built on fully initialized components.

Evaluating Package-Level Variables

After all dependent packages have been imported, Go evaluates package-level variable declarations. These variables may include:

- Constant expressions
- Computed values
- Struct and slice initializations
- Function calls necessary for initialization

For example:

```
var config = loadConfig()    // evaluated before init()
var counter = 10               // simple initialization
```

These expressions are executed in the order they appear within each file. If a variable depends on another variable, the dependency is respected to avoid inconsistencies.

Package-level variable evaluation plays a crucial role in setting up default states, caching values, and performing lightweight initialization required for the package to function correctly.

Executing init() Functions

Finally, Go executes any **init()** functions defined within the package. A package may have multiple **init()** functions, located across different files. Go guarantees the following:

- All package-level variables are initialized before any **init()** function runs.
- **init()** functions are called in the order they appear across the files of the package.
- **init()** is executed only once per package.
- No arguments or return values are permitted, reinforcing that **init()** is strictly for setup activities.

Typical use cases of **init()** include:

- Registering components or handlers.

- Initializing connections or global resources.
- Validating package-level configuration.
- Preparing lookup tables or caches.

Let us understand through an example:

```
func init() {
    fmt.Println("Package initialized")
}
```

Because **init()** is called automatically, and cannot be invoked directly, developers must design it carefully. Overuse of **init()** can make a program flow difficult to follow, so it is best to reserve it for essential, side-effect-driven initialization.

How Go Modules Work

Go modules help define a root directory for the source code. Modules help in tracking the dependencies and their versions. This is a critical piece of information required, in maintaining large codebases. This helps guarantee reproducible builds.

Go modules are represented in mod files. The **go.mod** file contains information of the module path and the go version and the required dependencies.

When you import a new package as:

```
import <package-name>
```

And then execute the **go mod tidy** command, the go.mod file updates with the version, like:

```
require <package-name> v1.1.0
```

Modules enable developers to monitor exact versions of dependencies, guaranteeing that builds are consistent across machines, environments, and CI/CD pipelines. Instead of relying on global paths or shared workspaces, every project maintains its own dependency graph, making the build process more portable, and deterministic. This aligns with Go's philosophy of simplicity and clarity–developers always know exactly what version of a library is being used and how it fits into the project.

Managing Dependencies

Go modules use a "minimal version selection" mechanism. When a developer imports a new package, the module system fetches the minimum required version that satisfies all constraints. This avoids dependency explosions and reduces unexpected breakages seen in other ecosystems.

Some of the dependency commands are as follows:

```
go get example-url.com/lib@v2.3.0   # Add or update a dependency
go mod tidy                        # Remove unused dependencies, add
                                     missing ones
go mod vendor                      # Vendor dependencies locally
```

With modules, the Go compiler ensures that:

- Builds use the exact versions specified in go.mod.
- Results are reproducible across operating systems and machines.
- The dependency graph remains stable unless explicitly modified.

This reliability is particularly important in production-grade Go systems, such as microservices, distributed systems, and command-line tools where stable builds are critical.

Nested Modules and Multi-Module Repos

Large organizations sometimes use monorepos containing multiple modules. Go supports this through nested module directories, each with its own **`go.mod`**. This separation promotes clearer boundaries and avoids unintended cross-dependencies.

The module system strongly encourages Semantic Versioning (SemVer). Major version changes require either:

a /v2, /v3, ... suffix in the module path or, a new module path entirely

Custom Packages

While Go's standard library provides a powerful foundation, real-world applications typically require organizing functionality into custom packages. Creating your own packages allows you to break large codebases into smaller, focused modules that are easier to maintain, test, and reuse. Go's package system encourages clean boundaries, explicit dependencies, and clear control over what is exposed to other parts of a program.

Custom packages help achieve:

- **Modularity:** Group related types, functions, constants, and interfaces.
- **Encapsulation:** Control visibility with exported (uppercase) and unexported (lowercase) identifiers.
- **Reusability:** To create building blocks that can be used across multiple applications.

- **Maintainability:** Split large codebases into coherent layers (such as **auth**, **storage**, **config**, **utils**).

By structuring code into well-defined packages, Go push developers towards clean architecture and separation of concerns.

Creating a Custom Package

A custom package is a directory containing one or more **.go** files, each beginning with the same package clause. You can follow along the example to create a custom Go Package:

The directory structure will look like:

```
project/
    main.go
    mathutils/
        add.go
        subtract.go
```

The first file is the **add.go** file. This has the functionality to sum two numbers. The file looks like:

```
package mathutils

func Add(a, b int) int {
    return a + b
}
```

The second file is the **subtract.go** file which takes care of the difference of two numbers. The file is implemented as:

```
package mathutils

func Subtract(a, b int) int {
    return a - b
}
```

Both files belong to the **mathutils** package. Any exported identifiers (those beginning with a capital letter) are visible to other packages that import it.

To use this custom package, import it using its module path (not the relative directory path).

In **main.go**:

```
package main

import (
    "fmt"
```

```
        "project/mathutils"
    )

    func main() {
        fmt.Println(mathutils.Add(10, 5))
        fmt.Println(mathutils.Subtract(10, 5))
    }
```

Go requires that files and imports follow module-aware paths. This ensures that tooling such as **`go build`** and **`go test`** can locate dependencies reliably.

Organizing Packages Effectively

Good package design involves more than scattering code across different directories–it requires deliberate decisions about structure, naming, abstraction, and dependency flow. Well-organized packages make a Go codebase easier to understand, extend, and maintain over time. The following guidelines represent the best widely accepted practices in the Go ecosystem.

Package Focus

Each package should have a single responsibility.

Examples of a good design:

- **`Config`**: Configuration data loading and parsing
- **`auth`**: Authentication logic
- **`storage`**: Database access
- **`httpserver`**: HTTP handlers and routing

Avoid:

- "Junk drawer" packages like **`utils`** with unrelated helpers.
- Deep, complex nested hierarchies.

Package Names

Go encourage short, concise, and meaningful package names:

Preferred names:

- bytes
- json
- strings
- cache

Names which can be avoided:

- stringhelpers
- myawesomepackage
- processingmodulev2

Package names should be in lowercase, single-word, and convey purpose.

Avoid Circular Dependencies

Go does not allow cycles between packages.

Example of a problematic structure:

```
package p1 imports p2
package p2 imports p1
```

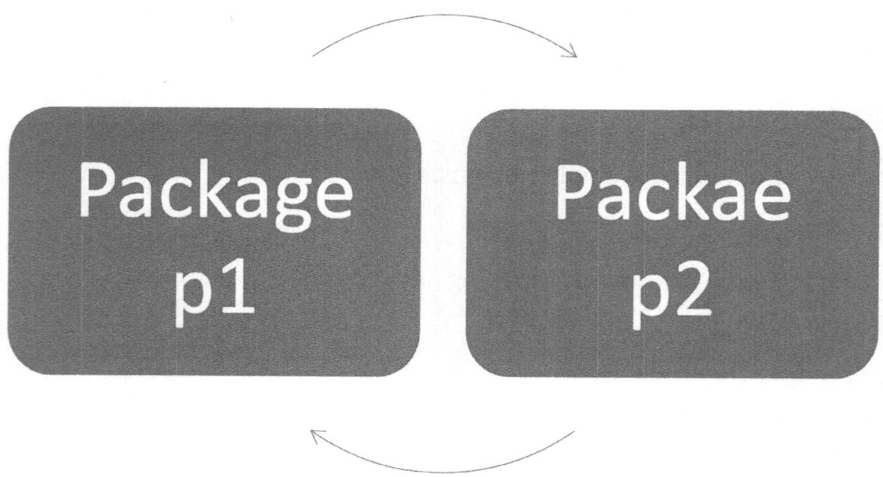

Figure 3.3: *Cyclic Package Dependency*

Effective package design ensures that dependencies flow in one direction, often by defining interfaces to decouple modules and separate concerns. Each package should encapsulate a single, well-defined responsibility, abstracting its logic behind a stable API. This structure improves clarity, reduces coupling, and avoids circular dependencies, which Go explicitly prohibits.

Building, Installing, Testing, Versioning, and Publishing Custom Packages

Creating a custom package is only the first step in delivering reusable Go functionality. Once a package is organized into a coherent structure, developers must understand how to build, install, test, version, and publish their work using Go's toolchain and module system. These activities are essential not only for internal development within a single codebase, but also for distributing libraries across teams or publishing them to the open-source community. This section explores these processes in depth, focusing on how Go's tooling simplifies the lifecycle of a package—from local development to public release.

Building Custom Packages

After defining the package and its exported identifiers, the next step is compiling the code. The build system of Go operates at the package level, automatically resolving module dependencies and determining the order of compilation.

The **`go build`** command compiles a package into an executable (if **`package main`**) or verifies that a library package compiles correctly.

For example, consider the following custom package:

```
// mathutil/mathutil.go
package mathutil

// Add returns the sum of two integers.
func Add(a, b int) int {
    return a + b
}
```

To build all packages within the module, a developer can run:

```
go build ./...
```

This command recurses through the module, compiling each package to ensure correctness. For library packages, no binary is created by default; instead, Go verifies that all files type- is checked and build successfully.

Installing Custom Packages

Go allows developers to install executables built from **`main`** packages into the system's binary directory (usually **`$GOBIN`** or **`$GOPATH/bin`**). Although library packages are not "installed" in the traditional sense, they become available in the module cache, once downloaded or referenced.

For example, if the developer adds a command that uses the earlier package:

```
package main

import (
    "fmt"
    "example.com/mathutil"
```

```
)

func main() {
    fmt.Println(mathutil.Add(2, 3))
}
```

Running:

```
go install ./cmd/calc
```

It produces a binary named calc, which can be executed from the command line. This workflow is common when packages support CLI tools or microservices.

Testing Custom Packages

Testing is a first-class component of Go development. Every package can include files ending in **_test.go** that define unit tests, benchmarks, and examples. This structure ensures that every package is validated independently.

Consider a test for the **Add** function:

```
package mathutil

import "testing"

func TestAdd(t *testing.T) {
    result := Add(20, 10)
    if result != 30 {
        t.Errorf("Expected 30, got %d", result)
    }
}
```

Running Tests:

```
go test ./...
```

This command executes all tests across all packages. Go automatically detects test files and organizes them into test binaries.

Testing Philosophy in Go

Go encourages:

- Short, isolated tests that validate small units of functionality.
- Clear error messages.
- Deterministic behavior.
- Same-package tests for internal logic, and external tests using **package mypkg_test** when testing only exported APIs.

The simplicity of the testing framework encourages thorough testing of custom packages before publishing.

Versioning Custom Packages

Versioning is essential when distributing packages to external users. Go Modules use Semantic Versioning (`SemVer`), which encodes compatibility guarantees into version numbers:

```
vMAJOR.MINOR.PATCH
```

- **MAJOR:** Incompatible changes.
- **MINOR:** Backward-compatible additions.
- **PATCH:** Bug fixes only.

For example:

```
v1.0.0   // first stable release
v1.1.0   // new features, no breaking changes
v2.0.0   // breaking changes
```

Setting a Version Tag

If the package repository is hosted on GitHub:

```
git tag v1.0.0
git push origin v1.0.0
```

Once tagged, users can add:

```
go get github.com/example/mathutil@v1.0.0
```

Go automatically resolves the module version and stores it in the module cache.

Publishing Custom Packages

Publishing a package makes it available for consumption by other developers, teams, or the Go community. The process involves:

1. Hosting the repository (GitHub, GitLab, Bitbucket, AWS CodeCommit, and so forth).
2. Ensuring the module path matches the repository URL.
3. Tagging releases following semantic versioning.
4. Allowing users to import the package via:

```
import "github.com/example/mathutil"
```

Repository Structure for Publishing

A typical published Go library might follow:

```
mathutil/
    go.mod
    mathutil.go
    mathutil_test.go
README.md
LICENSE
```

A clear **README** and license are essential for publicly distributed packages.

Module Discovery

For module discovery the following command initiates it:

```
go get github.com/example/mathutil
```

Once executed, Go will follow the following sequence of events:

1. Query the repository.
2. Fetch the module.
3. Verify tags and versions.
4. Add the module to the dependency graph.

The module proxy system of Go speeds up downloads, caches modules, and ensures immutability of published versions.

File Handling Using os, io, and bufio

Efficient file handling is a fundamental capability in Go, enabling applications to read, write, and manipulate files with precision and performance. The standard library of Go provides a well-structured collection of packages—primarily **os**, **io**, and **bufio**—that work together to deliver a flexible and powerful file-handling ecosystem. Each package serves a distinct purpose: **os** manages interaction with the operating system; **io** defines core interfaces for data streaming; and, **bufio** introduces buffering to improve I/O efficiency.

The os Package: Low-Level File Operations

The **os** package provides the foundational tools for interacting directly with the operating system's file system. It allows developers to create files, open existing ones, remove files, and inspect metadata—operations essential for controlling file lifecycle and structure.

Opening and Creating Files

os.Open opens a file in read-only mode, while **os.Create** creates or truncates a file for writing. Both return an ***os.Filevalue**, which implements key interfaces such as **io.Reader**, **io.Writer**, and **io.Closer**.

```
file, err := os.Open("data.txt")
if err != nil {
    // handle error
}
defer file.Close()
file, err := os.Create("output.txt")
if err != nil {
    // handle error
}
defer file.Close()
```

File Permissions and Flags

For more granular control, developers may use **os.OpenFile**, which accepts Unix-style permission bits and flags such as **os.O_RDONLY**, **os.O_WRONLY**, **os.O_CREATE**, and **os.O_APPEND**.

```
file, err := os.OpenFile("app.log", os.O_APPEND|os.O_CREATE|os.O_
WRONLY, 0644)
```

File Metadata

Functions like **file.Stat()** provide metadata including file size, modification time, and permissions.

The io Package: Core I/O Abstractions

While **os** handles system-level file operations, the io package defines the standard interfaces used across Go for reading and writing streams of data. These interfaces include:

- **io.Reader**: It reads data into a byte slice.
- **io.Writer**: This writes data from a byte slice.
- **io.Closer**: It closes resources.
- **io.ReaderAt, io.WriterAt**: This reads/writes at specific offsets.
- **io.Copy**: It copies data between sources and destinations.

Streaming Reads and Writes

Since **`*os.File`** implements **`io.Reader`** and **`io.Writer`**, it integrates seamlessly with higher-level functions.

```
n, err := io.Copy(dst, src)
```

This pattern allows the same abstractions to work for files, network connections, in-memory buffers, and more.

The bufio Package: Buffered I/O for Performance

Unbuffered reading and writing—especially on large files—can lead to performance bottlenecks. The **bufio** package wraps **`io.Reader`** and **`io.Writer`** types with internal buffers, significantly improving efficiency by reducing the number of system calls.

Buffered Reading

`bufio.NewReader` provides methods such as **`ReadString`**, **`ReadBytes`**, and **`ReadLine`** for convenient text processing.

```
reader := bufio.NewReader(file)
line, err := reader.ReadString('\n')
```

Buffered Writing

`bufio.NewWriter` accumulates data in memory before flushing it to disk.

```
writer := bufio.NewWriter(file)
writer.WriteString("Hello, World!")
writer.Flush()
```

Scanner for Line-by-Line Reading

`bufio.Scanner` simplifies reading input line by line—ideal for logs, configuration files, or structured text.

```
scanner := bufio.NewScanner(file)
for scanner.Scan() {
    fmt.Println(scanner.Text())
}
```

How These Packages Work Together

A typical file-handling workflow combines the strengths of all three packages:

- Use **os** to open or create the file.
- Use **bufio** to wrap the file in a buffered reader or writer.
- Use **io** utilities, such as **io.Copy**, to stream data efficiently between sources.

Having a layered design gives the developer a complete control over the performance, readability, and resource management.

```
src, _ := os.Open("input.txt")
dst, _ := os.Create("output.txt")

buffered := bufio.NewWriter(dst)
io.Copy(buffered, src)
buffered.Flush()
```

Here, **io.Copy** handles the data transfer, while **bufio** optimizes the write operations.

Error Handling and Resource Management

Proper error checking is essential. The idiomatic patterns of Go include:

- Checking every returned error.
- Using **defer file.Close()** immediately after opening.
- Validating scanner errors using **scanner.Err()**.
- Flushing buffered writers to prevent data loss.

These patterns ensure that file operations behave predictably under failure conditions.

Choosing the Right Approach

The choice between **os, io,** and **bufio** depends on the workload.

- **Use os when:**
    - You need low-level control over file modes, flags, or metadata.
    - You are managing the file lifecycle (creation, deletion, renaming).
- **Use io when:**
    - You want generic, composable operations across streams.
    - You need efficient copying or transformations.

- **Use bufio when:**
  - You expect many small reads or writes.
  - You need high-level convenience functions such as line scanning.

Logging and Formatting with `fmt` and `log`

Formatting text output and generating structured logs are the essential tasks in any Go application, whether developers are debugging programs, producing command-line output, or monitoring production systems. Go's standard library provides two key packages–**`fmt`** and **`log`**–each designed for different layers of application output. While **`fmt`** focuses on human-readable formatting and printing, **`log`** provides structured, timestamped messages suitable for debugging and operational monitoring. Understanding how, and when to use each package helps developers maintain clarity, consistency, and reliability across their Go applications.

The `fmt` Package: Human-Readable Formatting

The **`fmt`** package offers a rich set of functions for formatting strings, printing values, and displaying data structures in a readable way. It is commonly used for CLI output, quick debugging, text generation, and formatting values with precision.

Printing to Standard Output

The most frequently used functions include:

- **`fmt.Print()`**: It prints text without a trailing newline.
- **`fmt.Println()`**: This prints text with automatic spacing and a newline.
- **`fmt.Printf()`**: It prints formatted text using verbs.

Examples:

```
fmt.Println("Server started on port", port)
fmt.Printf("User: %s, Age: %d\n", name, age)
```

Formatting Verbs

The **`fmt`** package provides formatting verbs for strings (**`%s`**), integers (**`%d`**), floats (**`%f`**), types (**`%T`**), and structures (**`%+v`**, **`%#v`**). These verbs give developers fine-grained control over how data is presented.

```
fmt.Printf("Coordinates: x=%d, y=%d\n", point.X, point.Y)
fmt.Printf("Struct details: %+v\n", config)
```

Creating Formatted Strings

When the output is needed without immediate printing, **`fmt.Sprintf()`** returns a formatted string.

```
message := fmt.Sprintf("Processing file: %s", filename)
```

This is especially useful in logging systems, templating, and UI rendering.

The Log Package: Structured Logging for Applications

While **`fmt`** focuses on general formatting, the **`log`** package provides features tailored for application-level logging. By default, it writes messages to standard error with timestamps, making logs clearer, and more useful for debugging and observability.

Basic Logging

```
log.Println("Application started")
log.Printf("Loaded configuration: %s", configPath)
```

Each log entry includes:

- A timestamp
- The log message
- A newline

This makes it immediately suitable for production environments.

Log Fatal and Panic

The **`log`** package also provides functions for handling critical errors:

- **`log.Fatal()`**: It logs the message and exits the program.
- **`log.Panic()`**: This logs the message and triggers a panic.

```
if err != nil {
    log.Fatal("Failed to initialize database:", err)
}
```

These functions help ensure that runtime failures are captured with clear visibility.

Customizing Log Output

In Go development, you can customize log formatting using flags:

- **`log.Ldate`**

- **`log.Ltime`**
- **`log.Lshortfile,`** and the list continues.

```
log.SetFlags(log.Ldate | log.Ltime | log.Lshortfile)
```

You can also direct logs to files:

```
file, _ := os.Create("app.log")
log.SetOutput(file)
```

This is useful for CLI tools, servers, and background services that require persistent logs.

Choosing between `fmt` and `log`

Although both packages support printing and formatting, each has a specific role:

Use `fmt` when:

- Output is intended for user-facing CLI messages.
- You are formatting plain strings or generating structured text.
- Logs do not need timestamps or severity levels.

Use `log` when:

- You are capturing operational or runtime events.
- You need timestamps, metadata, or output redirection.
- You want consistent logging across multiple packages or services.

Integrating Logging with Other Go Components

Logging becomes especially valuable when combined with features such as:

- Goroutines (capturing concurrency-related failures)
- Web servers (request/response logs)
- File handling (logging read/write operations)
- Networking (connection failures and retries)

Dependency Management with Go Modules

Go modules provide a modern, reliable way to manage dependencies, eliminating the old GOPATH system, and enabling consistent builds across different machines. A module is a compilation of Go packages anchored by a go.mod file. It documents the module path and its requisite dependencies.

A module begins with a **go.mod** file:

```
module github.com/drishti/myapp

go 1.22

require (
    github.com/google/uuid v1.5.0
)
```

Here, Go records the module name, language version, and external dependencies.

- **Initializing a Module**

  To start a module:

  `go mod init myapp`

  Or, for published projects, follow this command:

  `go mod init github.com/yourname/project`

  Once initialized, Go automatically updates **go.mod** and **go.sum** whenever you add or modify imports.

- **Adding, Updating, and Tidying Dependencies**

  Just import a package:

  `import "github.com/google/uuid"`

  Then run:

  `go build`

  Go will fetch the dependency and update **go.mod**.

- **Updating a Dependency**

  `go get github.com/google/uuid@latest`

- **Cleaning up Unused Entries**

  `go mod tidy`

  This ensures that your module files match your actual code.

- **go.sum: Ensuring Integrity**

  The **go.sum** file stores cryptographic checksums for every dependency version your project uses. Go verifies these checksums during builds, guaranteeing reproducible and tamper-free dependency retrieval.

  The **go.mod** and **go.sum** must be committed to version control.

- **Replace Directives (Local Development)**

  The `replace` directive lets you swap a dependency with a local version:

  ```
  replace github.com/example/math => ../local-math
  ```

  This is useful for testing changes across multiple modules without publishing new versions.

- **Building and Reproducibility**

  Go modules make builds consistent:

  - All dependencies are versioned.
  - Checksums prevent unexpected changes.
  - Go automatically downloads what you need.

  This ensures that your project builds the same way for everyone.

- **Publishing Modules**

  To publish a reusable module:

  - Push the repository to a hosting service.
  - Tag a version:

    ```
    git tag v1.0.0
    git push origin v1.0.0
    ```

  Go will then make the module available via its proxy network.

- **Semantic Versioning**

  Modules follow semantic versioning:

  - `vMAJOR`: Breaking changes
  - `vMINOR`: New features, no breaks
  - `vPATCH`: Bug fixes

  For major versions above 1, the version must appear in the module path:

  ```
  module github.com/yourname/project/v2
  ```

  This prevents accidental breaking changes.

AI-Assisted Refactoring and Code Suggestions

As Go applications keep growing in scale and complexity, refactoring becomes a crucial practice for improving readability, performance, and maintainability. Modern AI-assisted coding tools–such as ChatGPT, GitHub Copilot, and Amazon Q Developer (formerly CodeWhisperer)– play an increasingly valuable role in this process. These tools do more than generate snippets; they analyze existing code, detect structural issues, and propose targeted improvements that align with Go's idioms and best practices. By understanding program context, dependency patterns, and common pitfalls, AI systems can suggest cleaner abstractions, more efficient algorithms, and safer concurrency models.

AI-driven refactoring is particularly powerful in Go because of the language's strong emphasis on clarity, simplicity, and orthogonal design principles. Assistants can identify overly long functions, unnecessary coupling between packages, misuse of goroutines, or verbose implementations that could be simplified using Go's built-in features. As a result, developers gain not only cleaner code, but also a deeper insight into the Go's design philosophy. AI tools complement human judgment, allowing developers to maintain control over architectural decisions while benefiting from automated pattern recognition, and knowledge distilled from thousands of real-world Go repositories.

Several detailed examples illustrating how AI assistants help refactor Go code more effectively, are elucidated in the following section.

Refactoring Multi-Responsibility Functions into Modular Components

AI tools excel at detecting functions that perform too many operations–a common violation of Go's single-responsibility principle. Consider the following initial implementation:

Before (Original Code)

```
func ProcessUser(name string, age int) error {
    if name == "" || age <= 0 {
        return fmt.Errorf("invalid input")
    }

    processed := strings.ToUpper(name) + fmt.Sprintf("_%d", age)

    f, err := os.Create("output.txt")
    if err != nil {
        return err
    }
    defer f.Close()

    _, err = f.WriteString(processed)
    if err != nil {
```

```
        return err
    }

    return nil
}
```

AI quickly identifies that validation, processing, and I/O tasks are mixed together. It proposes a cleaner, and a modular structure.

AI-Refactored Version

```
func ValidateUser(name string, age int) error {
    if name == "" || age <= 0 {
        return fmt.Errorf("invalid input")
    }
    return nil
}

func ProcessUserData(name string, age int) string {
    return strings.ToUpper(name) + fmt.Sprintf("_%d", age)
}

func WriteToFile(filename, data string) error {
    f, err := os.Create(filename)
    if err != nil {
        return err
    }
    defer f.Close()

    _, err = f.WriteString(data)
    return err
}

func ProcessUser(name string, age int) error {
    if err := ValidateUser(name, age); err != nil {
        return err
    }

    data := ProcessUserData(name, age)
    return WriteToFile("output.txt", data)
}
```

AI-Generated Improvements

- Functions are now reusable and testable.
- Each function has a clear responsibility.

- File operations are isolated for better error handling.
- Follows idiomatic Go modular design.

Improving Algorithmic Efficiency by Rewriting Recursive Functions

AI assistants frequently detect performance bottlenecks, especially expensive recursion.

Before (Recursive Fibonacci)

```
func Fib(n int) int {
    if n <= 1 {
        return n
    }
    return Fib(n-1) + Fib(n-2)
}
```

This implementation is elegant, but inefficient (exponential time).

AI-Refactored Version (Iterative)

```
func Fib(n int) int {
    if n <= 1 {
        return n
    }

    a, b := 0, 1
    for i := 2; i <= n; i++ {
        a, b = b, a+b
    }
    return b
}
```

AI-Generated Improvements

- Eliminates redundant recursive calls.
- Converts to an **`O(n)`** iterative solution.
- Reduces stack pressure and prevents overflow.

Detecting Concurrency Issues and Preventing Goroutine Leaks

Concurrency is a core strength of Go, but misuse of goroutines or channels can lead to leaks. AI tools can identify missing cancellation paths or improper synchronization.

Before (Potential Goroutine Leak)

```
func QueryData(ch chan string) {
    go func() {
        data := fetchFromDB()
        ch <- data
    }()
}
```

If **`fetchFromDB()`** hangs or the channel is not being read, the goroutine may leak.

AI-Refactored Version

```
func QueryData(ctx context.Context, ch chan<- string) {
    go func() {
        select {
        case <-ctx.Done():
            return
        case ch <- fetchFromDB():
        }
    }()
}
```

AI-Generated Improvements

- Introduces **`context.Context`** for cancellation.
- Avoids blocked channel writes.
- Ensures safe goroutine termination.

Reducing Parameter Clutter by Introducing Config Structs

AI can detect noisy function signatures that become error-prone or, hard to maintain.

Before (Too Many Parameters)

```
func CreateAccount(name string, email string, phone string, age
int, active bool) *Account {
    return &Account{name, email, phone, age, active}
}
```

AI-Refactored Version

```
type AccountOptions struct {
    Name   string
    Email  string
    Phone  string
    Age    int
    Active bool
}

func CreateAccount(opt AccountOptions) *Account {
    return &Account{
        Name:   opt.Name,
        Email:  opt.Email,
        Phone:  opt.Phone,
        Age:    opt.Age,
        Active: opt.Active,
    }
}
```

AI-Generated Improvements

- Reduces parameter order mistakes.
- Supports extensibility without breaking existing code.
- Promotes clarity and idiomatic API design.

Resolving Cyclic Dependencies across Packages

Circular dependencies violate Go's modularity rules and prevent builds. AI tools detect these patterns and propose interface-based refactoring.

Before (Circular Imports)

```
package user
import "myapp/auth"

package auth
import "myapp/user"
```

AI-Refactored Version

```
// In package auth:
type UserFetcher interface {
    GetUser(id string) (*User, error)
```

```
}

func Authenticate(fetcher UserFetcher, id string) error {
    user, err := fetcher.GetUser(id)
    if err != nil {
        return err
    }
    // authentication logic
    return nil
}
```

AI-Generated Improvements

- Removes cycles using dependency inversion.
- Provides a clean seam for testing with mocks.
- Preserves package responsibilities.

How AI Enhances Go Refactoring

Across all examples, AI tools consistently help developers:

- **Enforce Idiomatic Go Patterns**

  Such as proper error handling, clean package boundaries, and predictable concurrency.

- **Propose Structural Improvements Instead of Localized Edits**

  AI can detect that a function should be split—or that a file should be reorganized—not just rewritten line by line.

- **Identify Common Go Pitfalls**

  Examples include nil pointer dereferences, goroutine leaks, unchecked errors, and inefficient loops.

- **Suggest Architecture-Level Enhancements**

  AI can transform recursive solutions into iterative ones, introduce interfaces for abstraction, and simplify complex control flows.

Conclusion

This chapter has explored how Go encourages clean, modular, and maintainable code through its function and package system. You learned how functions form the core building blocks of Go programs—including parameters, multiple return values, recursion, variadic arguments, and anonymous functions that enable flexible, functional-style patterns. We then expanded into the modular structure of Go with packages and modules, understanding how package clauses, imports, naming conventions, exported identifiers, and directory layout shape a project's architecture.

You have also examined Go's deterministic initialization process–how dependencies load recursively, how package-level variables are evaluated, and how **`init()`** functions execute. The chapter covered how Go modules manage dependencies, ensure reproducible builds, and support versioning across single or multi-module repositories. You practiced creating custom packages, organizing them effectively, and building, testing, versioning, and publishing them using the toolchain of Go.

Finally, the chapter introduced essential file-handling concepts using **`os`**, **`io`**, and **bufio**, along with logging utilities from **`fmt`** and **`log`**. With these foundations–and AI-assisted tooling to support refactoring and structure–you now have the skills to build well-organized, scalable Go applications.

In the next chapter, we will look into the error model of Go, its debugging tools, and runtime insights, that work together to create robust, predictable, and production-ready applications.

CHAPTER 4
Error Handling and Debugging in Go

Introduction

Go treats reliability as a core part of software design, favouring clear, explicit mechanisms for handling of failures and diagnosing issues. Instead of traditional exceptions, Go uses simple error values, controlled panic-recovery flows, and well-structured logging, to help developers understand and manage unexpected behaviour. This chapter introduces these foundational concepts, and demonstrates how Go's error model, debugging tools, and runtime insights work together to create robust, predictable, and production-ready applications. AI-assisted tools are also introduced as powerful aids for interpreting failures, optimizing error paths, and strengthening the overall software resilience.

Structure

In this chapter, we will cover the following topics:

- Introduction to the Error Philosophy of Go
  - Errors as Values: A Foundational Idea
  - Explicit Error Propagation
  - Avoiding the Pitfall of Over-Reliance on Exceptions
  - Simplicity over Magic
  - The Impact on Software Reliability
- Understanding the Error Type of Go
  - The Error Interface
  - Creating Basic Errors
  - Custom Error Types for Richer Context
  - Errors as First-Class Return Values

  - Errors as Behaviour, Not Just Messages
- Idiomatic Error Handling Techniques
  - The Explicit Error Check
  - Creating and Wrapping Contextual Errors
- Panic, Defer, and Recover: Controlled Failure Handling
  - Panic: Signalling an Unexpected Failure
  - Defer: Ensuring Cleanup and Resource Finalization
  - Recover: Regaining Control after a Panic
  - Panic, Defer and Recover, Working Together
- Logging, Structured Errors, Runtime Pitfalls, and Debugging
  - Logging for Clarity and Diagnostics
  - Structured Errors with `errors` and `fmt`
  - Common Runtime Pitfalls
  - Debugging Techniques and Tooling in Go
- AI-Assisted Debugging and Reliability Improvement
  - Using AI Tools to Analyze Error-Prone Code Paths
  - Detecting Concurrency Bugs with AI
  - AI-Enhanced Panic Analysis
  - LLM-Driven Error Wrapping and Observability Improvements
  - Automated Refactoring for Reliability
  - AI for Predictive Debugging and Proactive Reliability
  - Integrating AI-Assisted Debugging into the Go Workflow

Introduction to the Error Philosophy of Go

Error handling sits at the center of Go's design philosophy. Unlike the languages that rely on exceptions and implicit control flow, Go embraces a model where errors are values: first-class, explicit, and visible in the function signatures that developers work with every day. This approach may feel unusual to the newcomers, but it creates a culture of clarity and predictability that aligns with Go's goals of simplicity, maintainability, and robust system-level programming.

At its core, the error philosophy of Go reflects three guiding principles:

- Errors are a part of normal execution, not exceptional events.
- Handling errors should be explicit and unambiguous.

- Error paths must be as readable and maintainable as success paths.

Understanding these principles is essential to writing idiomatic, production-grade Go applications.

Why Go Rejects Exceptions

Many mainstream languages–Java, Python, C++, JavaScript–use exceptions as the primary mechanism for a failure propagation. These systems let developers throw an exception in one location and catch it elsewhere, potentially many layers deeper in the call stack. While powerful, this model introduces a hidden control flow, and can make it difficult to reason about a program's behavior without scanning the entire call tree.

Go intentionally avoids this:

- No try/catch blocks.
- No stack-unwinding semantics.
- No separation between "normal" and "exceptional" errors.

The creators of Go wanted a language where reading a function gives you a complete picture of both success and failure behavior. By returning errors explicitly, Go ensures that anyone reading the signature of a function knows exactly what can go wrong, and what must be handled.

This intentional simplicity is one of the reasons Go is a foundation for cloud systems, distributed infrastructure, and microservices–domains, where predictability and stability matter far more than clever abstractions.

Errors as Values: A Foundational Idea

Go treats errors as simple values that implement the built-in error interface:

```
type error interface {
    Error() string
}
```

This design enables several powerful patterns:

- Errors can be constructed, wrapped, returned, or ignored–just like any other value.
- Libraries can define custom error types with extra metadata.
- Developers can perform error comparison, inspection, and unwrapping using standard utilities.

Most importantly, treating errors as values shall force developers into confronting failure cases directly. Instead of dreading exceptions thrown at runtime, Go encourages writing control flow around the failure paths from the beginning.

Explicit Error Propagation

Idiomatic Go error handling centers on a simple pattern:

```
result, err := doSomething()
if err != nil {
    return err
}
```

This repetitive pattern has drawn criticism from developers who are used to exception-based systems. But, the repetition is a deliberate trade-off: it ensures that errors can never silently bubble up the stack without the developer's awareness.

Some advantages include:

- **Local Reasoning**: You see exactly where errors originate and where they go.
- **Predictable Flow**: No hidden jumps or non-local exits from functions.
- **Consistent Style**: Teams follow shared conventions automatically.

This approach leads to code that is easier to review, maintain, and audit—especially in large codebases and safety-critical systems.

Avoiding the Pitfall of Over-Reliance on Exceptions

Languages with exceptions often encourage patterns like:

- Throwing exceptions for minor or expected failures.
- Catching exceptions too broadly.
- Allowing exceptions to propagate accidentally.
- Mixing business logic with exception handling.

The result is frequently fragile software that behaves unpredictably in edge cases.

Go's design explicitly avoids this by making error handling:

- **Predictable**, because every error is returned explicitly.
- **Local**, because errors must be addressed or forwarded immediately.
- **Transparent**, because no hidden control flow exists.

This leads to software that behaves consistently in production and is easier to reason about in large, distributed systems.

Simplicity over Magic

The philosophy of Go prioritizes readability over cleverness:

- No implicit stack unwinding.
- No special "exception" zones.
- No `try/catch/finally` constructs.
- No destructors or automatic cleanup logic.

Instead, Go gives developers simple primitives:

- Explicit errors
- defer for cleanup
- panic/recover for truly exceptional cases

Strong conventions are shared across the entire ecosystem. These primitives compose well and scale predictably.

By avoiding magic, Go ensures that even deeply complex systems can be understood by reading the code line-by-line—an invaluable property for debugging and reliability.

The Impact on Software Reliability

The error philosophy of Go directly contributes to system stability:

- Failing operations are handled immediately.
- Errors include contextual information.
- Callers can wrap errors to preserve the stack context.
- Monitoring systems receive structured, meaningful messages.
- Developers naturally write retry logic, fallbacks, and cleanup steps.

Because errors are explicit, Go codebases typically have:

- Fewer uncaught failures;
- More consistent error semantics;
- Clearer logging and observability patterns; and,
- Easier integration with SRE practices.

This makes Go popular in companies building large-scale distributed software organizations.

Understanding the Error Type of Go

At the heart of the error handling model of Go, is the built-in **error** type—an interface so minimal, that at first glance it appears deceptively simple. Yet, this simplicity is intentional: Go treats errors as descriptive values, and not as exceptional control-flow constructs, enabling developers to write clear, controlled, and predictable failure-handling logic.

This section explains the mechanics of the **error** type, how it enables idiomatic error handling, and why it forms the foundation of Go's philosophy of robustness.

The Error Interface

Go defines **error** as a built-in interface:

```
type error interface {
    Error() string
}
```

Any type that implements the **Error()** string method automatically satisfies this interface. This means you can represent errors using:

- Standard library error values
- Custom struct types
- Sentinel values
- Wrapped errors
- Dynamically generated messages

By treating errors as interfaces, rather than opaque exception objects, Go allows developers to craft flexible, descriptive, and domain-specific error types.

Creating Basic Errors

The simplest way to create an error is using the errors package:

```
import "errors"

var ErrNotFound = errors.New("resource not found")
```

This creates a sentinel error—a stable, reusable error value that can be compared directly.

Sentinel errors are commonly used for well-known failure states, such as:

- **io.EOF**
- **http.ErrNoCookie**

- Custom domain-specific conditions

They allow an easy comparison:

```
if err == ErrNotFound {
    // handle specifically
}
```

However, for more complex use cases, Go supports richer error types.

Custom Error Types for Richer Context

Since an error is just an interface, you can attach structured data to it:

```
type ParseError struct {
    Line int
    Msg  string
}

func (e *ParseError) Error() string {
    return fmt.Sprintf("parse error on line %d: %s", e.Line, e.Msg)
}
```

Custom errors are indispensable when:

- You want to include metadata (line numbers, file names, user IDs).
- You need more expressive logging or debugging information.
- Error-handling logic varies based on the type of error.

Custom types also make the error inspection straightforward:

```
var pe *ParseError
if errors.As(err, &pe) {
    fmt.Println("Error on line:", pe.Line)
}
```

This pattern enables production-grade error diagnostics without sacrificing readability.

Errors as First-Class Return Values

In Go, a function that may fail typically returns this signature:

```
func doWork() (Result, error)
```

The caller must inspect the error:

```
res, err := doWork()
if err != nil {
    return err
}
```

For dynamic errors that include runtime information, Go provides **`fmt.Errorf`**:

```
err := fmt.Errorf("failed to process %s: %w", filename, cause)
```

The **`%w`** verb allows error wrapping, preserving the underlying error for later retrieval.

This enables a stack-like accumulation of context, while still preserving structured inspection:

```
if errors.Is(err, os.ErrNotExist) {
    // underlying error is still detectable
}
```

Error wrapping is essential for debugging large systems, where errors from deep within the call stack must carry enough context to diagnose the issue without exposing low-level details to the user.

Go provides two key functions:

- **`errors.Is`**

  This checks for error equivalence. The command is as follows:

  ```
  if errors.Is(err, ErrNotFound) {
      // true if err == ErrNotFound or wraps it
  }
  ```

- **`errors.As`**

  It extracts specific error types. The command is as follows:

  ```
  var pe *ParseError
  if errors.As(err, &pe) {
      fmt.Println(pe.Line)
  }
  ```

These utilities replace the fragile string matching, and make error handling more precise and maintainable.

Why Go Uses Strings for Error Messages

A common question:

*Why does the **`Error()`** method return a string instead of a structured type?*

The answer lies in the design goals set be Go:

- Errors should be human-readable.
- Errors should be log-friendly.
- Errors should carry meaning, even without additional context.

- Developers should be free to add metadata through custom types when needed.

By default, Go keeps error messages simple, but never restricts developers from extending them.

Errors as Behaviour, Not Just Messages

Because errors are interfaces, new behaviours can be attached through methods. Consider an error that suggests the retry behaviour:

```
type RetryableError struct {
    Err error
}

func (r *RetryableError) Error() string {
    return r.Err.Error()
}

func (r *RetryableError) Retryable() bool {
    return true
}
```

This pattern allows error-driven logic:

```
var r *RetryableError
if errors.As(err, &r) && r.Retryable() {
    retry()
}
```

This turns errors into powerful decision-making tools without violating the simplicity of Go.

Readable errors are crucial in production as they have:

- Log aggregation systems rely on them.
- Monitoring pipelines identify patterns within them.
- SREs depend on them to detect regressions.
- AI-assisted debugging tools analyze them for diagnosis.

Since Go errors are simple strings, they integrate seamlessly with the existing observability stacks.

Later sections in this chapter will show how to format structured error messages, embed metadata, and integrate errors with logging.

Idiomatic Error Handling Techniques

Idiomatic error handling in Go emphasizes clarity, explicit control flow, and predictable program behaviour. Rather than relying on exceptions, or implicit propagation mechanisms, Go requires errors to be treated as ordinary values—returned, inspected, and acted upon at each step in a function's execution. This design encourages disciplined thinking around failure paths, and contributes directly to the language's emphasis on robustness and readability. This section examines the standard patterns used throughout Go codebases to manage errors effectively and consistently.

The Explicit Error Check

The most recognizable feature of Go's error philosophy is the explicit **`if err != nil`** check. This pattern appears throughout the standard library, and serves as the primary mechanism for determining whether an operation has failed.

```
value, err := compute()
if err != nil {
    return err
}
```

This construct makes error handling both visible and immediate. Instead of hiding failures behind exception frames or asynchronous handlers, Go requires that each potential error be confronted directly. As a result, the reader of the code gains a clear understanding of every point where execution might diverge due to a failure.

One of the most effective idioms in Go is the early return. By handling errors at the moment they occur, the functions avoid unnecessary nesting, and remain easier to read:

```
func process(filename string) error {
    f, err := os.Open(filename)
    if err != nil {
        return fmt.Errorf("opening %s: %w", filename, err)
    }
    defer f.Close()

    // continue processing
    return nil
}
```

The early-return pattern reduces cognitive load. Instead of wrapping entire functions in larger conditional blocks, the flow of logic remains linear for the success path. This style aligns with the preference of Go for simplicity and maintainability in real-world systems.

Creating and Wrapping Contextual Errors

Go encourages errors to carry enough context to be meaningful on their own, especially when surfaced in logs or returned to higher layers. The **`fmt.Errorf`** function, paired with the **`%w`** verb, enables the developer to enrich an error message while preserving access to the underlying cause.

```
content, err := readConfig()
if err != nil {
    return fmt.Errorf("loading configuration: %w", err)
}
```

Wrapped errors allow higher-level callers to understand what went wrong while still being able to inspect why it went wrong through **`errors.Is`** and **`errors.As`**. This duality is particularly important in modular systems where multiple operations may fail for similar reasons, but need distinct contextual descriptions.

In situations where a function must signal specific, well-defined failure states, Go uses sentinel errors—predefined error variables that can be compared directly. They provide stable and recognizable markers for control flow.

```
var ErrEmptyQueue = errors.New("queue is empty")
```

This approach is appropriate for limited sets of predictable conditions, such as "**`not found`**," "**`unavailable`**," or "**`already exists`**." While overuse of sentinel errors can make an API rigid, when applied carefully, they do allow higher-level logic to respond to particular situations without relying on ambiguous string comparisons.

Modern Go error handling encourages precise inspection using the **`errors`** package. This allows sophisticated behaviour without compromising the value-based model of error propagation.

`errors.Is` checks whether an error is equal to or wraps a specific sentinel error:

```
if errors.Is(err, ErrEmptyQueue) {
    // handle empty queue case
}
```

`errors.As` extracts an error of a particular type:

```
var pe *ParseError
if errors.As(err, &pe) {
    fmt.Println("Parsing failed on line", pe.Line)
}
```

These tools promote clarity and type-safety in error analysis and avoid patterns—such as substring matching—that are brittle, and difficult to maintain in production systems.

Idiomatic Go encourages error patterns that remain consistent regardless of the complexity of the surrounding module structure. Whether a package contains a single source file or spans numerous components, the way it produces, wraps, and returns errors should follow the same conventions. Consistency ensures that consumers of the package can rely on predictable error behaviour, and makes cross-team collaboration more efficient. In larger projects, adherence to idiomatic error patterns also aids automated error-analysis tools and observability systems.

Despite its minimalistic foundation, Go's error system is designed to be expressive when needed. Developers may introduce custom error types to store metadata, choose wrapping to preserve causal chains, or use sentinel errors for clear categorization of failure modes. The idioms described above allow errors to carry the right amount of information without overwhelming the code with abstractions. This balance between simplicity, and power is a core reason why Go's error model scales effectively from small scripts to distributed, production-grade systems.

Panic, Defer, and Recover: Controlled Failure Handling

The error-handling model of Go relies primarily on explicit error values, but there are scenarios where a different mechanism is required–situations in which normal program execution cannot or should not be continued. For these cases, Go provides the **`panic`**, **`defer`**, and **`recover`** primitives. Together, they form a controlled failure-handling system, designed not to replace regular error checking, but to handle exceptional events, enforce cleanup logic, and help diagnose unexpected states.

While superficially similar to exceptions in other languages, the approach by Go is intentionally constrained. Panics are reserved for severe, program-level errors–conditions such as out-of-bounds indexing, invalid program states, or unrecoverable initialization failures. Their use is deliberate and minimal, and developers are encouraged to treat panics as a last resort, rather than a general error-handling strategy.

Panic: Signaling an Unexpected Failure

A **`panic`** causes the program to unwind its stack and eventually terminate unless the panic is intercepted by a matching **`recover`**. Panics should arise only in abnormal situations that normal error returns cannot adequately describe.

```
func riskyOperation(value int) {
    if value < 0 {
        panic("negative value encountered")
    }
    // continue execution
}
```

A panic immediately stops the current function's execution, begins stack unwinding, and triggers the invocation of any deferred functions along the way. Because panics halt ordinary control flow, they are unsuitable for routine failure paths, and are used sparingly in standard Go libraries.

Common legitimate uses for panics include:

- Violations of internal invariants
- Failed runtime assertions
- Unexpected nil dereferences
- Programmer mistakes or logically impossible states

In these scenarios, the presence of a panic surfaces a failure that cannot be meaningfully recovered from at the call site.

Defer: Ensuring Cleanup and Resource Finalization

The **defer** statement schedules a function to execute after the surrounding function returns—whether through a normal return, a panic, or a recovered state. This ensures that essential cleanup logic is executed reliably.

```
func handleFile(path string) (err error) {
    f, err := os.Open(path)
    if err != nil {
        return err
    }
    defer f.Close() // guaranteed to run

    // process file...
    return nil
}
```

Defer plays a significant role in:

- Releasing file handles.
- Unlocking mutexes.
- Flushing buffered output.
- Validating postconditions.
- Logging function exit conditions.

Deferred calls are executed even during panic; therefore, they provide a critical safety net for the programs that interact with external resources.

The ability to stack multiple deferred calls gives developers fine-grained control over cleanup sequencing. Deferred calls execute in reverse order, reflecting a Last-in, First-out (LIFO) model.

Recover: Regaining Control after Panic

The **recover** feature facilitates the regulated interception of panics. Within a deferred function, **recover** intercepts the panic value and restores regular execution.

```
func safeExecute(fn func()) (err error) {
    defer func() {
        if r := recover(); r != nil {
            err = fmt.Errorf("execution failed: %v", r)
        }
    }()
    fn()
    return nil
}
```

The recovered value–often a string or error–provides diagnostic information that can be logged or rewrapped. Although recovery allows a function to prevent a panic from terminating the program, its use should remain focused and intentional. Recovering every panic indiscriminately can obscure severe logic errors, and accordingly make debugging more difficult.

Appropriate uses for recovery include:

- Converting panics into error values at API boundaries.
- Protecting goroutines from uncontrolled failure.
- Gracefully shutting down servers or background workers.
- Logging details about unexpected states before exiting.

In these contexts, recover acts as a containment mechanism, ensuring that a single failing component does not destabilize the entire application.

Panic, Defer, and Recover Working Together

These three features form a coherent system that balances control and safety.

- **panic** initiates stack unwinding when abnormal conditions arise.
- **defer** ensures that cleanup logic executes consistently, regardless of how a function exits.
- **recover** selectively intercepts panics to prevent any catastrophic failure.

A common pattern in robust Go programs involves wrapping potentially unsafe operations in a recoverable boundary:

```
func protected() {
    defer func() {
        if r := recover(); r != nil {
            log.Printf("unexpected failure: %v", r)
        }
    }()
    executeCriticalLogic()
}
```

This pattern prevents a single panic from propagating through the entire call stack, while still surfacing the issue for debugging or logging.

Logging, Structured Errors, Runtime Pitfalls, and Debugging

Robust Go applications rely on clear visibility into how a program behaves at runtime. Once errors are detected—or even before they emerge—developers must have the reliable mechanisms to log the diagnostic information, represent errors meaningfully, identify system-level pitfalls, and debug issues with precision. Go provides a well-integrated ecosystem for these tasks using its **fmt**, **log**, and **errors** packages, combined with runtime diagnostics and optional third-party tools. Together, these capabilities form the backbone of observability and troubleshooting in production-grade Go systems.

Logging for Clarity and Diagnostics

Logging is more than printing text to the console; it is the process of capturing structured, contextual information about program behaviour. The **log** package in the standard library offers a simple, yet powerful interface for generating logs with timestamps, prefixes, and severity indicators.

The basic logger writes messages to standard error and includes automatic timestamps, which assists in correlating program activity with system metrics or external events.

```
log.Println("server started")
log.Printf("user %s authenticated", username)
```

The logger can be customized using **log.SetPrefix()** and **log.SetFlags()** to add metadata:

```
log.SetPrefix("AUTH: ")
log.SetFlags(log.Ldate | log.Ltime | log.Lshortfile)
```

This produces highly contextual logs, which are indispensable when diagnosing intermittent or environment-specific failures.

While the standard library focuses on simplicity, modern software systems often require structured logs that can be ingested by observability platforms such as ELK, Loki, CloudWatch, or Stackdriver. Structured logs typically capture the data in formats like JSON:

```
type LogEntry struct {
    Level   string `json:"level"`
    Message string `json:"message"`
    Time    string `json:"time"`
}

b, _ := json.Marshal(LogEntry{
    Level:   "INFO",
    Message: "initializing subsystem",
    Time:    time.Now().Format(time.RFC3339),
})
fmt.Println(string(b))
```

Although Go's standard library does not enforce structured logging, many teams adopt libraries such as Zap, Zerolog, or Logrus to improve performance and consistency. Regardless of the chosen tool, the objective remains the same: logs must be readable by both humans and machines, and that they must help pinpoint issues efficiently.

Structured Errors with `errors` and `fmt`

The philosophy recognized by Go encourages explicit, and meaningful error values. The **`errors`** and **`fmt`** packages provide the building blocks for constructing descriptive and maintainable error messages.

The simplest error is constructed using **`errors.New`**:

```
err := errors.New("invalid configuration")
return err
```

However, more descriptive error chains are created through wrapping:

```
if err := loadConfig(); err != nil {
    return fmt.Errorf("failed to load configuration: %w", err)
}
```

The **`%w`** verb allows callers to inspect wrapped errors with **`errors.Is`** or **`errors.As`**, enabling both human-readable and machine-verifiable error handling.

Structured Error Values

Well-designed Go errors convey:

- What failed?
- Why has it failed?
- Where it has failed?
- What to do next (and when will it be applicable)?

Consider a structured approach using the custom types:

```
type ValidationError struct {
    Field string
    Cause string
}

func (v ValidationError) Error() string {
    return fmt.Sprintf("validation failed on field %s: %s", v.
Field, v.Cause)
}
```

Such errors allow richer inspection:

```
var vErr ValidationError
if errors.As(err, &vErr) {
    log.Printf("client error: %s", vErr.Field)
}
```

This level of structure is essential when applications scale or when error information must flow across API boundaries.

Annotating Errors for Observability

Error values can be additionally decorated to include:

- Stack traces (via third-party libraries like pkg/errors).
- Error codes for API contracts.
- Correlation IDs for distributed systems.
- Remediation suggestions for internal tools.

This transforms errors into actionable artifacts rather than opaque signals.

Common Runtime Pitfalls

Even well-written Go programs encounter subtle challenges rooted in concurrency, memory management, and type behavior. Recognizing these pitfalls early helps developers avoid elusive bugs.

Nil Pointer Dereferences

One of the most frequent runtime crashes in Go arises from dereferencing nil.

```
Var p *Person
fmt.Println(p.Name) // panic: nil pointer dereference
```

Effective nil checking, careful constructor patterns, and explicit initialization are essential defensive techniques.

Goroutine Leaks

These are goroutines that never exit accumulate silently, and can exhaust memory over time. Common causes include:

- Missing **`range`** termination on channels.
- Blocking on unbuffered channels.
- Forgetting to close channels.
- Infinite loops waiting on conditions that never occur.

Monitoring goroutine counts using **`runtime.NumGoroutine()`**, or profiling via **`pprof`** helps detect leaks before they reach production.

Race Conditions

Simultaneous access to shared state without synchronization results in erratic behavior. Go offers the **`-race`** detector, which identifies the races at runtime:

```
go run -race main.go
```

The race detector is one of the strongest debugging tools by Go for parallel programs.

Slice Pitfalls

Slices can behave unexpectedly when their underlying arrays grow or shrink:

- Appending to a slice may reallocate it.
- Modifying a subslice may modify the original slice.
- Passing slices to functions can introduce unintended side effects.

Understanding slice semantics prevents many subtle bugs.

Deadlocks with Mutexes and Channels

Improper locking or waiting patterns can freeze a program permanently.

Common examples include:

- Forgetting to unlock a mutex after returning early.
- Mutual lock acquisition in different orders.

- Channel sends without corresponding receives.

Static analysis and careful design reviews greatly reduce these issues.

Debugging Techniques and Tooling in Go

Go provides a mixture of built-in debugging capabilities, along with external tools to diagnose and resolve issues effectively.

`fmt.Printf` remains one of the simplest debugging tools:

```
fmt.Printf("value=%+v\n", v)
```

Although not suitable for production, quick prints often help isolate logic errors.

For more controlled debugging, the **`log`** package includes file/line metadata which simplifies tracing control flow during execution.

The **`runtime`** package exposes internal details of the Go runtime:

- **`runtime.Caller()`** to obtain file/line info.
- **`runtime.Stack()`** to capture stack traces.
- **`runtime.GOMAXPROCS()`** to tune CPU usage.
- **`runtime.NumGoroutine()`** to detect goroutine leaks.

These capabilities are invaluable during investigation of concurrency issues.

Since panics include stack traces by default, they assist in identifying:

- Code paths leading to failure
- Sequence of function calls
- States that triggered an unexpected behavior

Developers often temporarily rely on panic output during deep debugging.

Delve (**`dlv`**) is the primary debugger of Go, providing features such as:

- Step-by-step execution
- Variable inspection
- Setting breakpoints
- Examining goroutine states

Example usage:

```
dlv debug ./cmd/app
```

Delve integrates with VS Code, GoLand, and command-line workflows.

AI-Assisted Debugging and Reliability Improvement

As Go applications grow in complexity–integrating concurrency, network communication, cloud services, and third-party dependencies–traditional debugging often becomes insufficient. Manual log inspection, trial-and-error fixes, or reading stack traces may still work for small programs, but scalable systems demand faster and more intelligent approaches.

In this section we shall explore how AI tools augment debugging, error analysis, and reliability engineering, accompanied by concrete examples rooted in real Go patterns.

Using AI Tools to Analyze Error-Prone Code Paths

LLMs excel at finding subtle bugs by analyzing control flow, error propagation behavior, concurrency interactions, and edge cases that humans often overlook.

Example: Silent Error Ignoring

Consider the following problematic snippet:

```
func ReadConfig(path string) ([]byte, error) {
    data, _ := os.ReadFile(path) // ignoring error!
    return data, nil
}
```

An AI tool can immediately flag:

- The error from **os.ReadFile** is ignored.
- Returning nil for the error misleads callers.
- On failure, data becomes useless and may propagate upstream.

AI-Generated Insight (Typical Output)

*"You are discarding the error returned by **os.ReadFile**. This may lead to nil data being used downstream. Return the actual error to maintain integrity of the error chain."*

Refactored Version (after AI Suggestion)

```
func ReadConfig(path string) ([]byte, error) {
    data, err := os.ReadFile(path)
    if err != nil {
        return nil, fmt.Errorf("read config %s: %w", path, err)
    }
```

```
    return data, nil
}
```

AI assistance has reduced debugging time by surfacing a correctness issue that could have resulted in cascading runtime failures.

Detecting Concurrency Bugs with AI

Race conditions, deadlocks, goroutine leaks, and blocked channels are some of the most difficult bugs in Go. AI tools can interpret the usage patterns, and detect likely the concurrency flaws before execution.

Example: Goroutine Leak

```
func FetchAll(urls []string) chan []byte {
    out := make(chan []byte)
    for _, u := range urls {
        go func() {
            resp, _ := http.Get(u)
            body, _ := io.ReadAll(resp.Body)
            out <- body
        }()
    }
    return out
}
```

AI-Generated Warning

"The returned channel is never closed. Any consumer ranging over it will block forever. Also, the closure inside the loop does not capture the loop variable correctly."

AI-Driven Refactor

```
func FetchAll(urls []string) <-chan []byte {
    out := make(chan []byte)

    go func() {
        defer close(out)
        for _, u := range urls {
            url := u // capture variable
            resp, err := http.Get(url)
            if err != nil {
                continue
            }
            body, err := io.ReadAll(resp.Body)
            if err != nil {
                continue
            }
```

```
                out <- body
                resp.Body.Close()
            }
        }()

        return out
    }
```

AI tools spotted:

- A goroutine leak (channel never closed).
- Incorrect variable capture.
- Missing body close.

Static analysis tools alone may not catch all the three simultaneously; LLM reasoning helps bridge that gap.

AI-Enhanced Panic Analysis

When panic stack traces the surface in logs or terminal output, AI tools can explain them in plain language, or connect them to the likely root causes.

Example: Interpreting a Panic Trace

Suppose a panic appears:

```
panic: runtime error: invalid memory address or nil pointer
dereference
goroutine 42 [running]:
main.(*Cache).Get(0x0, ...)
```

AI Explanation

"The method ***(*Cache).Get*** *is being called on a nil receiver, meaning the Cache instance was never initialized. Look for construction paths where* ***NewCache()*** *is not called, or dependency injection failures.»*

AI Suggestion Patch

```
func NewCache() *Cache {
    return &Cache{
        data: make(map[string]string),
    }
}
```

And, add validation wherever Cache is used:

```
if c == nil {
    return "", errors.New("cache is not initialized")
}
```

The AI ties together type information, pointer analysis, and error semantics to offer both, diagnosis and remediation.

LLM-Driven Error Wrapping and Observability Improvements

AI tools often suggest adding a context to errors–something developers skip in the initial implementations.

Original Code

```
func SaveUser(u User) error {
    return db.Insert(u)
}
```

AI-Recommended Version

```
func SaveUser(u User) error {
    if err := db.Insert(u); err != nil {
        return fmt.Errorf("save user %s: %w", u.ID, err)
    }
    return nil
}
```

The enhancement improves the observability, making logs actionable, and alongside improving post-mortem debugging.

Automated Refactoring for Reliability

AI models can produce structured refactors which can fix multiple reliability issues simultaneously.

Example: From Unreliable to Robust I/O

Original Implementation:

```
func CopyFile(src, dst string) error {
    in, _ := os.Open(src)
    defer in.Close()

    out, _ := os.Create(dst)
    defer out.Close()

    io.Copy(out, in)
    return nil
}
```

Issues:

- Ignored errors from **`os.Open`**, **`os.Create`**, and **`io.Copy`**.
- **`defer in.Close()`** may panic if **`in`** is nil.
- Output file may be partially written.
- No **`fsync`** or permission checks.

AI-Refactored Version

```go
func CopyFile(src, dst string) error {
    in, err := os.Open(src)
    if err != nil {
        return fmt.Errorf("open source file: %w", err)
    }
    defer in.Close()

    out, err := os.Create(dst)
    if err != nil {
        return fmt.Errorf("create destination file: %w", err)
    }
    defer func() {
        cerr := out.Close()
        if err == nil { // preserve original error
            err = cerr
        }
    }()

    if _, err := io.Copy(out, in); err != nil {
        return fmt.Errorf("copy contents: %w", err)
    }

    if err := out.Sync(); err != nil {
        return fmt.Errorf("sync output file: %w", err)
    }

    return nil
}
```

The AI strengthens:

- Error propagation
- Deferred close error handling
- Durability (**c** call)
- Contextual logging

This is an example of AI transforming a fragile function into a production-grade code.

AI for Predictive Debugging and Proactive Reliability

LLMs can surface patterns that hint at future failures:

- Goroutines launched inside loops without bounds
- Unprotected shared maps
- Unbounded channels
- Retry loops with backoff missing
- JSON decoding without field validation
- File descriptors not closed in corner cases
- Timeouts missing on network operations

Example: Suggesting Timeouts

```
resp, err := http.Get(url)
```

AI may suggest:

*"Use **`http.Client`** with timeouts to avoid indefinite blocking."*

Refactor

```
client := http.Client{
    Timeout: 5 * time.Second,
}
resp, err := client.Get(url)
```

This shifts the code toward reliability and production-readiness.

Integrating AI-Assisted Debugging into the Go Workflow

To fully leverage AI in debugging:

- Use AI to analyze failing tests and suggest corrections.
- Paste stack traces or logs into the AI for explanations.
- Ask for refactoring best practices (error wrapping, concurrency patterns).
- Run AI-driven code reviews before merging pull requests.

- Use AI to verify that you are following Go best practices (which includes resource cleanup, safe concurrency).

Conclusion

The approach of Go to be reliable surrounds on clarity and predictability, and this chapter has explored how its explicit error-handling philosophy shapes a resilient software design. By examining the error type and Go's preference for returning the errors as values, the chapter additionally, emphasized on how this model keeps the control flow transparent, and avoids the hidden complexity, which is often associated with exception-driven languages. Idiomatic techniques—such as early exits, contextual error wrapping, and consistent error propagation—form the foundation of a robust Go code.

The chapter further examined controlled failure mechanisms using panic, defer, and recover, highlighting not only their appropriate use cases but also how they differ from the standard error-handling patterns. Logging, structured error representation, and debugging practices were explored in depth, showing how the standard library in Go equips engineers to diagnose the issues quickly and improve observability. Common runtime and concurrency pitfalls were analysed along with strategies to prevent leaks, race conditions, and starvation scenarios.

Finally, the chapter has successfully demonstrated how AI-assisted tools can enhance debugging and reliability workflows. By analysing stack traces, identifying suspicious patterns, recommending refactors, and generating targeted diagnostics, AI systems support developers in resolving complex defects more efficiently. These capabilities, when combined with Go's disciplined error-handling model, enable the creation of applications that are both maintainable and production-ready.

In the next chapter, the focus will be on Concurrency in Go. We shall focus on how Go's lightweight goroutines, channel-based communication model, and synchronization primitives collectively create a sophisticated and robust concurrency system.

CHAPTER 5
Concurrency in Go

Introduction

Concurrency lies at the heart of Go's design philosophy, thus enabling developers to build systems that are highly responsive, scalable, and capable of handling millions of operations in parallel. This chapter explores how Go's lightweight goroutines, channel-based communication model, and synchronization primitives come together to form an elegant, and powerful concurrency framework. By examining how these components interact under real-world workloads—along with the modern AI-assisted techniques for tuning and debugging—readers will gain a deep understanding of how to write concurrent programs that are not only correct, but equally efficient, predictable, and production-ready.

Structure

In this chapter, we will cover the following topics:

- Introduction to Concurrency in Go
- Creating and Managing Goroutines
  - Understanding Goroutines
  - Creating Goroutines
  - Goroutines and Loop Variable Capture
- Channels: Buffered versus Unbuffered
  - Unbuffered Channels: Synchronous Communication
  - Buffered Channels: Asynchronous Communication
  - Choosing between Buffered and Unbuffered Channels
  - The Mechanics of Blocking and Synchronization
  - Buffered Channels and Backpressure
  - Common Pitfalls and Misconceptions

- Synchronization and Communication Patterns
    - Producer–Consumer Coordination
    - Pipeline Communication
    - Fan-Out and Fan-In
    - Controlling Access with Token Channels
    - Using Channels for Notifications and Signaling
    - Avoiding Shared State through Message Passing
    - Graceful Shutdown with Channel-Based Coordination
- Race Conditions and Prevention Using Sync Package
    - Understanding Race Conditions in Go
    - Overview of the Sync Package
    - Using sync.Mutex to Prevent Race Conditions
    - Potential Pitfalls of Mutexes
    - Reader/Writer Locking with sync.RWMutex
    - Synchronization with sync.WaitGroup
    - Condition Variables with sync.Cond
    - Avoiding Races through sync.Map and Lock-Free Designs
    - Memory Synchronization and Happens-before Relationships
    - Combining the Concurrency Tools of Go Effectively
- Profiling and Optimizing Concurrency with AI Suggestions
    - Worker Pools as a Concurrency Optimization Strategy
    - AI-Assisted Diagnosis and Root Cause Analysis
    - Practical Guide: How to Use AI Tools for Concurrency Optimization

Introduction to Concurrency in Go

Concurrency sits at the heart of Go's design philosophy, and is one of the primary reasons why the language has become a favorite for building scalable network servers, cloud-native platforms, data pipelines, and distributed systems. From the beginning, the creators of Go recognized that the modern software must perform many tasks at once–handling requests, processing data, monitoring resources, or communicating across networks–often in environments where efficiency, correctness, and reliability are non-negotiable. Instead of treating concurrency as an advanced or optional capability, Go elevates it to a first-class construct, providing the mechanisms that are both powerful and intuitive.

Go employs a concurrency paradigm influenced by Communicating Sequential Processes (CSP), wherein autonomous units of work operate in isolation and interact via clearly specified channels. This method circumvents numerous drawbacks linked to conventional multithreading, including intricate locking mechanisms, unpredictable race events, and nuanced synchronization problems. By advocating for communication over shared memory, Go facilitates the creation of programs that are more comprehensible, simpler to test, and less susceptible to the kind of errors commonly associated with concurrent systems.

Equally central to the concurrency story of Go is the **concept of `channels`**–typed conduits through which goroutines send and receive values. Channels provide a structured, deterministic mechanism for coordination and data exchange. They enforce synchronization implicitly, ensuring that the communication happens safely without exposing shared state. By combining goroutines and channels, Go enables a programming style in which workflows are broken into independent components that operate in parallel and pass messages as needed, thereby, mirroring real-world pipelines and distributed architectures.

Beyond these foundational components, Go introduces additional concurrency tools that support various communication and coordination patterns. The **`select`** statement enables goroutines to wait on multiple channel operations simultaneously, making it easy to implement fan-in, fan-out, cancellation, and timeout behavior. The **`sync`** package provides low-level primitives–such as mutexes, wait groups, and atomic operations–for scenarios where shared memory is unavoidable, or more efficient. The **`context`** package offers a structured cancellation and timeout propagation across goroutine hierarchies, promoting resilient, well-behaved concurrent systems. Together, these tools form a comprehensive concurrency toolkit suitable for everything: from simple background workers to high-throughput microservices.

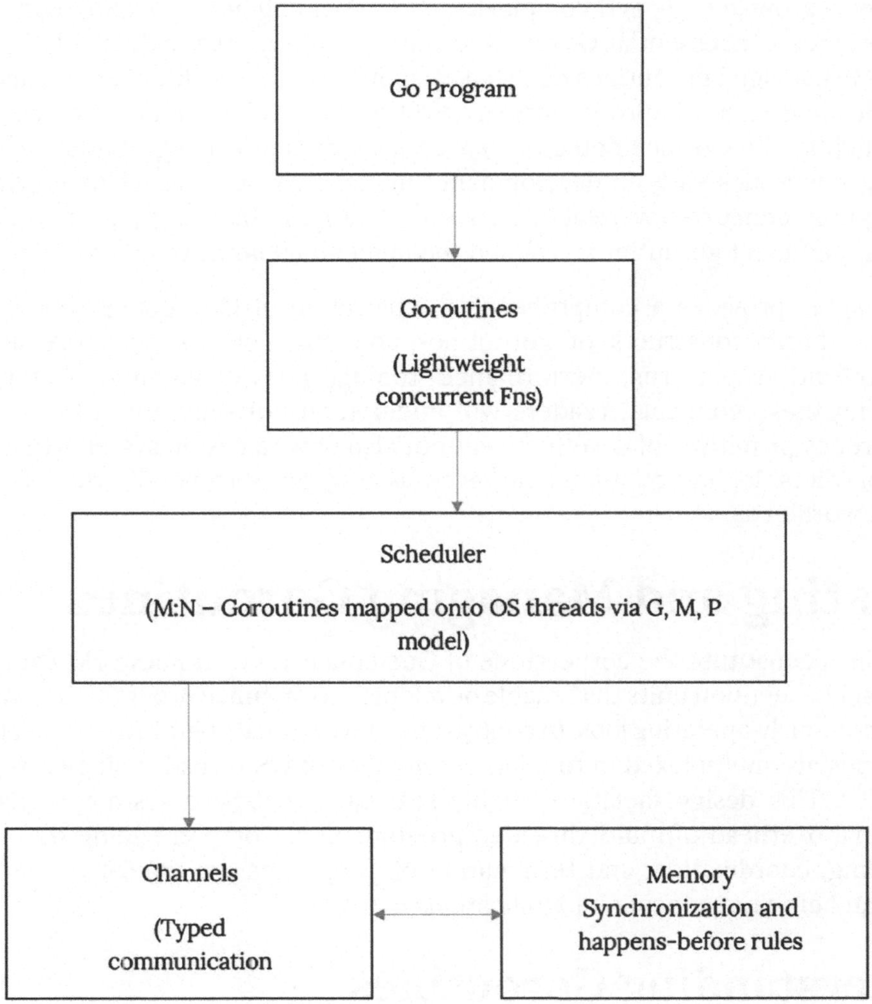

Figure 5.1: *Go Concurrency Overview Model*

The concurrency model of Go also aligns naturally with the demands of modern distributed platforms. In systems such as microservices, event-driven architectures, real-time data processing frameworks, and container orchestrators, concurrency is not a luxury, but instead a fundamental capability. The approach by Go empowers developers to express parallelism directly and succinctly, often resulting in a code that is clearer and less error-prone than equivalent implementations in more traditional languages. The minimalistic syntax of the language, and well-designed runtime eliminate much of the boilerplate that typically surrounds concurrent programming, making sophisticated parallel execution accessible even to developers with limited experience in multithreading.

As systems grow in scale and complexity, understanding how to exploit concurrency efficiently becomes essential. Go offers strong guarantees but also demands disciplined usage. Mismanaged goroutines can lead to subtle memory leaks, channel misuse can cause deadlocks, and improper synchronization can still introduce race conditions. Tools such as the Go race detector, `pprof` profiler, and tracing utilities help reveal concurrency issues early in development. Increasingly, AI-assisted debugging tools also support concurrency-related analysis, identifying blocking patterns, deadlock risks, or inefficient goroutine usage and recommending improvements.

This chapter provides a comprehensive exploration of Go's concurrency model—from the basic constructs of goroutines and channels to the more advanced synchronization patterns, performance tuning, and debugging strategies. By mastering these concepts, readers will understand not only how to leverage the concurrency primitives of Go effectively, but also how to design systems that remain clear, predictable, and maintainable—even as they grow to handle the large-scale, parallel workloads.

Creating and Managing Goroutines

Goroutines constitute the cornerstone of Go's concurrency framework. They denote lightweight execution units that enable developers to organize programs as assemblies of autonomously operating jobs. In contrast to conventional operating-system threads, goroutines are multiplexed onto a limited number of OS threads using Go's runtime scheduler. This design facilitates highly scalable, responsive systems without the traditional overhead of multi-threaded programming. Comprehending the creation, scheduling, coordination, and termination of goroutines are crucial for developing robust and efficient concurrent applications in Go.

Understanding Goroutines

A goroutine is conceptually similar to a function running concurrently with the rest of the program. However, the internal mechanics distinguish it sharply from the traditional threads. At launch, a goroutine begins with a very small stack—often just a few kilobytes—rather than the megabyte-level stacks used by OS threads. The Go runtime expands or shrinks this stack dynamically based on the needs of the executing function, allowing thousands or even millions of goroutines to execute within a single process.

Under the hood, the Go scheduler uses the **G-M-P** model:

- **G**: The goroutine itself (the work item)
- **M**: An operating-system thread
- **P**: A logical processor that executes goroutines and manages run queues

This model permits highly efficient work stealing, load balancing, and preemptive scheduling. As of recent Go versions, asynchronous preemption ensures that long-running or CPU-bound goroutines cannot block the system indefinitely. Although the runtime handles scheduling automatically, developers must remain aware that goroutines may block on channels, locks, system calls, or I/O operations, causing the scheduler to reschedule other runnable goroutines instead.

Goroutines are ideal for the workloads involving I/O, networking, and pipelines. They enable non-blocking concurrency patterns while preserving a simple, synchronous code style. However, they still require a disciplined management–improper signaling, channel misuse, or missing termination paths can lead to memory waste, resource contention, and latent concurrency bugs.

Creating Goroutines

A goroutine is created using the go keyword followed by a function call:

```
go doWork()
```

Go immediately schedules **`doWork()`** to execute concurrently. This launch does not block the caller; both, the newly created goroutine, and the launching function are executed independently.

Goroutines can be created from named functions or anonymous functions. Anonymous goroutines are particularly flexible and allow temporary logic to be embedded inline:

```
go func() {
    fmt.Println("Running in a goroutine")
}()
```

Although convenient, anonymous goroutines require careful consideration of captured variables, resource lifetimes, and synchronization. Because closures capture *variables* instead of *values*, a common pitfall arises when creating goroutines inside loops.

Goroutines and Loop Variable Capture

Consider the following code:

```
for i := 0; i < 5; i++ {
    go func() {
        fmt.Println(i)
    }()
}
```

Every goroutine prints the same value because each closure refers to the same memory location for **`i`**. The variable's value changes during the loop, but each goroutine reads it only when it eventually runs—which may be only after the loop completes.

The idiomatic correction passes the loop variable as an explicit argument:

```
for i := 0; i < 5; i++ {
    go func(v int) {
        fmt.Println(v)
    }(i)
}
```

Passing values avoids non-deterministic behavior, and remains consistent with Go's emphasis on clarity and correctness.

Channels: Buffered versus Unbuffered

Concurrency is one of the hallmark strengths of Go, and channels lie at the center of its model for communication and coordination between goroutines. While goroutines allow lightweight parallel execution, channels enable these goroutines to exchange data safely without explicit locks. Understanding channels is essential to writing idiomatic Go, and one of the most fundamental distinctions to grasp is the behavior difference between **buffered** and **unbuffered channels**.

At first glance, the distinction may look small—the presence or absence of a buffer. But in practice, it profoundly influences the program flow, synchronization, performance, and application design. In this section, we will explore both types of channels in depth, examine when each is appropriate, identify common misconceptions, and walk through patterns that take advantage of their characteristics.

Unbuffered Channels: Synchronous Communication

An **unbuffered channel** is the most straightforward channel type in Go. It is created without specifying a capacity, for example:

```
ch := make(chan int)
```

This creates a channel with a zero internal storage, meaning that every send operation (**`ch <- value`**) must synchronize directly with a corresponding receive operation (**`<-ch`**). The key concept is *synchronous communication*: both the sender and the receiver must be ready at the exact same moment. Neither side proceeds until the other side has completed the operation.

This synchronous behavior turns unbuffered channels into a powerful tool for coordination. They do more than move data—they create a handoff point between goroutines. When a value is sent, the sending goroutine pauses until another goroutine picks it up. Likewise, a receiving goroutine pauses until someone sends a value. This pattern can be extremely useful when you need to enforce ordering, guarantee that a message has been processed, or ensure that two goroutines stay aligned in the execution.

A simple example illustrates this clearly:

```
func main() {
    ch := make(chan string)

    go func() {
        ch <- "task done" // waits until receiver is ready
    }()

    msg := <-ch // waits for sender
    fmt.Println(msg)
}
```

This tight handshake ensures deterministic sequencing. No matter how goroutines are scheduled, the program cannot reach the **`fmt.Println`** call until the message has been sent, and the sender cannot proceed past the send until the receiver picks up the value.

Because of this, unbuffered channels are frequently used for:

- Synchronization or signaling.
- Worker coordination.
- Ensuring that a task is completed before continuing.
- Avoiding race conditions through timed data exchange.

Unbuffered channels give your program a predictable rhythm, similar to two hands passing a baton, where both participants must meet at the same moment.

Buffered Channels: Asynchronous Communication

A buffered channel introduces storage capacity:

```
ch := make(chan int, 5)
```

This channel can hold *up to five values* without requiring an immediate receiver. Once the buffer is full, the behavior becomes synchronous—sends block until space is freed. But until then, the sender can continue executing independently.

Buffered channels enable asynchronous communication between goroutines. A producer can send faster than the consumer receives, at least temporarily, without waiting. This allows the production and consumption rates to differ for short periods, making buffered channels excellent for smoothing out spikes in the workload.

Consider this simple producer-consumer example:

```
func main() {
    ch := make(chan int, 3)

    go func() {
        for i := 1; i <= 3; i++ {
            ch <- i // does not block until buffer is full
        }
    }()

    time.Sleep(time.Second)
    fmt.Println(<-ch)
    fmt.Println(<-ch)
    fmt.Println(<-ch)
}
```

Here, the producer finishes its work immediately, even though the consumer only starts reading one second later. The buffer absorbs the delay, allowing the goroutines to operate without tightly coupled timing.

This makes buffered channels valuable in:

- Work queues.
- Pipelines that process data in stages.
- Batching operations.
- Decoupling producers and consumers.
- Improving throughput in high-volume systems.

In contrast to unbuffered channels that enforce order, buffered channels allow for elasticity.

Choosing between Buffered and Unbuffered Channels

Choosing between the two is not arbitrary. Each has specific advantages depending on your concurrency pattern.

When to Use Unbuffered Channels:

- You need a strict synchronization between goroutines.
- You want to signal completion or readiness.

- You need a deterministic sequencing.

You want to avoid the complexities and unpredictability associated with queues or buffers.

Unbuffered channels are easier to reason about when synchronization is more important than throughput. They naturally prevent producers from overwhelming consumers.

When to Use Buffered Channels:

- You want to improve the performance by reducing blocking.
- You are working with tasks or data that can be queued briefly.
- You want to handle bursts of input gracefully.
- You are building pipelines, fan-out/fan-in architectures, or producer–consumer flows.

Buffered channels allow goroutines to work independently without stopping each other unnecessarily. They introduce flexibility, but also bring potential risks, such as unbounded growth if buffer sizes are misjudged or deadlocks when consumers do not read as expected.

The Mechanics of Blocking and Synchronization

To truly understand buffered and unbuffered channels, it is important to study how blocking works in each case.

Unbuffered Channel Behavior:

- A **send** operation blocks until a receiver is ready.
- A **receive** operation blocks until a sender is ready.
- No values sit "in transit"; the exchange is immediate.

Buffered Channel Behavior:

- A **send** operation blocks only when the buffer is full.
- A **receive** operation blocks only when the buffer is empty.
- Values may remain in the buffer for some time before being consumed.

This difference changes the performance and responsiveness of your application. Buffered channels allow burst traffic to flow more smoothly, minimizing stalls. However, they also introduce a temporary storage area, which can hide the bottlenecks or failures until the buffer fills up.

Buffered Channels and Backpressure

Backpressure refers to how a system naturally slows production when consumption cannot keep up. Unbuffered channels provide immediate backpressure because every send blocks until the receiver is ready. Buffered channels delay backpressure until the buffer fills.

This distinction is important in distributed systems, streaming applications, and real-time data pipelines. If backpressure is required for correctness—say, to prevent memory overuse or ensure that external systems do not get overwhelmed—then unbuffered channels or small buffers are of a better fit.

If throughput and performance are more important, a larger buffer allows fast producers to keep running, while slower consumers catch up.

Common Pitfalls and Misconceptions

"Buffered channels always improve performance" – Not true.

Large buffers can improve throughput, but they can also hide underlying issues like unbalanced workers or infinite loops. Overuse leads to unpredictable memory use and potential deadlocks when the buffer fills and goroutines block unexpectedly.

"Unbuffered channels are too slow" – Not necessarily.

Unbuffered channels can be faster when synchronization is necessary because they avoid extra memory allocation and state management for buffer slots. Many Go concurrency patterns intentionally use the unbuffered channels for clarity and correctness.

"Buffered channels eliminate the need for mutexes" – Only sometimes.

Channels handle data passing, but they do not protect shared memory unless that memory is accessed solely through the channel.

"Deadlocks happen only with unbuffered channels" – False.

Buffered channels can lead to deadlocks as soon as the buffer fills and no receiver is available.

Synchronization and Communication Patterns

While goroutines make it easy to run functions concurrently, real power emerges only when these goroutines interact correctly. In any non-trivial concurrent program, multiple goroutines must coordinate their progress, exchange data, signal state changes, and avoid interfering with one another. Go's concurrency model, built on channels and the sync package, offers rich synchronization and communication patterns that let developers build predictable, safe, and scalable parallel workflows. This section explores these patterns in depth, explaining when each applies, and how Go encourages clear thinking about independent execution.

At its core, synchronization is about ensuring that different goroutines reach certain states at appropriate times. Communication, in turn, involves transferring of the actual data or control information. Although these concepts often overlap, understanding their roles separately helps in selecting the right pattern for each task. For example, sending a value over a channel both transfers data *and* synchronizes sender and receiver; calling a **`WaitGroup`**'s **`Done`** method synchronizes completion without sending any data. Go encourages developers to think consciously about which mechanism fits the problem best instead of reaching for a single, generic solution.

Producer–Consumer Coordination

One of the most common patterns involves separating work creation from work execution. A producer generates tasks and sends them into a channel, while one or more consumers receive tasks and process them. Although the external form resembles a queue, the behavior reflects the channel type. An unbuffered channel forces producers and consumers to stay in lockstep, whereas a buffered channel gives producers a room to run ahead briefly.

Consider the following example:

```
tasks := make(chan int, 5)
done  := make(chan struct{})

go func() {
    for i := 1; i <= 10; i++ {
        tasks <- i
    }
    close(tasks)
}()

go func() {
    for t := range tasks {
        fmt.Println("Processing", t)
    }
    done <- struct{}{}
}()

<-done
```

Here, the channel acts as both a communication medium, and a synchronization point. The consumer stops automatically when the producer closes the channel. Instead of relying on shared memory or explicit locks, the channel orchestrates progress in a structured, readable sequence. The elegance of this pattern lies in the fact that both goroutines operate independently, yet remain safely connected through the flow of tasks.

Pipeline Communication

Many concurrent applications benefit from splitting work into multiple stages, each handled by separate goroutines. This design forms a pipeline in which each stage accepts input from one channel, performs transformations, and forwards the result to the next stage through another channel. Pipelines allow several stages of computation to run simultaneously, improving throughput and making the code easier to reason about.

A typical pipeline might look like this:

```
stage1 := make(chan int)
stage2 := make(chan int)
stage3 := make(chan int)

// producer
go func() {
    for i := 1; i <= 5; i++ {
        stage1 <- i
    }
    close(stage1)
}()

// transform
go func() {
    for v := range stage1 {
        stage2 <- v * 2
    }
    close(stage2)
}()

// consumer
go func() {
    for v := range stage2 {
        stage3 <- v + 1
    }
    close(stage3)
}()
```

```
for output := range stage3 {
    fmt.Println("Output:", output)
}
```

Each goroutine in this pipeline communicates exclusively through channels, forming a clear flow of data. Synchronization occurs naturally because a stage cannot read from a channel until the previous stage has produced values. Meanwhile, closing channels signals the end-of-data conditions, allowing stages to terminate gracefully. This style of communication is central in streaming systems, ETL jobs, and real-time processing services.

Fan-out and Fan-in

Another important set of patterns involves distributing work among multiple goroutines, and later collecting their results. Fan-out is the process of launching several workers to handle tasks in parallel. Fan-in is the complementary aggregation of results from those workers. Together, these patterns allow a program to use available CPU cores more effectively, and to structure a parallel execution in a controlled way.

Here is a simple demonstration:

```
jobs := make(chan int)
results := make(chan int)

// fan-out
for w := 0; w < 3; w++ {
    go func() {
        for j := range jobs {
            results <- j * j
        }
    }()
}

// producer
go func() {
    for i := 1; i <= 5; i++ {
        jobs <- i
    }
    close(jobs)
}()

// fan-in
go func() {
    for i := 1; i <= 5; i++ {
        fmt.Println(<-results)
    }
```

```
        close(results)
    }()
```

In this design, multiple worker goroutines participate in the same workload. The job channel synchronizes when a worker can pick up a task, while the results channel coordinates the gathering of outputs. Although it appears simple, this pattern scales remarkably well and is regularly used in services that require heavy computation or parallel I/O operations. The channels, in effect, form a structured concurrency contract: workers will neither starve nor step on the data of each other, and the main goroutine receives all the results without contention.

Controlling Access with Token Channels

Token channels provide a lightweight mechanism for managing limited resources, such as connection slots, rate limits, or concurrency caps. Instead of using locks or semaphores, a buffered channel holds "tokens," each representing permission to start a new task. A goroutine removes a token before proceeding and returns it when done. This pattern uses the channel's capacity as a natural resource counter.

An example simplifies the idea:

```
sem := make(chan struct{}, 3) // only 3 concurrent operations
allowed

for i := 0; i < 10; i++ {
    go func(id int) {
        sem <- struct{}{} // acquire
        fmt.Println("Running job", id)
        time.Sleep(time.Second)
        <-sem // release
    }(i)
}
```

The channel enforces synchronization implicitly. Even though ten goroutines start, only three run at a time. The others wait until space becomes available. This pattern avoids traditional locking entirely and expresses concurrency limits using the semantics of channel buffering. It is widely used in web crawlers, API clients, and systems where unbounded concurrency would be harmful.

Using Channels for Notifications and Signaling

Not all synchronization patterns require sending meaningful values; sometimes the intention is simply to indicate that something has happened. Unbuffered channels that carry empty structs are commonly used for this purpose. They provide a simple, clear signal: a goroutine sends a value when it has completed its work, and another goroutine waits for this signal before proceeding.

A straightforward example is as follows:

```
done := make(chan struct{})

go func() {
    // some work here
    done <- struct{}{}
}()

<-done // wait for signal
```

This pattern is particularly valuable when coordinating shutdown sequences, or when ensuring that cleanup tasks are completed before the program exits. Unlike other synchronization primitives, signaling channels integrate naturally with the rest of Go's communication ecosystem. They also participate easily in **select** statements, enabling timeouts, cancellation, or multi-way communication.

Avoiding Shared State through Message Passing

One of the philosophical pillars of the design of Go is the idea that concurrency should revolve around the communicating state rather than sharing it. Channels help avoid race conditions by ensuring that data is owned by exactly one goroutine at a time. Instead of several goroutines reading and writing shared variables, ownership of a value is passed explicitly through a channel. Once a goroutine receives data, it becomes wholly responsible for that data until it hands it off to someone else.

For situations involving mutable structures, this pattern can eliminate the need for mutexes entirely. Consider a goroutine that manages a map:

```
type query struct {
    key string
    reply chan string
}

store := make(chan query)
data := map[string]string{"x": "alpha", "y": "beta"}

go func() {
    for q := range store {
        q.reply <- data[q.key]
    }
}()
```

```
reply := make(chan string)
store <- query{key: "x", reply: reply}
fmt.Println(<-reply)
```

All access to the map occurs through a single goroutine, which serializes reads and writes. Other goroutines do not interact with the map directly–they communicate with it. This model mirrors the actor pattern found in other concurrent languages and promotes clarity: the map remains safe because its owner never changes except by deliberate message passing.

Graceful Shutdown with Channel-Based Coordination

Stopping a concurrent system cleanly is just as important as starting one. Channels offer a structured way to signal shutdown events. A dedicated "quit" channel can broadcast the intention to stop, and each goroutine checks this channel during its normal operation. Since the quit signal travels through the same communication system as regular data, shutdown becomes predictable and maintainable.

A sample approach looks like this:

```
quit := make(chan struct{})

go func() {
    for {
        select {
        case <-quit:
            fmt.Println("Stopping goroutine")
            return
        default:
            // normal work
        }
    }
}()

time.Sleep(time.Second)
close(quit)
```

Once the quit channel is closed, all goroutines that are listening to it can exit cleanly. Hence, whether the application consists of two goroutines or hundreds, the same mechanism scales simply because it aligns with Go's natural communication style.

Race Conditions and Prevention Using sync Package

Concurrency is one of Go's greatest strengths, but with it comes the challenge of managing shared state safely. When two or more of the goroutines attempt to read and write shared data without proper coordination, the program can enter a race condition–a situation where the outcome depends on the unpredictable timing of concurrent operations. Race conditions are complex to detect as they may only appear under certain workloads, CPU scheduling decisions, or network conditions. As a result, the same program may behave correctly thousands of times before producing incorrect results, corrupted data, or subtle nondeterministic bugs.

In Go, race conditions most commonly occur when goroutines access shared memory simultaneously. This can happen in simple scenarios–such as updating a counter–or in more complex workflows involving multiple goroutines reading and writing across slices, maps, or shared structs. While the language encourages message-passing concurrency through channels, shared memory remains an important part of many applications, particularly in performance-critical sections where copying data may be expensive. Go provides the sync package as a comprehensive suite of tools to manage concurrency safely, offering mechanisms that prevent race conditions while allowing developers to maintain high throughput, and low-latency execution.

Understanding Race Conditions in Go

A race condition exists when:

1. Two or more goroutines access the same variable concurrently.
2. At least one of the goroutines modifies that variable.
3. There is no synchronization ensuring deterministic ordering.

A simple example illustrates this issue clearly:

```
var counter = 0

func main() {
    for i := 0; i < 1000; i++ {
        go func() {
            counter++ // unsafe
        }()
    }
    time.Sleep(time.Second)
    fmt.Println(counter)
}
```

The expected result might be 1000, yet the printed value often fluctuates. The increment operation (**`counter++`**) is not atomic; it expands into a read, modify, and write sequence. If two goroutines execute this sequence at the same time, one update may override another, causing data loss.

Go's race detector (**`go run -race`**) can identify such issues at runtime. However, detection does not resolve the problem. To eliminate the underlying race condition, the program must introduce synchronization. This is where the sync package becomes essential.

Overview of the `sync` Package

Go's **`sync`** package provides low-level concurrency primitives designed to control access to shared state:

- **`sync.Mutex`:** Mutual exclusion lock
- **`sync.RWMutex`:** Reader/writer lock
- **`sync.WaitGroup`:** Coordination of goroutine lifecycles
- **`sync.Once`:** Ensure initialization happens just once
- **`sync.Cond`:** Condition variables for signaling
- **`sync.Map`:** Concurrent map implementation
- **`sync.Pool`:** Object reuse to optimize allocation

Each of these tools serves a different purpose. Some protect the critical sections, others coordinate the execution progress, and some help structure the memory access patterns. Together, they give developers reliable mechanisms for preventing data races while retaining performance.

Using `sync.Mutex` to Prevent Race Conditions

The simplest and most widely used tool for preventing race conditions is **`sync.Mutex`**. A mutex enforces mutual exclusion, ensuring that only one goroutine at a time can execute a protected code block.

Basic Mutex Usage:

```
var (
    counter = 0
    mu      sync.Mutex
)

func increment() {
    mu.Lock()
```

```
        counter++
        mu.Unlock()
    }
```

The **Lock()** call blocks other goroutines until the current goroutine releases the lock with **Unlock()**. This guarantees that the read-modify-write sequence is executed atomically.

Potential Pitfalls of Mutexes

While Mutex is effective, improper use can create new issues:

- **Deadlocks** if a goroutine forgets to unlock.
- **Performance bottlenecks** if locks are held for too long.
- **Contention spikes** when too many goroutines compete.
- **Nested locks** that may lead to ordering problems.

To avoid deadlocks, the defer keyword is often used:

```
mu.Lock()
defer mu.Unlock()
```

This does incur minimal overhead, but greatly improves safety, especially in functions with error handling paths.

Mutex Granularity

Correct granularity is essential:

- **Coarse-grained locking** (single lock for large structure) reduces complexity, but limits parallelism.
- **Fine-grained locking** (multiple locks for different fields) increases parallelism, but risks deadlock and complexity.

Finding the right balance is part of designing concurrent Go systems.

Reader/Writer Locking with sync.RWMutex

Some data structures are read more frequently than they are written. For such cases, **sync.RWMutex** allows multiple readers to access data concurrently while still permitting exclusive access for writers.

```
type SafeConfig struct {
    mu  sync.RWMutex
    cfg map[string]string
}

func (s *SafeConfig) Get(key string) string {
```

```
    s.mu.RLock()
    defer s.mu.RUnlock()
    return s.cfg[key]
}

func (s *SafeConfig) Set(key, value string) {
    s.mu.Lock()
    defer s.mu.Unlock()
    s.cfg[key] = value
}
```

Here, multiple Get calls can run in parallel, but Set operations enforce exclusive access. This dramatically improves throughput in read-heavy workloads.

However, misuse can lead to starvation—writers may wait indefinitely if readers continue to acquire shared locks. The implementation by Go tries to minimize this issue, but developers must still design with awareness.

Synchronization with `sync.WaitGroup`

Although not directly used for preventing data races, **`WaitGroup`** plays a critical role in coordinating goroutine execution. Without proper synchronization, a program may terminate before all goroutines complete, leading to incomplete writes, partial updates, or corrupted state.

```
var wg sync.WaitGroup

for i := 0; i < 10; i++ {
    wg.Add(1)
    go func() {
        defer wg.Done()
        // safe concurrent work
    }()
}

wg.Wait()
```

`WaitGroup` ensures that all goroutines finish before the program continues, preventing timing-related errors that mimic race conditions.

Condition Variables with `sync.Cond`

`sync.Cond` provides condition-based synchronization, allowing goroutines to wait for or signal state changes. This is essential for producer-consumer pipelines, and coordination patterns where goroutines need to sleep until a condition becomes true.

```
var (
    mu   sync.Mutex
    cond = sync.NewCond(&mu)
    data = make([]int, 0)
)

func producer() {
    mu.Lock()
    data = append(data, 42)
    cond.Signal()
    mu.Unlock()
}

func consumer() {
    mu.Lock()
    for len(data) == 0 {
        cond.Wait()
    }
    value := data[0]
    data = data[1:]
    mu.Unlock()
    fmt.Println("Consumed:", value)
}
```

Misuse of condition variables can cause missed signals, deadlocks, or infinite waits. Their correct usage requires consistent locking discipline, but they offer an efficiency superior to busy-waiting.

Avoiding Races through `sync.Map` and Lock-Free Designs

The **`sync.Map`** type offers a concurrency-safe map implementation, suitable for use cases where:

- Keys are frequently created once and read many times.
- The set of keys is not known at compile time.
- Performance under heavy read/write contention is critical.

```
var m sync.Map

m.Store("id", 123)
value, ok := m.Load("id")
```

Internally, **`sync.Map`** uses sophisticated lock-free techniques and amortized strategies to minimize contention. It should be used only when traditional maps with mutexes become bottlenecks.

Memory Synchronization and Happens-before Relationships

Preventing race conditions requires more than simply locking; developers must understand memory visibility. A "happens-before" relationship ensures that writes by one goroutine become visible to another at a defined synchronization point. In Go:

- Mutex unlock → happens-before → next corresponding lock.
- Channel send → happens-before → corresponding receive.
- Close of a channel → happens-before → receive of zero value.
- Writing to a variable without synchronization → no happens-before guarantee → potential race.

Correct memory ordering ensures deterministic behavior in concurrent programs. The sync/atomic package further provides tools for low-level, lock-free synchronization, though it requires a careful use.

Combining the Concurrency Tools of Go Effectively

Preventing race conditions is not solely about choosing the right primitive; it is about understanding the program intent. Common strategies include:

- Protecting shared memory with mutexes.
- Replacing shared memory with channels (share-by-communicating).
- Implementing reader-heavy workloads with RWMutex.
- Using **`WaitGroup`** and **`Cond`** for coordinated concurrency.

Well-designed Go systems blend these tools to achieve high throughput, correctness, and maintainability.

Profiling and Optimizing Concurrency with AI Suggestions

Optimizing concurrency in Go requires a deep understanding of how goroutines are scheduled, how channels behave under different loads, and how shared resources interact across CPU cores. While Go's runtime offers a rich suite of profiling tools to expose these behaviors, interpreting the resulting data can be challenging—especially when performance bottlenecks emerge from subtle interleavings or non-deterministic race conditions. In modern development environments, AI-assisted tools provide a powerful overlay on top of Go's profiling ecosystem, enabling faster diagnosis, clearer explanations, and smarter architectural improvements.

Go's built-in tools—particularly **pprof**—allow detailed sampling of CPU time, memory allocations, goroutine scheduling, blocking events, and mutex contention. This data provides the foundation for debugging and optimizing concurrency.

```
import (
    "log"
    "net/http"
    _ "net/http/pprof"
)

func main() {
    go func() {
        log.Println("pprof available on :6060")
        http.ListenAndServe(":6060", nil)
    }()
    runConcurrentSystem()
}
```

By combining runtime profiling with goroutine dumps, block profiles, and trace visualizations, developers obtain a holistic picture of the execution flow. Yet, raw profiling artifacts can be overwhelming. AI tools step in by translating flame graphs, stack dumps, and traces into digestible insight.

Profiling uncovers systemic patterns that degrade performance in concurrent applications:

- **Goroutine proliferation** due to unbounded spawning.
- **Mutex contention** caused by coarse locking.
- **Blocked channels** indicating backpressure or starvation.
- **Scheduler imbalance** where some goroutines dominate CPU time.
- **Improper timeout/Cancel priority** leading to retry storms.
- **Race conditions** triggered by unsynchronized data access.

While these issues are identifiable through **pprof**, the key challenge is interpreting their meaning within the architecture. This is where AI-enhanced analysis becomes a force multiplier.

Worker Pools as a Concurrency Optimization Strategy

Another common concurrency optimization pattern in Go is the **worker pool**, which limits uncontrolled goroutine creation by reusing a fixed set of workers to process tasks from a queue. Without worker pools, systems often suffer from goroutine proliferation, excessive context switching, and memory pressure.

Worker pools provide several benefits:

- **Bounded concurrency**, preventing resource exhaustion.
- **Predictable scheduling behavior**, improving cache locality.
- **Reduced goroutine churn**, lowering GC and scheduler overhead.
- **Natural backpressure**, as producers block when the task queue is full.

From a profiling perspective, worker pools often reduce:

- Goroutine count spikes in `pprof`.
- Mutex contention caused by oversubscription.
- Scheduler thrashing due to excessive runnable goroutines.

AI-Assisted Insights for Worker Pools

AI tooling can analyze profiling data and suggest:

- Optimal worker pool sizes based on CPU cores and workload characteristics.
- Whether a bounded pool or dynamic pool (with scaling workers) is more appropriate.
- Detection of underutilized pools (idle workers) or saturated pools (queue backlog).
- Channel buffer sizing to balance throughput and latency.

By correlating pprof traces with runtime metrics, AI systems can recommend architectural changes—such as replacing unbounded goroutine spawning with structured worker pools—turning reactive debugging into proactive system design.

AI-Assisted Diagnosis and Root Cause Analysis

AI systems can process profiling artifacts, logs, and stack traces to provide intuitive explanations and prioritization. They excel in three areas:

Explaining Complex Profiling Reports

Profiling reports often include thousands of frames or multiple layers of call stacks—far too noisy for quick human interpretation. AI can:

- Summarize flame graphs.
- Highlight hotspots where goroutines frequently block.

- Explain why particular channels cause backpressure.
- Detect cyclical patterns in call paths.
- Identify misconfigured goroutine lifecycles.

For example, pasting a goroutine dump:

```
goroutine 1834 [chan send]:
main.processEvent(...)
    /app/worker.go:72
```

into an AI tool results in an explanation such as:

"These goroutines are blocked on a send operation. This likely indicates a slow consumer or insufficient channel buffer. Consider increasing buffer size or introducing additional consumers."

This analysis replaces hours of manual trace-following.

Predicting Race-Prone Code Paths

AI models trained on concurrency patterns recognize common race signatures, such as:

- Shared state updated without synchronization.
- Variables captured incorrectly in goroutine closures.
- Misuse of read/write locks.
- Unsynchronized access inside select cases.
- Potential for double-closing channels.

By examining code snippets or the output of go test -race, AI can forecast vulnerabilities even before runtime.

Recommending Optimized Concurrency Structures

AI-assisted suggestions often include architectural improvements, such as:

- Switching from per-request goroutines to worker pools.
- Replacing unbuffered channels with appropriately sized buffers.
- Batching work units to reduce channel chatter.
- Introducing **`sync.Cond`** or **`sync.Map`** for specialized workflows.
- Restructuring pipelines for better parallelism.
- Using atomic operations where appropriate.
- Dividing shared state into sharded locks.

These recommendations accelerate the path from profiling data to an optimized solution.

Practical Guide: How to Use AI Tools for Concurrency Optimization

The following workflow illustrates how AI can be systematically integrated into the tuning process:

Step 1: Collect Profiling Data

- **Start by gathering artifacts:**

```
go test -cpuprofile cpu.out
go tool pprof cpu.out
```

Or run a live **pprof** session from your application.

- **Export:**
  - CPU profiles
  - Memory profiles
  - goroutine dumps
  - Trace files
  - Mutex/block profiles

Step 2: Feed Relevant Data into an AI System

Most AI coding assistants accept:

- Flame graph summaries
- goroutine stack traces
- pprof textual output
- Code snippets
- Log patterns
- Lock ordering violations

If data is large, isolate the top 20–50 lines of the hottest regions. AI thrives on reduced but meaningful input.

Step 3: Ask Targeted Questions

Although AI can provide broad suggestions, targeted prompts yield the best results:

Examples:

"Explain why these goroutines are blocked and suggest concurrency improvements."

"Analyze this pprof CPU output and identify bottlenecks."

"Given this mutex trace, how can I reduce lock contention?"

"Suggest a better design pattern for this channel pipeline."

"Can this code create a race condition? How do I fix it?"

"Do all goroutines have a clear exit path once work is done or on failure?"

Step 4: Apply AI-Suggested Refactorings

AI often proposes specific improvements.

- **Example: Suggested Buffer Tuning**

  Original:

  ```
  jobs := make(chan int)
  ```

  AI recommendation:

  "Increase the channel buffer to decouple producers and consumers."

  Refactored:

  ```
  jobs := make(chan int, 100)
  ```

- **Example: Worker Pool Introduction**

  Before AI suggestion:

  ```
  for _, task := range tasks {
      go handle(task)
  }
  ```

  After AI suggestion:

  ```
  pool := make(chan struct{}, 20)

          for _, task := range tasks {
              pool <- struct{}{}
              go func(t Task) {
                  handle(t)
                  <-pool
              }(task)
          }
  ```

Step 5: Re-Profile and Validate

AI optimization is hypothesis-driven. Verification is still grounded in measurement:

- Rerun **`pprof`**.

- Compare CPU/heap graphs.
- Ensure that goroutine counts stabilize.
- Assess reduced contention.

If the change is ineffective, return to the AI with updated data.

Step 6: Iterate Until Scalability Goals are Met

Concurrency tuning is inherently iterative. AI accelerates this loop by reducing analysis time, offering design patterns, and connecting profiling behavior to architectural solutions.

Profiling builds visibility. AI builds understanding. Together, they form a modern approach to the concurrency optimization in Go—one that blends systematic measurement with intelligent guidance. AI tools amplify the strengths of Go's profiling ecosystem by interpreting runtime artifacts, identifying concurrency patterns, and proposing practical code improvements. This synergy leads to systems that scale efficiently, avoid subtle races, and maintain predictable performance under load.

Conclusion

This chapter has provided a comprehensive exploration of Go's concurrency model—one of the language's defining strengths. It began by examining Go's philosophy of treating concurrency as a core feature, rather than an afterthought, and how goroutines serve as lightweight executable units managed by the runtime, rather than the operating system. By understanding goroutines as cheap, independently scheduled functions, readers gained an insight into why the Go applications scale naturally across multiple cores and high-volume workloads without excessive complexity.

The chapter then introduced channels as the backbone of safe communication between goroutines. Through an in-depth analysis of buffered and unbuffered channels, it illustrated how data flows between concurrent components, how blocking behavior ensures synchronization, and how design choices around channel capacity influence throughput and responsiveness. These concepts were reinforced through real-world communication patterns, demonstrating that channels are not merely data pipes, but structural tools for orchestrating concurrent behavior.

From there, the discussion moved into synchronization techniques and mechanisms for avoiding unintended interactions. Patterns such as fan-out/fan-in, worker pools, and pipeline architectures were unpacked to show how complex systems can be decomposed into predictable concurrent stages. The chapter has emphasized the importance of clear communication boundaries and deliberate synchronization choices, particularly when shared memory or stateful operations are involved. The select statement was presented as a powerful way to manage multiple communication paths, implement timeouts, and build responsive, fault-tolerant systems.

A substantial portion was dedicated to identifying and preventing race conditions—a common hazard in concurrent programming. Through the use of Go's synchronization primitives such as **`sync.Mutex`**, **`sync.RWMutex`**, and **`sync.WaitGroup`**, readers learned strategies for ensuring correctness when shared state cannot be avoided. Tools such as Go's race detector and execution tracing were introduced as essential aids for diagnosing the elusive concurrency bugs that might only appear under specific workloads, or hardware conditions.

The chapter concluded by exploring profiling and optimization techniques, including the role of AI-assisted tools in analyzing concurrency performance. Readers have seen how advanced systems like ChatGPT, Amazon Q, and static-analysis codemods can surface bottlenecks, identify deadlock-prone structures, recommend goroutine lifecycle improvements, and flag inefficient communication patterns. With these combined insights—spanning theory, tooling, and modern AI support—readers are now equipped with the knowledge required to design, debug, and optimize highly concurrent Go applications with confidence and precision.

In the next chapter, the focus is on databases and context management. The chapter covers how Go's low-level database/sql standard package and higher-level ORMs like GORM interface with relational and NoSQL systems. Along with database mechanics, it teaches Go's strong context model, which controls request lifecycles, timeouts, cancellations, and tracing—vital for designing dependable, production-ready services.

CHAPTER 6
Database Interaction and Context Management in Go

Introduction

As modern Go applications increasingly rely on the external data sources for persistence, analytics, and real-time processing, understanding how to integrate databases with the concurrency-oriented design of Go becomes essential. This chapter provides a comprehensive exploration of how Go interacts with both relational and NoSQL systems through its low-level database/sql standard package, and higher-level Object-Relational Mappings (ORMs) like Go Object-Relational Mapping (GORM). Alongside database mechanics, it introduces Go's powerful context model, which governs the request lifecycles, timeouts, cancellations, and tracing—the crucial capabilities for building reliable, production-ready services. Readers will learn not only how to connect, query, and manage transactions across multiple database engines, but also how to design resilient data layers that behave predictably under load, shut down gracefully, and support observability. Together, these tools form the backbone of real-world Go APIs that are fast, scalable, and operationally robust.

Structure

In this chapter, we will cover the following topics:

- Introduction to the **`database/sql`** Package
- Connecting to PostgreSQL and MySQL Databases
    - Choosing the Appropriate Database Driver
    - Constructing Connection Strings
    - Understanding **`sql.DB`** as a Connection Pool

- Connection Lifecycle and Context Support
  - Security Considerations for SQL Connections
  - Advanced PostgreSQL Considerations
  - Advanced MySQL Considerations
  - Testing Connections in Local and CI Environments
- Querying and Scanning Rows Efficiently Using GORM for ORM and Migrations
  - Querying and Scanning Rows Efficiently with database/sql
  - Executing Simple Queries
  - Iterating Over Multiple Rows
  - Best Practices for Efficient Row Scanning
  - Using GORM for ORM Operations and Schema Migrations
  - Schema Management and Migrations in GORM
  - Combining Manual SQL and GORM Effectively
- Managing Transactions and Error Handling
- Mastering Context: Request-Scoped Data, Cancellation, and Timeout Control
  - Deadlines and Timeouts: Avoiding Runaway Operations
  - Cancellation: Cleaning up Resources Responsively
  - Request-Scoped Metadata: Adding Meaning without Globals
  - Putting It All Together: Context as Architecture
- Designing Production-Grade Data Layers: Context-Aware Operations, Pool Tuning, and Graceful Shutdowns
  - Context-Aware Database Operations
  - Connection Pool Tuning in Production
  - Graceful Shutdowns: Managing the Data Layer During Termination
  - Integrating Context, Pool Tuning, and Shutdowns into a Unified Architecture
- Integrating Database and Context Management in Real-World Go APIs
  - Architecture of a Context-Aware Data Layer
  - Context-Aware Query Execution in Handlers and Repositories
  - Context Propagation with Deadlines and Timeouts
  - Managing Complex Operations: Transactions with Context
  - Observability and Context: Logging, Tracing, and Metadata
  - Connection Pool Behavior in Real APIs

- Graceful Shutdown in API Servers
- Putting Everything Together: Example API Architecture
- The Benefits of Unified Database-Context Integration

Introduction to the `database/sql` Package

The **`database/sql`** package serves as the foundational abstraction layer for interacting with relational databases in Go. Rather than functioning as a standalone database driver, it provides a general-purpose interface that allows Go applications to communicate with a wide variety of SQL databases through a consistent, idiomatic API. Actual database support is implemented by driver packages–such as **`github.com/lib/pq`** for PostgreSQL or **`github.com/go-sql-driver/mysql`** for MySQL–which register themselves with **`database/sql`** and supply the low-level protocol details, connection handling logic, and driver-specific features. This separation of concerns enables the developers to write portable data-access code while retaining flexibility in choosing, or switching underlying database engines.

At its core, the **`database/sql`** package introduces three primary types that define its operational **model: `sql.DB`**, **`sql.Conn`**, and **`sql.Tx`**. A **`sql.DB`** instance represents a pool of zero or more active connections, rather than a single connection. It manages connection creation, lifetime, reuse, and pooling strategies automatically, making it both lightweight and safe for concurrent use. Under the hood, it also handles timeouts, idle connections, and reconnection logic, allowing higher-level application code to focus entirely on executing queries and managing results. For scenarios requiring more deterministic control–such as pinning work to a single connection–**`sql.Conn`** provides an explicit handle to an individual database connection. Meanwhile, **`sql.Tx`** models a transactional context that ensures atomic execution of a sequence of SQL statements.

The package introduces a uniform set of methods for executing queries and inspecting the results. The **`Exec`** and **`Querymethods`** allow for executing SQL statements directly, while **`QueryRow`** is optimized for retrieving a single record. Results are returned as lightweight wrappers (**`sql.Rows`** and **`sql.Row`**) that expose scanning methods for mapping column data into Go variables. Importantly, the API strongly encourages explicit error handling at each stage: issuing queries, iterating over returned rows, and closing result sets. This explicit model aligns with Go's philosophy of clarity and control, ensuring that resource management and error paths remain predictable even in complex workflows.

Prepared statements are another critical feature facilitated by the package. Through **`DB.Prepare`** or **`Tx.Prepare`** the application can create reusable statement objects that are optimized by the database engine for repeated execution. This approach promotes performance for high-traffic queries and improves security by separating SQL structure from user-supplied parameters, thereby reducing exposure to injection flaws. Because prepared statements participate in the connection lifecycle, the package ensures that they remain tied to the connection or transaction that created them.

Finally, the **database/sql** package is designed with concurrency in mind. A single DB instance can be shared safely across goroutines, allowing large-scale applications to coordinate queries without manual locking. Connection pooling **behavior**–such as the maximum number of open connections, maximum idle connections, and connection lifetime–is configurable through methods like **SetMaxOpenConns**, giving developers a fine-grained control over performance tuning and resource usage. Combined with Go's concurrency model and context propagation semantics, **database/sql** forms the backbone of the production-grade data access layers for modern Go applications.

Connecting to PostgreSQL and MySQL Databases

Relational databases such as PostgreSQL and MySQL remain central components of modern backend systems, and Go's **database/sql package** offers a clean, efficient foundation for interfacing with both. While **database/sql** defines a universal API, it delegates actual connectivity to external drivers that implement database-specific protocols. Connecting to PostgreSQL or MySQL, therefore, requires importing the appropriate driver, configuring the connection string, establishing the connection pool, and validating communication with the database engine. Understanding these steps is necessary for building reliable data layers that perform well under concurrent workloads.

Choosing the Appropriate Database Driver

Go developers typically rely on two widely adopted driver implementations:

- **PostgreSQL:**

  ```
  github.com/lib/pq (classic driver, mature and stable)
  github.com/jackc/pgx/v5 (newer, faster, feature-rich driver often
  preferred for high-performance applications)
  ```

- **MySQL:**

  ```
  github.com/go-sql-driver/mysql (the de facto standard MySQL
  driver)
  ```

Each driver implements the **database/sql/driver** interfaces, registers itself under a unique name (similar to "**postgres**" or "**mysql**"), and exposes driver-specific functionality when needed. In most cases, the default capabilities exposed through the sql package suffice, providing compatibility with a wide range of relational workflows.

Constructing Connection Strings

Connection strings define how Go should authenticate and communicate with the database. Although formats differ between PostgreSQL and MySQL, the underlying parameters remain similar: host, port, username, password, database name, and optional SSL or timeout settings.

PostgreSQL example (`lib/pq`):

```
connStr := "host=localhost port=5432 user=appuser password=secret
dbname=appdb sslmode=disable"
db, err := sql.Open("postgres", connStr)
if err != nil {
      log.Fatal("Failed to open PostgreSQL connection:", err)
}
```

MySQL example:

```
dsn := "appuser:secret@tcp(localhost:3306)/appdb?parseTime
=true&charset=utf8mb4"
db, err := sql.Open("mysql", dsn)
if err != nil {
      log.Fatal("Failed to open MySQL connection:", err)
}
```

Although **`sql.Open`** initializes a **`*sql.DB`** instance, it does not validate the connection immediately. Instead, it creates a handle to the connection pool. To verify that credentials and network settings are correct, it is essential to call **`db.Ping()`** or **`db.PingContext()`**.

```
if err := db.Ping(); err != nil {
      log.Fatal("Database unreachable:", err)
}
```

This explicit ping step helps detect misconfigurations early and allows the application to surface descriptive startup errors.

Understanding `sql.DB` as a Connection Pool

A **`sql.DB`** object is not a single connection, but a managed pool of reusable connections. This design allows Go applications to support many simultaneous requests efficiently, distributing database load across the available pool.

Pooling parameters such as maximum idle connections, maximum open connections, and connection lifetime significantly influence throughput and resource utilization.

```
db.SetMaxOpenConns(20)          // Limit total concurrent connections
db.SetMaxIdleConns(10)          // Maintain warm idle connections
db.SetConnMaxLifetime(time.Hour) // Avoid stale connections
```

For applications that handle high concurrency or frequent database operations—such as REST APIs or microservices—tuning these values ensures stable throughput while preventing database overload.

PostgreSQL and MySQL behave differently under heavy pooling. PostgreSQL, for instance, creates a dedicated server process for each active connection, so excessive open connections can exhaust system memory. MySQL operations are lighter, but still require thoughtful pool management to avoid starvation or slowdowns.

Connection Lifecycle and Context Support

Establishing secure, robust connection logic requires integrating Go's context semantics for cancellation and timeout control. Both PostgreSQL and MySQL drivers fully support **`QueryContext`**, **`ExecContext`**, and **`PrepareContext`**. These context-aware variants ensure that long-running or stalled queries do not block application progress.

```
ctx, cancel := context.WithTimeout(context.Background(), 2*time.
Second)
defer cancel()

row := db.QueryRowContext(ctx, "SELECT name FROM users WHERE
id=$1", 42)
```

If the query fails to return within two seconds, the context triggers cancellation, and releases the underlying connection back to the pool. This behavior is essential for maintaining system responsiveness under unreliable network conditions or complex transactional workloads.

Security Considerations for SQL Connections

Production environments require carefully structured connection strategies:

- Disable SSL only for local development.
  For PostgreSQL, **`sslmode=disable`** should never be used in production unless connections are tunneled through a secure private network.

- Avoid embedding credentials in source code.
  Prefer environment variables or secrets managers.

- Pre-validate connection pooling limits.
  Overly generous pool sizes can overwhelm the database engine.
- Enable MySQL options such as **`parseTime=true`**.
  Without this setting, MySQL drivers may treat timestamps as byte slices rather than native **`time.Time`**.

To help reduce boilerplate and enforce secure defaults, many developers use AI-assisted tools to generate environment-safe configuration scaffolding, connection wrappers, and secrets-handling logic. These suggestions help avoid common misconfigurations and improve maintainability.

Advanced PostgreSQL Considerations

PostgreSQL exposes extended functionality that benefits high-performance Go applications, especially when using the **`pgx`** driver:

- Connection pooling via **`pgxpool`**.
- Support for PostgreSQL-specific types (UUID, JSONB, arrays).
- Binary protocol support for faster I/O.
- Advanced authentication like SCRAM-SHA-256.

Example using `pgxpool`:

```
config, err := pgxpool.ParseConfig("postgres://appuser:secret@
localhost:5432/appdb")
if err != nil {
	log.Fatal(err)
}

pool, err := pgxpool.NewWithConfig(context.Background(), config)
if err != nil {
	log.Fatal(err)
}
defer pool.Close()
```

While still interoperable with **`database/sql`**, **`pgx`** often offers lower latency and higher throughput for intensive workloads, making it ideal for analytics systems, event processors, and large-scale APIs.

Advanced MySQL Considerations

MySQL deployments frequently leverage capabilities such as:

- Connection attributes for distributed tracing.
- Failover handling via multiple host definitions.

- Prepared statement reuse.
- Time zone and encoding management.

For example, a production-grade DSN may include additional configuration:

```
dsn := "appuser:secret@tcp(mysql-primary:3306)/appdb" +
       "?parseTime=true&tls=true&timeout=5s&loc=UTC"
```

The driver ecosystem of MySQL also includes specialized load balancers (such as ProxySQL) that integrate seamlessly with the Go applications, enabling high-availability and read-write splitting strategies.

Testing Connections in Local and CI Environments

A robust development workflow requires safe, reproducible testing capabilities. Go developers frequently use Docker-based databases for local work and continuous integration pipelines.

Example using PostgreSQL on Docker:

```
docker run --name pgtest -p 5432:5432 -e POSTGRES_PASSWORD=secret
-d postgres:15
```

Integration testing typically uses ephemeral databases, with AI tools providing automated generation of test harnesses, cleanup logic, and table migration scripts. Context-aware queries combined with transaction rollbacks ensure independent, repeatable tests.

Querying and Scanning Rows Efficiently Using GORM for ORM and Migrations

Efficient data retrieval is central to building high-performance Go applications. Whether an application relies on the low-level primitives of the **`database/sql`** package or the expressive abstractions provided by GORM, the principles remain the same: minimize unnecessary work, handle results predictably, and structure queries in a maintainable, testable way. This section examines how to execute SQL queries, and scan results manually for maximum control, followed by an exploration of GORM as a higher-level ORM framework that automates common database tasks, including schema migrations.

Querying and Scanning Rows Efficiently with `database/sql`

The **`database/sql`** package provides a minimal, powerful API for issuing SQL commands. It is intentionally low-level, requiring an explicit handling of query execution, row iteration, type conversion, and error management. This design forces clarity and control, ensuring that application behavior remains predictable even under high concurrency or complex data flows.

Executing Simple Queries

The most common query pattern involves retrieving a single row using **`QueryRowContext`**. Since the method does not return an error immediately, the error must be inspected during the **`Scan`** call.

```
var name string
var age int

err := db.QueryRowContext(ctx,
    "SELECT name, age FROM users WHERE id=$1", userID,
).Scan(&name, &age)

if err != nil {
    if err == sql.ErrNoRows {
        // Handle missing record
    }
    return err
}
```

This pattern is highly efficient because it avoids allocating a result set when only one row is needed.

Iterating over Multiple Rows

For larger result sets, **`QueryContext`** returns a **`*sql.Rows`** cursor.

```
rows, err := db.QueryContext(ctx,
    "SELECT id, email FROM subscribers WHERE active = true")
if err != nil {
    return err
}
defer rows.Close()

for rows.Next() {
    var id int
```

```
        var email string
        if err := rows.Scan(&id, &email); err != nil {
            return err
        }
        // Process row
    }

    if err := rows.Err(); err != nil {
        return err
    }
```

This pattern is optimized for streaming large datasets because Go reads rows incrementally, rather than loading the entire result into memory. This makes it suitable for analytics dashboards, background processing, and continuous data ingestion.

Best Practices for Efficient Row Scanning

Several principles ensure predictable, performant scanning operations:

- Declare variables once, outside the loop, to minimize allocations.
- Scan into Go native types, letting the driver perform appropriate decoding.
- Use context-aware queries (**`QueryContext`**) to support cancellation and timeouts.
- Always defer **`rows.Close()`** immediately after a successful query creation.
- Check **`rows.Err()`** after iteration to capture any streaming errors.

Applications that follow these patterns exhibit strong performance characteristics even as dataset sizes grow.

Using GORM for ORM Operations and Schema Migrations

While **`database/sql`** offers low-level control, many applications benefit from a higher-level abstraction that simplifies common CRUD patterns and schema evolution. GORM, the most widely adopted ORM in the Go ecosystem, provides a full-featured API for modeling relational data, performing queries, managing transactions, and applying migrations. It removes repetitive boilerplate, thereby enabling developers to express database interactions in a more declarative style.

Defining Models in GORM

A model in GORM maps directly to a database table. Struct tags control the column properties, primary keys, indexes, constraints, and naming conventions.

```
type User struct {
    ID        uint      `gorm:"primaryKey"`
    Name      string    `gorm:"size:100;not null"`
    Email     string    `gorm:"uniqueIndex"`
    Age       int
    CreatedAt time.Time
}
```

GORM follows conventional defaults, but allows full customization using tags. For example, specifying **`gorm:"size:100"`** ensures that GORM generates **`VARCHAR(100)`** for SQL dialects that support variable-length strings.

Opening a Database Connection with GORM

GORM builds on top of database drivers while offering additional abstractions:

```
dsn := "host=localhost user=appuser dbname=appdb password=secret
sslmode=disable"
db, err := gorm.Open(postgres.Open(dsn), &gorm.Config{})
if err != nil {
    log.Fatal("Failed to connect:", err)
}
```

Internally, GORM creates a **`*sql.DB`** connection pool, which can be tuned similarly to manual setups:

```
sqlDB, _ := db.DB()
sqlDB.SetMaxIdleConns(10)
sqlDB.SetMaxOpenConns(50)
sqlDB.SetConnMaxLifetime(time.Hour)
```

Querying with GORM

GORM provides multiple querying mechanisms; each balancing readability with flexibility.

Retrieving Single Rows:

```
var user User
err := db.First(&user, 42).Error
if err != nil {
    // Record not found or DB error
}
```

GORM Automatically Constructs:

```
SELECT * FROM users WHERE id = 42 LIMIT 1;
```

Filtering with Conditions:

```
var users []User
db.Where("age > ?", 18).
```

```
    Order("created_at desc").
    Limit(20).
    Find(&users)
```

Selecting Specific Columns:

```
db.Model(&User{}).Select("name", "email").Scan(&results)
```

This avoids fetching unnecessary data, and also improves memory efficiency.

Joining Related Data, GORM Supports Eager Loading:

```
db.Preload("Orders").First(&user)
```

Allowing structured queries without manually writing JOIN statements.

Schema Management and Migrations in GORM

A major advantage of GORM is its built-in migration engine. Migrations allow the database schema to evolve as the application requirements change.

Auto-Migration

Auto-migration creates or updates tables to match model definitions:

```
err := db.AutoMigrate(&User{}, &Order{})
if err != nil {
    log.Fatal("Migration failed:", err)
}
```

Auto-migration can:

- Create new tables.
- Add missing columns.
- Create indexes.
- Apply constraints.

Auto-migration does not remove existing columns to prevent accidental data loss.

Versioned Migrations

For large teams or production systems, migration scripts should be version-controlled using libraries such as:

- **`golang-migrate/migrate`**
- **`pressly/goose`**
- **`dbmate`**

GORM integrates with these tools by generating SQL schemas via the Migrator interface.

Combining Manual SQL and GORM Effectively

Many production systems use both manual SQL and GORM:

- GORM is ideal for standard CRUD, relationship handling, and migrations.
- Manual SQL is preferred for complex analytical queries, bulk operations, or database-specific optimizations.

GORM's `db.Raw()` enables hybrid use:

```
type Result struct {
    Count int
}

db.Raw("SELECT COUNT(*) AS count FROM orders WHERE status = ?",
"pending").
   Scan(&Result{})
```

This preserves the flexibility of raw SQL while benefiting from the scanning and model mappings by GORM.

Query performance improves significantly when:

- Column selection is narrow.
- Prepared statements are reused.
- Indexes support common filters.
- Scanning is done into simple structs.
- Queries run with timeouts via context.
- GORM debug mode (**`db.Debug()`**) is used for query inspection.

Developers often complement these strategies with AI-assisted analysis tools, which help identify potential N+1 queries, missing indexes, inefficient joins, or redundant query patterns. AI refactoring tools frequently detect these issues earlier than manual reviews, leading to a better database performance overall.

Managing Transactions and Error Handling

Transactions form the backbone of reliable data operations in Go applications that interact with relational databases. Whether one is inserting related records, updating multiple tables, or performing conditional changes that must succeed or fail as a single unit, transactional guarantees ensure data integrity. Go's **database/sql** package provides a clean, predictable model for managing transactions explicitly, giving developers full control over when work is committed or rolled back. Rather than relying on implicit transaction management—as seen in some ORMs or dynamic languages—Go encourages a deliberate approach: begin a transaction, execute a sequence of operations, verify its correctness, and finalize with a commit or rollback based on the outcome. This explicit pattern significantly reduces ambiguity, and forces consistent error handling discipline.

A transaction begins with the **Begin()** or **BeginTx()** method, which returns a ***sql.Tx** object representing an active transactional context. All queries—reads or writes—issued within this transaction occur in isolation from the broader database state until committed. The idiomatic form involves three distinct steps: start a transaction, defer a rollback to ensure a cleanup on unexpected failures, and explicitly call **Commit()** only if all operations succeed. This pattern ensures that even if a function returns prematurely—due to an error or a logic branch—the database is left in a consistent state.

```
func CreateOrder(ctx context.Context, db *sql.DB, order Order,
items []Item) error {
    tx, err := db.BeginTx(ctx, nil)
    if err != nil {
        return fmt.Errorf("cannot begin transaction: %w", err)
    }
    defer tx.Rollback() // Safe even if commit happens

    // Insert the order
    res, err := tx.ExecContext(ctx,
        `INSERT INTO orders (customer_id, total_amount) VALUES
($1, $2)`,
        order.CustomerID, order.Total,
    )
    if err != nil {
        return fmt.Errorf("inserting order failed: %w", err)
    }

    orderID, _ := res.LastInsertId()

    // Insert order items
    for _, item := range items {
        _, err := tx.ExecContext(ctx,
            `INSERT INTO order_items (order_id, product_id,
quantity, price)
             VALUES ($1, $2, $3, $4)`,
            orderID, item.ProductID, item.Quantity, item.Price,
        )
```

```
            if err != nil {
                return fmt.Errorf("inserting item failed: %w", err)
            }
        }

        // All operations succeeded—commit the results
        if err := tx.Commit(); err != nil {
            return fmt.Errorf("commit failed: %w", err)
        }

        return nil
    }
```

This example demonstrates the transactional discipline Go promotes. The deferred **tx.Rollback()** ensures that the database is not left in a partially updated state if any error occurs. Only after all statements succeed does the function attempt **Commit()**. The use of %w for error wrapping allows callers to inspect the original database errors using **errors.Is()** or **errors.As()**, forming the foundation for robust upstream error classification.

Error handling in transactional code deserves specific attention. Transactions amplify the consequences of failures because problems that occur deep within a series of actions may not surface until related writes have already been attempted. To mitigate such risks, Go encourages early checks, explicit propagation of errors, and clear rollback semantics. Additionally, transactions should be kept as short as possible. Long-running transactions increase the likelihood of locking conflicts, slow down other queries, and may trigger deadlocks in high-throughput systems. Designing queries carefully—performing validation or lookups before starting the transaction—often yields more predictable behavior.

Another important consideration is how transactions interact with the application's context. Using **ExecContext** and **QueryContext** within **BeginTx** ensures that a transaction respects deadlines and cancellation signals. When the context expires, the transaction automatically fails, leading to a clean rollback. This becomes especially important in HTTP-driven systems where server-side handlers must enforce request-scoped timeouts to avoid holding database resources longer than intended.

```
ctx, cancel := context.WithTimeout(context.Background(), 3*time.
Second)
defer cancel()

tx, err := db.BeginTx(ctx, &sql.TxOptions{Isolation: sql.Level
Serializable})
if err != nil {
    log.Println("begin failed:", err)
}
```

Here, the isolation level is configured explicitly. While many applications rely on the default isolation provided by the database, certain workloads–such as financial transfers–may require stricter guarantees. The transactional API allows this fine-grained control without complexity.

Error handling extends beyond transactional boundaries. A well-designed system distinguishes between retryable and non-retryable errors. For instance, serialization errors **(SQLSTATE 40001)** in PostgreSQL often indicate transient conflicts under high concurrency and can be retried safely. Go's structured error wrapping supports building retry loops that examine error codes and re-attempt operations when appropriate.

Libraries like GORM simplify transaction handling through helpers such as **db.Transaction(func(tx *gorm.DB) error { ... })**, but the conceptual model remains the same: a function returns nil to commit or an error to trigger rollback. Even when using ORM abstractions, understanding the underlying semantics helps diagnose complex issues such as nested transactions, partial updates, and unexpected constraint violations.

```
err := db.Transaction(func(tx *gorm.DB) error {
    if err := tx.Create(&order).Error; err != nil {
        return err
    }
    for _, item := range items {
        if err := tx.Create(&item).Error; err != nil {
            return err
        }
    }
    return nil // commit
})
if err != nil {
    log.Println("transaction error:", err)
}
```

Ultimately, managing transactions in Go is not just about writing correct SQL statements–it is about designing a predictable control flow, building strong error-handling paths, and ensuring that failures are not compromised over data consistency. Hence, whether using **database/sql** directly, or an abstraction layer like GORM, the principles remain constant: explicit control, clear commit semantics, reliable rollback, and thorough error classification. These foundations form the basis for constructing durable, production-ready data systems in Go.

Mastering Context: Request-Scoped Data, Cancellation, and Timeout Control

With the increasing complexity in Go applications–spanning HTTP servers, background workers, database layers, and distributed systems–the need for structured control over execution lifecycles becomes unavoidable. Go's context package addresses this need by providing a standardized mechanism for managing deadlines, cancellation signals, and request-scoped metadata across function boundaries. Instead of relying on ad hoc flags, global variables, or custom cancellation logic, the **`context.Context`** type introduces a uniform contract: every operation that may block, wait, or depend on upstream state should accept a context and respect its lifecycle. This philosophy permeates the entire Go ecosystem, and understanding it deeply is essential for writing responsive, predictable, and resource-safe applications.

At its core, a context represents the state of a request. When an HTTP request arrives, for example, the server automatically generates a context that carries the deadlines and cancellation semantics tied to the connection of the client. As the request moves through middleware, handlers, services, and the data layer, this context ensures that all parts of the system remain synchronized with the lifecycle of that request. If the user closes the browser tab, if the load balancer enforces a timeout, or if the server intentionally cancels a long-running operation, the cancellation of the context propagates instantly to all participating components. By aligning system behavior with real-time conditions, context prevents wasted computation, stale work, and unnecessary database or network load.

Deadlines and Timeouts: Avoiding Runaway Operations

One of the most powerful aspects of context is its ability to define time limits on work. A timeout ensures that the caller will not wait indefinitely for slow I/O, blocked queries, or network partitions. Without such limits, even a single misbehaving downstream dependency can exhaust server resources. Using **`context.WithTimeout`** or **`context.WithDeadline`**, a developer can precisely express how long a particular operation is permitted to run. Code that honors these deadlines returns early with a descriptive error, rather than occupying threads or goroutines indefinitely.

```
ctx, cancel := context.WithTimeout(context.Background(), 2*time.
Second)
defer cancel()
```

```
rows, err := db.QueryContext(ctx, "SELECT * FROM large_table")
if err != nil {
    return fmt.Errorf("query timed out or failed: %w", err)
}
```

Here, the database driver listens for the context's cancellation signal. If the query exceeds two seconds–perhaps due to table locks or a network stall–it returns immediately. This behavior is essential for systems that must maintain consistent response times and protect themselves against slow downstream services.

Deadlines become even more critical in distributed architectures. When a service calls another, it must propagate the remaining time budget so that downstream services do not attempt to exceed the constraints of the caller. Go's context is explicitly designed for this propagation. By passing the same context through RPC clients, message processors, and database calls, a system maintains end-to-end awareness of latency expectations.

Cancellation: Cleaning up Resources Responsively

Timeouts are only one side of context management. Cancellation–either manual or automatic–is equally fundamental. By invoking the cancel function returned from **context.WithCancel**, an operation signals that all participating goroutines must stop work and release resources. This makes cancellation a vital tool for coordinating concurrent operations, especially when one result makes the others redundant.

Consider a scenario where an application performs multiple parallel queries, and only needs the fastest response:

```
ctx, cancel := context.WithCancel(context.Background())
defer cancel()

results := make(chan string, 2)

go func() {
    r, _ := fastQuery(ctx)
    results <- r
    cancel()  // stop the slower ones
}()

go func() {
    r, _ := slowQuery(ctx)
    results <- r
}()
```

```
answer := <-results
return answer
```

Once the first query completes, the cancellation propagates to all other oroutines. This mechanism prevents duplicate work and ensures that the system does not expend unnecessary CPU cycles, memory, or network traffic. Without context propagation, concurrent workers would need manual synchronization logic, significantly increasing the complexity and risk of resource leaks.

Request-Scoped Metadata: Adding Meaning without Globals

Beyond deadlines and cancellation, context plays an important role in transporting request-scoped metadata across layers of an application. Instead of storing such metadata in globals or passing dozens of parameters, context allows it to be safely attached using **context.WithValue**.

A common use case is storing correlation IDs or authenticated user information:

```
type key int
const requestIDKey key = 0

func addRequestID(ctx context.Context, id string) context.Context {
    return context.WithValue(ctx, requestIDKey, id)
}

func requestID(ctx context.Context) string {
    v := ctx.Value(requestIDKey)
    if v == nil {
        return ""
    }
    return v.(string)
}
```

Such metadata helps with tracing, logging, and observability. It allows every part of the application—including the database layer—to associate events with the request that triggered them. However, Go's documentation strongly cautions developers to keep context values small and use them sparingly. They are not intended as a replacement for structs or configuration objects. Instead, context values should store only data directly tied to the lifecycle of a request, and only when passing additional parameters through a deep call chain would otherwise create clutter or unnecessary coupling.

The integration between the context package and **database/sql** is especially important. All database operations—queries, prepared statements, transaction calls—should use their Context-aware variants. When an HTTP request ends, the cancellation propagates down to the database layer, which then cancels active queries, releases locks, and terminates network waits.

```
func findUser(ctx context.Context, db *sql.DB, id int64) (*User,
error) {
    row := db.QueryRowContext(ctx,
        "SELECT id, email, name FROM users WHERE id=$1", id,
    )

    var u User
    if err := row.Scan(&u.ID, &u.Email, &u.Name); err != nil {
        return nil, err
    }
    return &u, nil
}
```

This pattern enables graceful system behavior. If a client disconnects mid-request, the server no longer attempts to finish the expensive database work. This approach naturally leads to improved latency, reduced lock contention, and lower resource waste.

Contexts are also vital for graceful shutdowns. During shutdown, servers often stop accepting new requests but must allow active ones to complete. By creating a root context with a timeout, and passing it through all shutdown routines, the application ensures that deadlines are respected consistently across network listeners, goroutine pools, and database connections.

Putting It All Together: Context as Architecture

When used properly, context becomes more than an API—it becomes an architectural foundation. It shapes how data flows through layers, dictates how cancellations propagate across goroutines, and maintains control over resource lifecycles. It encourages consistent behavior across subsystems and provides strong guarantees about execution timing and cleanup.

Systems built without proper context propagation often exhibit unpredictable behavior: database connections remain open long after a client disconnects, background goroutines continue running despite canceled requests, and errors propagate without clarity. In contrast, systems built with disciplined context usage demonstrate controlled responsiveness, predictable shutdown behavior, and scalable performance under varying load conditions.

Mastering Go's context package, therefore, is not only a matter of technical correctness—it is a prerequisite for designing reliable, production-grade systems that behave well under real-world conditions. Hence, whether handling a short-lived API call, orchestrating multiple concurrent tasks, or coordinating services in a distributed environment, context is the mechanism that keeps operations bounded, meaningful, and aligned with the lifecycle of the request.

Designing Production-Grade Data Layers: Context-Aware Operations, Pool Tuning, and Graceful Shutdowns

Designing a data layer suitable for production environments requires far more than simply opening a database connection and issuing SQL queries. A robust data layer must balance performance, reliability, and responsiveness, especially under unpredictable workloads and distributed system constraints. Go provides powerful primitives—**`context.Context`**, **`database/sql`**, connection pooling mechanisms, and composable abstractions—that help developers build data-access systems capable of meeting production demands. When engineered thoughtfully, these tools ensure that the application handles failures gracefully, utilizes resources effectively, and maintains consistent latency even as concurrency scales.

At the heart of modern Go data-layer architecture lies context-aware operations, which tightly couple database work with the lifecycle of a request or background task. Connecting context propagation with pooling strategy and graceful shutdown workflows ensures that every part of the system follows a clear operational contract: no work should continue longer than the caller intends, no resource should be leaked, and every critical component should shut down cleanly during redeployment or service rotation.

Context-Aware Database Operations

Using context throughout the data layer establishes deterministic behavior when handling deadlines, cancellations, or hierarchical workflows. Any database function that interacts with the datastore should adopt a signature modeled after:

```
func (r *Repo) GetUser(ctx context.Context, id int64) (*User, error)
```

This convention guarantees that all downstream operations abide by the constraints defined at the application boundary—be it an HTTP request, a message handler, or a scheduled task. The database/sql package provides **`QueryContext`**, **`ExecContext`**, and **`BeginTx`** to ensure that queries terminate when the context expires.

Why Context Matters in the Data Layer:

- **Prevents Runaway Queries:** A context deadline ensures that a slow query does not monopolize connections.

- **Aligns with Request Lifecycles:** If the user cancels a request, database operations stop immediately.
- **Enables Cascading Cancellation:** In multi-step workflows, failure or timeout at one step cancels all remaining steps.
- **Helps with Tracing and Observability:** Correlation IDs stored in context propagate automatically to logs and spans.

Example: Context-Aware Query Execution

```
func (r *Repo) FindActiveOrders(ctx context.Context, userID
int64) ([]Order, error) {
    ctx, cancel := context.WithTimeout(ctx, 3*time.Second)
    defer cancel()

    rows, err := r.db.QueryContext(ctx,
        `SELECT id, amount, status FROM orders WHERE user_id=$1
AND status='active'`,
        userID,
    )
    if err != nil {
        return nil, fmt.Errorf("query failed: %w", err)
    }
    defer rows.Close()

    var orders []Order
    for rows.Next() {
        var o Order
        if err := rows.Scan(&o.ID, &o.Amount, &o.Status);
err != nil {
            return nil, err
        }
        orders = append(orders, o)
    }
    return orders, rows.Err()
}
```

This pattern ensures that every query is bounded, cancellable, and respectful of operational limits.

Connection Pool Tuning in Production

The **`database/sql`** package of Go includes a sophisticated, built-in connection pool that manages concurrency, idle connections, and connection reuse. Poorly tuned pools frequently become bottlenecks in production systems; developers may observe timeouts, connection exhaustion, or unbounded goroutine growth when queries wait indefinitely for resources.

A production-grade data layer must configure:

- **`SetMaxOpenConns(n int):`**

  Maximum number of open connections to the database.

- **`SetMaxIdleConns(n int):`**

  Maximum number of idle connections retained for reuse.

- **`SetConnMaxLifetime(d time.Duration):`**

  Maximum lifetime of a connection before it must be recreated.

- **`SetConnMaxIdleTime(d time.Duration):`**

  Maximum idle time before a connection is retired.

Example: Tuning a PostgreSQL Pool

```
db, err := sql.Open("pgx", dsn)
if err != nil {
    log.Fatalf("db open failed: %v", err)
}

db.SetMaxOpenConns(50)
db.SetMaxIdleConns(25)
db.SetConnMaxLifetime(30 * time.Minute)
db.SetConnMaxIdleTime(5 * time.Minute)
```

Principles for Effective Pool Tuning:

- **Match limits to workload patterns**: High-throughput systems often require larger pools; CPU-bound services may need smaller ones.
- **Avoid overprovisioning**: Too many open connections can overwhelm the database server, leading to degraded performance.
- **Rotate connections periodically**: This prevents idle connections from becoming stale—especially important for cloud database load balancers.
- **Monitor connection usage**: Metrics such as queue wait time, open connections, and idle connections inform tuning decisions.
- **Favor short-lived queries**: Long-running queries monopolize connections; combining context timeouts with indexing strategy mitigates this.

  Connection pools form the backbone of a production-ready data layer; tuning them proactively ensures smooth scaling under high concurrency.

Graceful Shutdowns: Managing the Data Layer During Termination

Production systems cannot afford abrupt shutdowns. Restarting servers–whether due to deployments, autoscaling events, or maintenance–must occur without interrupting in-flight operations or corrupting data. Go's context model and SQL package together provide the tools necessary for graceful shutdown workflows.

The Lifecycle of a Graceful Shutdown:

1. **Stop accepting new requests**: The server halts listeners but continues serving active requests.
2. **Propagate a shutdown context**: Components receive a top-level context with a deadline.
3. **Let ongoing operations finish or timeout**: Long-running database queries or transactions complete naturally or exit when context expires.
4. **Close the database pool safely**: After all operations are done, **`db.Close()`** shuts down the remaining idle connections.

Example: Graceful Shutdown with Context

```
func main() {
    db := setupDB()

    srv := &http.Server{
        Addr:    ":8080",
        Handler: apiRouter(db),
    }

    go func() {
        if err := srv.ListenAndServe(); err != nil &&
err != http.ErrServerClosed {
            log.Fatalf("server failed: %v", err)
        }
    }()

    stop := make(chan os.Signal, 1)
    signal.Notify(stop, os.Interrupt, syscall.SIGTERM)

    <-stop
    log.Println("shutting down...")

    ctx, cancel := context.WithTimeout(context.Background(),
10*time.Second)
```

```
        defer cancel()

        if err := srv.Shutdown(ctx); err != nil {
            log.Println("server shutdown error:", err)
        }

        db.Close()
        log.Println("shutdown complete")
    }
```

This pattern ensures that any in-progress database operations can gracefully conclude. Since all database calls use **`QueryContext`** or **`ExecContext`**, cancellation propagates naturally once the server enters the shutdown phase.

Integrating Context, Pool Tuning, and Shutdowns into a Unified Architecture

A production-grade data layer is not merely a set of database functions—it is an architectural component that governs how data access interacts with lifecycle management, concurrency, high load, and system resilience. Integrating all three areas—context-aware operations, connection pooling, and graceful shutdowns—creates a predictable and maintainable system.

Key Architectural Principles:

- Every database operation must be context-driven.

  Hard Requirement: No Query or Exec calls should appear in production code.
- **Centralized Database Initialization:** A single package or struct manages pool settings, health checks, and configuration.
- **Consistent Shutdown Semantics:** All services use a shared shutdown context.
- **Error Wrapping and Observability:** Clear error messages, correlation ID propagation, and structured logs enhance debuggability.
- **Testing with Controlled Contexts:** Contexts with short deadlines simulate load conditions and ensure robustness.
- **Use AI-assisted profiling and refactoring.**

  Tools like ChatGPT can detect anti-patterns:
  - Queries missing context
  - Functions that never cancel
  - Poor pool configuration
  - Blocking goroutine hotspots

Integrating Database and Context Management in Real-World Go APIs

The true power of the database ecosystem by Go emerges when it is woven seamlessly into a real-world API. Production systems must respond to user requests predictably, enforce operational boundaries, instrument observability, and maintain reliability even under significant concurrency. Integrating database access with context propagation forms the backbone of these capabilities. Properly designed APIs ensure that every query is bounded by request lifetime, every cancellation flows to dependent operations, and every error carries enough context for meaningful debugging, while still performing efficiently under load.

Real-world Go APIs typically follow a layered architecture: an HTTP handler that receives a request, a service layer that defines application logic, and a repository layer that communicates with the database. Context flows through every layer, ensuring that business logic and database operations share the same cancellation and timeout semantics. By standardizing this flow, the API avoids resource leaks, mitigates unpredictable latency, and maintains consistent behavior across all endpoints.

This section demonstrates how to integrate **`database/sql`**, **`context.Context`**, connection pooling, observability, and repository abstractions into a cohesive API architecture suitable for production deployments. The examples use PostgreSQL and follow idiomatic Go conventions relevant to modern backend systems.

Architecture of a Context-Aware Data Layer

A robust API begins with clear boundaries between layers, and each layer must accept a **`context.Context`** parameter and forward it downstream. This contract ensures that:

- Request cancellation aborts lower-level operations.
- Timeouts protect database resources.
- Request identifiers propagate to logs and traces.
- Graceful shutdown works uniformly.

Handler Signature:

```
func (h *UserHandler) GetUser(w http.ResponseWriter, r *http.
Request) {
    ctx := r.Context()
    user, err := h.service.GetUser(ctx, userID)
    ...
}
```

Service Signature:

```
func (s *UserService) GetUser(ctx context.Context, id int64)
(*User, error) {
    return s.repo.GetUserByID(ctx, id)
}
```

Repository Signature:

```
func (r *UserRepo) GetUserByID(ctx context.Context, id int64)
(*User, error) {
    return r.fetchUser(ctx, id)
}
```

This consistent shape ensures that context never gets lost, or is recreated unnecessarily.

Context-Aware Query Execution in Handlers and Repositories

APIs often perform multiple queries per request. A context passed from the handler governs all downstream database calls. Using **QueryContext**, **ExecContext**, and **BeginTx** enforces this behavior.

Example: Context-Aware Repository Method

```
func (r *UserRepo) fetchUser(ctx context.Context, id int64)
(*User, error) {
    row := r.db.QueryRowContext(ctx,
        `SELECT id, name, email FROM users WHERE id=$1`, id)

    var u User
    if err := row.Scan(&u.ID, &u.Name, &u.Email); err != nil {
        return nil, fmt.Errorf("fetchUser scan: %w", err)
    }
    return &u, nil
}
```

If the client disconnects from the HTTP connection or if a timeout is reached, the context is canceled, and this query terminates early.

Context Propagation with Deadlines and Timeouts

Many APIs enforce timeouts at the handler level to guard against slow or overloaded database conditions.

Example: Setting Timeouts per Request

```
func (h *UserHandler) GetUser(w http.ResponseWriter, r *http.
Request) {
    ctx, cancel := context.WithTimeout(r.Context(), 2*time.Second)
    defer cancel()

    user, err := h.service.GetUser(ctx, userID)
    ...
}
```

This pattern ensures that:

- Slow queries do not hold the resources for too long.
- Database pools remain responsive.
- The service behaves predictably under load.

In larger applications, middleware often manages timeout creation so that every endpoint shares the same policies.

Managing Complex Operations: Transactions with Context

Real-world APIs frequently execute multi-step operations that must succeed or fail atomically–for example, creating an order, updating inventory, and logging events. Go provides **`BeginTx`** to ensure that transactions follow the same context rules as single queries.

Example: Context-Aware Transaction

```
func (r *OrderRepo) CreateOrder(ctx context.Context, o *Order)
error {
    tx, err := r.db.BeginTx(ctx, &sql.TxOptions{Isolation: sql.
LevelSerializable})
    if err != nil {
        return err
    }

    if _, err := tx.ExecContext(ctx,
        `INSERT INTO orders (user_id, amount) VALUES ($1, $2)`,
o.UserID, o.Amount); err != nil {
        tx.Rollback()
        return fmt.Errorf("insert order: %w", err)
    }
```

```
    if _, err := tx.ExecContext(ctx,
        `UPDATE inventory SET stock = stock - 1 WHERE product_
id=$1`, o.ProductID); err != nil {
        tx.Rollback()
        return fmt.Errorf("inventory update: %w", err)
    }

    return tx.Commit()
}
```

If the context cancels, both operations terminate immediately, and the transaction rolls back automatically when Commit is skipped.

Observability and Context: Logging, Tracing, and Metadata

Context is not only about cancellation—it also acts as a metadata container for passing request-specific values such as:

- Correlation IDs
- Authentication claims
- Trace spans
- Logging fields

Example: Passing Metadata

```
ctx = context.WithValue(ctx, requestIDKey, reqID)
```

Repository functions can log with full request context:

```
log.Printf("request=%s querying user %d", ctx.Value
(requestIDKey), id)
```

Distributed tracing libraries such as OpenTelemetry automatically bind spans to context, producing detailed traces across API and database boundaries.

Connection Pool Behavior in Real APIs

A highly concurrent API often runs hundreds or thousands of simultaneous database-bound requests. Proper pool sizing and usage become essential. When queries block waiting for a connection, request latency spikes and cancellations become more frequent.

Good API design includes:

- Early context timeout to abort waiting.
- Efficient queries and indexing.

- Avoiding long-lived transactions.
- Exposing pool metrics through /metrics endpoints.

Many Go production systems use Prometheus, which collects pool statistics such as:

- Open connections
- In-use connections
- Wait duration

These metrics guide tuning and fresh deployments.

Graceful Shutdown in API Servers

Modern cloud environments require frequent redeployments. An API must shut down without interrupting ongoing work or corrupting database operations. Go's HTTP server shutdown mechanism pairs seamlessly with MySQL/PostgreSQL drivers and context cancellation.

Shutdown Workflow:

1. The server receives a SIGTERM or similar signal.
2. It stops accepting new HTTP connections.
3. It waits for ongoing handlers to complete or timeout.
4. Each handler propagates cancellation to all database operations.
5. The **db pool** closes safely once no operations remain.

Example: Integrated Shutdown Logic

```
func main() {
    db := setupDB()
    srv := &http.Server{Addr: ":8080", Handler: router(db)}

    go func() { srv.ListenAndServe() }()

    stop := make(chan os.Signal, 1)
    signal.Notify(stop, os.Interrupt, syscall.SIGTERM)
    <-stop

    ctx, cancel := context.WithTimeout(context.Background(),
10*time.Second)
    defer cancel()

    srv.Shutdown(ctx)
    db.Close()
}
```

This design ensures that database operations never run “loose” during service termination.

Putting Everything Together: Example API Architecture

The following is a small example that demonstrates how handlers, services, and repositories connect through a context:

Handler:

```
func (h *UserHandler) ListUsers(w http.ResponseWriter, r *http.
Request) {
    ctx, cancel := context.WithTimeout(r.Context(), 3*time.
Second)
    defer cancel()

    users, err := h.service.ListUsers(ctx)
    ...
}
```

Service Layer:

```
func (s *UserService) ListUsers(ctx context.Context) ([]User,
error) {
    return s.repo.FetchAllUsers(ctx)
}
```

Repository Layer:

```
func (r *UserRepo) FetchAllUsers(ctx context.Context) ([]User,
error) {
    rows, err := r.db.QueryContext(ctx, `SELECT id, name FROM
users`)
    if err != nil {
        return nil, fmt.Errorf("FetchAllUsers: %w", err)
    }
    defer rows.Close()

    var users []User
    for rows.Next() {
        var u User
        rows.Scan(&u.ID, &u.Name)
        users = append(users, u)
    }
    return users, rows.Err()
}
```

This pattern remains stable across hundreds of endpoints, and is compatible with:

- PostgreSQL
- MySQL
- CockroachDB
- SQLite
- GORM or custom SQL layers

The Benefits of Unified Database-Context Integration

A real-world Go API that integrates context and database management enjoys several long-term advantages:

- Predictable timeout behavior.
- Clean cancellation across multi-step operations.
- No resource leaks from abandoned queries.
- Lower latency under heavy load.
- Better observability via tracing and structured logging.
- Reliable, graceful shutdown during deployments.
- Consistent API design and maintainability.

This architecture scales naturally from small services to high-throughput distributed systems.

Conclusion

This chapter has continued to explore the foundations and advanced practices of database interaction and context management in Go, forming the backbone of any production-grade backend service. It began with an introduction to the **`database/sql` package**, explaining how Go's minimalistic, interface-driven approach provides a flexible and efficient abstraction layer for communicating with relational databases. Readers then examined how to establish reliable connections to PostgreSQL and MySQL, configure DSNs, tune connection parameters, and validate database connectivity in real-world environments.

From there, we have discussed how to execute queries, scan results efficiently, and leverage GORM for a higher-level ORM experience, including migrations, model definitions, and structured CRUD workflows. Transaction management followed, with a focus on atomicity, rollback strategies, and error propagation—critical elements for ensuring data integrity in complex systems.

A significant portion of the chapter was dedicated to mastering Go's context package. We explored how to embed request-scoped values, enforce cancellation, and apply timeout boundaries to long-running operations. These techniques were then carried forward into designing production-ready data layers featuring context-aware database calls, connection pooling strategies, and graceful shutdown mechanisms essential for robust and observable microservices.

The chapter is concluded by integrating these concepts into complete, real-world API workflows, demonstrating how database operations and context propagation work together to build high-performance, fault-tolerant Go systems. With these tools and patterns, readers are now prepared to architect data-intensive services that remain stable under load, recover gracefully, and adhere to modern operational standards.

In the next chapter, we shall take a look into how Go's simplicity, performance, and standard library design make it exceptionally well suited for modern backend development. The focus of the next chapter is on Web Server and REST API Development.

CHAPTER 7
Web Server and REST API Development

Introduction

Building web servers and RESTful APIs is one of the most common and powerful uses of Go, and this chapter explores how the simplicity, performance, and standard library design of Go make it exceptionally well-suited for modern backend development. Using the net/http package as the foundation, we will examine how requests flow through a server, how routing and middleware shape application behavior, and how JSON becomes the primary format for exchanging data. Along the way, we will see how Go's emphasis on clarity and composability leads to clean, maintainable APIs—and how AI tools can accelerate endpoint generation, validation, and refinement without sacrificing control or reliability.

Structure

In this chapter, we will cover the following topics:

- HTTP Fundamentals in Go
    - The Core Abstractions: `Request`, `ResponseWriter`, and `Handler`
    - The HTTP Server Lifecycle
    - HTTP Methods and Semantics in Go
    - Request Body Handling and Streaming
    - Headers, Cookies, and Query Parameters
    - Concurrency is Built-In
    - AI Tools Assisting in Understanding HTTP Behavior
- Creating a Web Server with net/http
    - The Minimal Server: A Complete HTTP Service in a Few Lines
    - Handlers and Handler Functions

    - Building a Custom HTTP Server Struct
    - The Default Multiplexer versus Custom ServeMux
    - Handling Different HTTP Methods
    - Serving Static Files
    - Graceful Shutdown: Essential for Production
- Routing Requests and Handling Methods
    - The Role of ServeMux: Go's Core Router
    - Exact Match versus Subtree Match
    - Method-Specific Handling: Ensuring REST Consistency
    - Organizing Routes in Modular Applications
    - Using Closures to Capture Handler Dependencies
    - Creating Reusable Method Routers
    - Routing and Middlewares: Composition over Frameworks
- Middleware Patterns for Go Web Servers
    - Basic Middleware Structure
    - Designing Composable Middleware Chains
    - Common Middleware Patterns in Real Applications
    - Stateful Middleware and Response Interception
    - Middleware Performance Considerations
- JSON Requests and Responses with encoding/json
    - Security Considerations When Handling JSON
    - AI-Assisted JSON Handling
- Error Handling in Web Servers
    - Returning Structural Error Responses
    - Handling JSON Parsing Errors
    - Using Middleware for Centralized Error Handling
- AI-Assisted Generation of API Endpoints
    - How AI Helps in Designing API Endpoints
    - Using AI to Generate a Basic CRUD Endpoint
    - AI-Assisted Input Validation
    - AI-Assisted Error Response Standardization
    - AI-Assisted Generation of Query/Response Models

- Using AI for Complete Endpoint Flows
- Best Practices When Using AI for Endpoint Generation

HTTP Fundamentals in Go

Go was designed with networked systems in mind, and nowhere is this more apparent than in its elegant, high-performance HTTP support. The entire Go standard library includes first-class packages for creating clients, servers, multiplexers (routers), and middleware—all without requiring external dependencies. At the center of this design is the **`net/http`** package, a highly optimized and composable toolkit that makes building modern, production-grade web services both intuitive and efficient. Before diving into routing, middleware, and REST APIs, it is essential to understand the HTTP primitives that Go exposes and how they translate into request-response workflows.

The Core Abstractions: `Request`, `ResponseWriter`, and `Handler`

Go's HTTP ecosystem is built on three fundamental components: **`http.Request`**, **`http.ResponseWriter`**, and **`http.Handler`**.

- **`http.Request`**

  The **`http.Request`** struct encapsulates the entire incoming request—its headers, method, URL, query parameters, cookies, body stream, and more. It represents the client's intent and data.

  The key fields include:

  - **Method:** The HTTP method, such as **`GET`**, **`POST`**, **`PUT`**, **`DELETE`**.
  - **URL:** The URL requested, including query parameters.
  - **Header:** A map of incoming request headers.
  - **Body:** An **`io.ReadCloser`** that streams the request payload.
  - **`Context()`:** For cancellation, deadlines, and request-scoped values.

  Example Access Patterns:

```
func handler(w http.ResponseWriter, r *http.Request) {
    fmt.Println("Method:", r.Method)
    fmt.Println("User-Agent:", r.Header.Get("User-Agent"))
    fmt.Println("Path:", r.URL.Path)
}
```

- **`http.ResponseWriter`**

  `ResponseWriter` is an interface used to send data back to the client. It exposes methods to write:

  - HTTP headers
  - Status codes
  - Response body bytes

  Example:

  ```
  func handler(w http.ResponseWriter, r *http.Request) {
      w.Header().Set("Content-Type", "text/plain")
      w.WriteHeader(http.StatusOK)
      w.Write([]byte("Hello from Go!"))
  }
  ```

  Although this interface looks minimal, yet internally it manages buffers, connection persistence, chunking, and low-level protocol details.

- **`http.Handler`**

  At the core of Go's HTTP framework is the **`http.Handler`** interface:

  ```
  type Handler interface {
      ServeHTTP(ResponseWriter, *Request)
  }
  ```

  Any object that implements this method becomes a handler. Functions can also serve as handlers using the **`http.HandlerFunc`** adapter:

  ```
  http.HandleFunc("/hello", func(w http.ResponseWriter, r *http.
  Request) {
      w.Write([]byte("Hello!"))
  })
  ```

  This design enables clean composition, and makes middleware chaining possible.

The HTTP Server Lifecycle

Understanding how a Go HTTP server receives and processes requests helps developers structure APIs effectively.

When calling:

```
http.ListenAndServe(":8080", nil)
```

Go performs the following steps:

1. Opens a TCP listener on the specified address.

2. Accepts incoming connections concurrently using goroutines.
3. Parses HTTP requests from each connection.
4. Dispatches requests to handlers through the default multiplexer (**`http.ServeMux`**), unless a custom one is provided.
5. Invokes ServeHTTP on the matched handler.
6. Writes the response back to the client.
7. Manages keep-alive connections, reuse, and cleanup.

This flow is highly optimized: each request is handled in its own goroutine, allowing large-scale concurrency with minimal developer intervention. Since, goroutines are cheaper, Go servers naturally scale under high load.

HTTP Methods and Semantics in Go

Go encourages working directly with HTTP semantics. Each method–**`GET`**, **`POST`**, **`PUT`**, **`PATCH`**, **`DELETE`**–maps naturally to API operations.

Example of method checks:

```
func handler(w http.ResponseWriter, r *http.Request) {
    switch r.Method {
    case http.MethodGet:
        // fetch resources
    case http.MethodPost:
        // create resource
    default:
        http.Error(w, "method not allowed", http.StatusMethod
NotAllowed)
    }
}
```

Go's request handlers rarely abstract away HTTP concepts. This explicitness gives developers more control over idempotency, caching, and correct API design.

Request Body Handling and Streaming

One of the strengths of the HTTP implementation in Go is its streaming-friendly design. The Body field in **`http.Request`** is an **`io.ReadCloser`**, enabling:

- Reading large payloads incrementally.
- Forwarding streams directly to other services.
- Avoiding copying large buffers into memory.

Example of reading a body:

```
data, err := io.ReadAll(r.Body)
if err != nil {
    http.Error(w, "failed to read body", http.StatusBadRequest)
    return
}
defer r.Body.Close()
```

For high-volume applications, developers may choose to decode JSON directly from the stream, or even pass the stream to other handlers without loading it entirely.

Headers, Cookies, and Query Parameters

Go's HTTP library makes working with metadata straightforward.

- **Query Parameters:**
  `name := r.URL.Query().Get("name")`
- **Cookies:**
  `cookie, _ := r.Cookie("session")`
- **Setting Headers:**
  `w.Header().Set("X-Server", "GoHTTP")`

This explicit approach ensures full control over HTTP semantics without hidden behavior or middleware magic.

Concurrency is Built-in

One of the advantages of writing HTTP servers in Go is that concurrency is not added externally through frameworks–it is part of the runtime. Each HTTP request is handled in its own goroutine.

This means:

- Horizontal scaling is natural.
- Blocking operations do not block the entire server.
- Context-aware cancellation integrates seamlessly.

Because of this concurrency model, Go is well-suited for building latency-sensitive APIs, high-throughput gateways, and microservices.

Go also has HTTP Web-framework - Gin. It is a high-performance HTTP web framework written in Go (Golang). It is designed for building REST APIs and web applications quickly, with minimal boilerplate and excellent speed. It is built on top of Go's net/http package and uses a fast HTTP router based on a radix tree.

AI Tools Assisting in Understanding HTTP Behavior

While not covered in detail until later in the chapter, HTTP fundamentals are a key area where AI tools such as ChatGPT or Amazon Q Developer can help by:

- Generating sample server scaffolds.
- Explaining **`http.Request`** fields or tricky behavior (like connection reuse).
- Suggesting performance improvements such as connection pooling.
- Detecting inefficient request handling patterns.
- Automatically converting handler functions into structured routers.

These capabilities make onboarding Go's HTTP primitives much faster, especially for developers coming from frameworks where HTTP is heavily abstracted.

Creating a Web Server with `net/http`

Building a web server in Go begins with the **`net/http`** package, a core part of the standard library that provides all the fundamental primitives for serving HTTP traffic. Unlike many languages that rely heavily on external frameworks, Go offers a rich, production-ready HTTP stack out of the box. This design aligns with the language's philosophy of simplicity, clarity, and explicit control. By understanding the foundational elements of **`net/http`**, developers can construct REST APIs, microservices, proxies, and full-fledged web backends with minimal friction.

The Minimal Server: A Complete HTTP Service in a Few Lines

A Go web server starts by defining handlers–functions that satisfy the **`http.Handler`** interface–and then binding those handlers to URL paths. Even the simplest server demonstrates the elegance of Go's HTTP model:

```
package main

import (
    "fmt"
    "net/http"
)

func main() {
    http.HandleFunc("/", func(w http.ResponseWriter, r *http.
Request) {
```

```
        fmt.Fprintln(w, "Welcome to the Go Web Server!")
    })

    http.ListenAndServe(":8080", nil)
}
```

This program performs more work than its size suggests. Once executed, the server:

- Listens on TCP port 8080.
- Accepts concurrent connections.
- Parses incoming HTTP requests.
- Routes them through the default **`http.ServeMux`**.
- Invokes the handler function.
- Constructs and sends the HTTP response back to the client.

The framework already operates in a concurrent manner, as each request runs in its own goroutine, illustrating how naturally concurrency integrates with Go's approach to web development.

Handlers and Handler Functions

At the core of **`net/http`** lies the handler, represented by the **`http.Handler`** interface:

```
type Handler interface {
    ServeHTTP(ResponseWriter, *Request)
}
```

Any struct that implements ServeHTTP becomes a handler. This design offers flexibility, enabling stateful handlers, dependency injection, and middleware-like interceptors.

Using `HandlerFunc`

The vast majority of handlers are written as functions, made possible by the built-in adapter:

```
type HandlerFunc func(ResponseWriter, *Request)
```

This adapter allows plain functions to act as handlers, enabling expressive and concise definitions:

```
func greet(w http.ResponseWriter, r *http.Request) {
    fmt.Fprintln(w, "Hello from a handler function!")
}

func main() {
    http.HandleFunc("/greet", greet)
```

```
    http.ListenAndServe(":8080", nil)
}
```

The duality of **Handler** and **HandlerFunc** becomes deeply useful when building more sophisticated middleware chains, routing tables, and dependency-injected handlers.

Building a Custom HTTP Server Struct

While it is common to rely on the convenience function **http.ListenAndServe**, the full **http.Server** struct exposes extensive configuration options:

```
server := &http.Server{
    Addr:           ":8080",
    Handler:        myMux,
    ReadTimeout:    5 * time.Second,
    WriteTimeout: 10 * time.Second,
    IdleTimeout:   120 * time.Second,
    MaxHeaderBytes: 1 << 20,
}
```

Starting this server

```
if err := server.ListenAndServe(); err != nil {
    log.Fatalf("server error: %v", err)
}
```

Using this approach gives precise control over:

- Connection timeouts
- Header size limits
- Graceful shutdown behavior
- TLS configuration
- Custom multiplexers

For production systems, configuring these fields is essential to prevent slow clients, denial-of-service attempts, or resource exhaustion.

The Default Multiplexer versus Custom ServeMux

Go includes a default multiplexer (**http.DefaultServeMux**), which maps URL paths to handlers:

```
http.HandleFunc("/home", homeHandler)
```

However, applications with a more complex routing, needs benefit from creating their own:

```
mux := http.NewServeMux()

mux.HandleFunc("/home", homeHandler)
mux.Handle("/admin", &AdminHandler{})
```

Advantages of a dedicated ServeMux include:

- Avoiding global state.
- Cleaner encapsulation.
- Easier dependency injection.
- Clearer separation between public and private routes.

Custom multiplexers are also required when integrating with middleware stacks that must wrap an entire handler chain.

Handling Different HTTP Methods

A single URL path may support multiple HTTP methods, such as GET, POST, or PUT. Inside a handler, branching logic clarifies the intended behavior:

```
func userHandler(w http.ResponseWriter, r *http.Request) {
    switch r.Method {
    case http.MethodGet:
        w.Write([]byte("Fetching user data"))
    case http.MethodPost:
        w.Write([]byte("Creating user"))
    default:
        http.Error(w, "Method not allowed", http.StatusMethod
NotAllowed)
    }
}
```

This explicit handling encourages correct REST design by aligning behavior with HTTP semantics rather than obscuring them behind framework abstractions.

Serving Static Files

Static servers can be created directly from the standard library:

```
fs := http.FileServer(http.Dir("./public"))
http.Handle("/static/", http.StripPrefix("/static/", fs))
```

This approach supports:

- Directory browsing (when enabled).

- File caching via headers.
- Efficient file streaming.

Due to the zero-copy file handling by Go on many systems, static content can be served with impressive performance.

Graceful Shutdown: Essential for Production

Since Go 1.8, **`http.Server`** includes native support for graceful shutdowns. This feature ensures that ongoing requests are complete before the server terminates.

```
func main() {
    srv := &http.Server{Addr: ":8080"}

    go func() {
        if err := srv.ListenAndServe(); err != nil &&
err != http.ErrServerClosed {
            log.Fatalf("listen: %s\n", err)
        }
    }()

    stop := make(chan os.Signal, 1)
    signal.Notify(stop, os.Interrupt)

    <-stop
    ctx, cancel := context.WithTimeout(context.Background(),
5*time.Second)
    defer cancel()

    srv.Shutdown(ctx)
    fmt.Println("Server gracefully stopped")
}
```

This pattern is pivotal for production deployments on Kubernetes, Amazon ECS, Docker, or any environment that may terminate processes without warning.

Routing Requests and Handling Methods

Routing lies at the heart of any web application. It defines how an incoming HTTP request is mapped to a specific handler function, which, in turn, generates the response. While many languages depend heavily on external routing frameworks, Go takes a more minimalist and explicit approach. The **`net/http`** package provides the primitives for routing, and, through their simplicity, enables developers to construct flexible and high-performance routing layers without unnecessary abstraction. Understanding how routing works—along with how to correctly handle HTTP methods—is fundamental to building robust REST APIs and production web services in Go.

The Role of ServeMux: Go's Core Router

At the center of Go's routing model is the ServeMux, a request multiplexer. The multiplexer compares the incoming request's URL path with a list of registered patterns and dispatches the request to the most specific match. Each Go application may use either:

- The default multiplexer (**`http.DefaultServeMux`**); or,
- A custom multiplexer created via **`http.NewServeMux`**.

A typical registration looks like this:

```
mux := http.NewServeMux()

mux.HandleFunc("/users", listUsers)
mux.HandleFunc("/users/create", createUser)
mux.HandleFunc("/users/", userDetails)
```

The routing rules follow a longest-prefix match strategy, meaning that more specific paths override shorter, more general ones. For example, /users/create always takes precedence over /users/.

This deterministic routing model–simple, yet powerful–ensures that routing behavior remains explicit and predictable. Unlike web frameworks that rely on pattern inference or reflection, Go prioritizes clarity and minimal overhead.

Exact Match versus Subtree Match

Go supports two forms of path matching:

- **Exact Match:** This occurs when the registered pattern is an exact string match. The example is as follows:

  ```
  mux.HandleFunc("/status", statusHandler)
  ```
- **Subtree Match**: Only **`/status`** will match.

  A pattern ending with a slash / matches its entire subtree:

  ```
  mux.HandleFunc("/assets/", serveAssets)
  ```

This pattern matches:

- `/assets/`
- `/assets/logo.png`
- `/assets/css/style.css`

This is exceptionally useful for serving resource collections or nested REST endpoints.

However, Go does not support parameterized routes (such as **/users/:id**) natively. Instead, handlers must parse such values from the URL themselves or delegate to third-party routers such as Gorilla Mux or Chi if desired. Many high-performance production systems still rely entirely on the standard library by designing predictable, structured URL schemes.

Method-Specific Handling: Ensuring REST Consistency

HTTP defines multiple methods—**GET**, **POST**, **PUT**, **PATCH**, **DELETE**, among others. A well-structured API must differentiate between them. Go encourages an explicit method-based branching strategy within handlers:

```
func userHandler(w http.ResponseWriter, r *http.Request) {
    switch r.Method {
    case http.MethodGet:
        getUser(w, r)
    case http.MethodPost:
        createUser(w, r)
    case http.MethodDelete:
        deleteUser(w, r)
    default:
        http.Error(w, "Method not allowed", http.StatusMethod
NotAllowed)
    }
}
```

This approach reinforces REST semantics:

- **GET** retrieves data.
- **POST** creates new data.
- **PUT** updates or replaces.
- **PATCH** updates partially.
- **DELETE** removes resources.

By treating methods as first-class routing criteria, Go ensures that APIs remain predictable and well-structured.

Organizing Routes in Modular Applications

As applications grow, concentrating all routes in a single **main.go** file becomes unmanageable. A common organizational strategy involves encapsulating related routes within dedicated packages or modules.

Example: Grouping User-Related Routes

```
// in internal/user/routes.go

func RegisterUserRoutes(mux *http.ServeMux) {
    mux.HandleFunc("/users", listUsers)
    mux.HandleFunc("/users/", userHandler)
}
```

The **main.go** simply composes the routing configuration:

```
mux := http.NewServeMux()
user.RegisterUserRoutes(mux)
log.Fatal(http.ListenAndServe(":8080", mux))
```

This pattern naturally supports domain separation, clearer testing boundaries, and greater maintainability. It also pairs well with dependency injection, where handlers may be constructed with services, repositories, or configuration parameters.

Using Closures to Capture Handler Dependencies

Go's function literals are a powerful mechanism for routing. Closures allow handlers to capture services or configuration:

```
func UserHandler(repo UserRepository) http.HandlerFunc {
    return func(w http.ResponseWriter, r *http.Request) {
        id := r.URL.Query().Get("id")
        user, err := repo.Find(id)
        if err != nil {
            http.Error(w, "User not found", http.StatusNotFound)
            return
        }
        fmt.Fprintf(w, "User: %s", user.Name)
    }
}
```

Registering the handler:

```
mux.HandleFunc("/users/details", UserHandler(userRepo))
```

This pattern eliminates reliance on global variables and enables precise control over application wiring.

Creating Reusable Method Routers

Although Go recommends explicit branching, it is often useful to encapsulate method handling using custom routers:

```
func MethodRouter(handlers map[string]http.HandlerFunc) http.
HandlerFunc {
    return func(w http.ResponseWriter, r *http.Request) {
        if h, ok := handlers[r.Method]; ok {
            h(w, r)
        } else {
            http.Error(w, "Method Not Allowed", http.StatusMethod
NotAllowed)
        }
    }
}
```

Usage:

```
mux.HandleFunc("/items", MethodRouter(map[string]http.Handler-
Func{
    http.MethodGet: listItems,
    http.MethodPost: createItem,
}))
```

This provides a lightweight layer of abstraction while retaining Go's explicit style.

Routing and Middlewares: Composition over Frameworks

Middlewares can be stacked around routes by using handler chaining:

```
func AuthMiddleware(next http.Handler) http.Handler {
    return http.HandlerFunc(func(w http.ResponseWriter, r *http.
Request) {
        if !isAuthenticated(r) {
            http.Error(w, "Unauthorized", http.StatusUn
authorized)
            return
        }
        next.ServeHTTP(w, r)
    })
}
```

Applied to a route:

```
protected := AuthMiddleware(http.HandlerFunc(secretHandler))
mux.Handle("/secret", protected)
```

Routing, therefore, becomes both expressive and modular without hidden framework logic.

Middleware Patterns for Go Web Servers

Middleware stands crucial in shaping how a Go web server processes requests. At its core, middleware is a code that wraps an HTTP handler to execute logic before or after the main request-processing function runs. This pattern makes it possible to implement cross-cutting concerns—such as logging, authentication, rate limiting, compression, or recovery—without scattering code throughout handlers. Since Go does not prescribe a middleware system in its standard library, developers often rely on higher-order functions and handler chaining to build elegant and composable pipelines.

In Go, middleware, commonly takes the form of a function that accepts an **`http.Handler`**, and returns another **`http.Handler`**. This results in a wrapper that can intercept the request early, apply logic, call the next handler, and optionally run cleanup logic afterward. This simple but powerful concept mirrors the decorator pattern and underpins most middleware implementations across Go frameworks.

Basic Middleware Structure

A middleware chain can then be built by wrapping handlers in layers. This manual composition approach encourages transparency: developers see exactly what runs before their logic.

```
func LoggingMiddleware(next http.Handler) http.Handler {
    return http.HandlerFunc(func(w http.ResponseWriter, r *http.
Request) {
        log.Printf("Request: %s %s", r.Method, r.URL.Path)
        next.ServeHTTP(w, r)
    })
}
```

The simplicity of this pattern is one reason many Go web frameworks—such as Chi, Echo, and Gin—adopt middleware as a first-class concept while retaining compatibility with net/http. Even in these frameworks, the underlying principle remains handler wrapping.

Designing Composable Middleware Chains

In production systems, a single request may pass through multiple middleware layers: authentication, caching, request shaping, tracing, and panic recovery. Instead of applying each individually, developers can create a reusable chain constructor.

Example: A Middleware Chain

```
type Middleware func(http.Handler) http.Handler
```

```
func Chain(h http.Handler, middlewares ...Middleware)
http.Handler {
    for i := len(middlewares) - 1; i >= 0; i-- {
        h = middlewares[i](h)
    }
    return h
}
```

This small utility allows developers to declaratively stack middleware:

```
handler := Chain(
    finalHandler,
    LoggingMiddleware,
    RecoverMiddleware,
    AuthMiddleware,
)
```

The reverse iteration ensures that the outer middleware wraps the inner ones, forming a call hierarchy identical to layered abstractions in traditional web stacks.

Common Middleware Patterns in Real Applications

There are multiple patterns that enable structure in developing Go applications. In the following sub-sections, we look at the common middleware patterns.

Logging and Request Tracing

Logging middleware adds structured logs for incoming requests. Modern systems integrate correlation IDs or trace IDs to follow requests through distributed systems.

```
func TraceMiddleware(next http.Handler) http.Handler {
    return http.HandlerFunc(func(w http.ResponseWriter, r *http.
Request) {
        traceID := uuid.NewString()
        ctx := context.WithValue(r.Context(), "trace_id", traceID)
        log.Printf("[trace=%s] %s %s", traceID, r.Method, r.URL.
Path)
        next.ServeHTTP(w, r.WithContext(ctx))
    })
}
```

This gives observability and supports systems like OpenTelemetry.

Recovery Middleware

Go servers should not crash because of a panic in a handler. Recovery middleware guards against this by intercepting panics, and returning an internal server error instead.

```
func RecoverMiddleware(next http.Handler) http.Handler {
    return http.HandlerFunc(func(w http.ResponseWriter, r *http.
Request) {
        defer func() {
            if err := recover(); err != nil {
                log.Printf("panic: %v", err)
                http.Error(w, "internal error", http.Status
InternalServerError)
            }
        }()
        next.ServeHTTP(w, r)
    })
}
```

This is vital for production reliability.

Authentication and Authorization

Authentication middleware validates the identity of a user before allowing access to restricted endpoints. It can extract tokens, validate JWTs, or read session cookies.

Example: A Simple API Key Check

```
func AuthMiddleware(next http.Handler) http.Handler {
    return http.HandlerFunc(func(w http.ResponseWriter, r *http.
Req
uest) {
        if r.Header.Get("X-API-Key") != "secret123" {
            http.Error(w, "unauthorized", http.Status
Unauthorized)
            return
        }
        next.ServeHTTP(w, r)
    })
}
```

More advanced versions integrate OAuth2 providers or RBAC systems.

Stateful Middleware and Response Interception

Middleware sometimes needs to modify responses—for example, to add security headers, enable compression, or rewrite output. Since **`http.ResponseWriter`** does not expose its buffer; middleware can use wrapper types.

Example: Adding Response Headers

```
func SecurityHeaders(next http.Handler) http.Handler {
    return http.HandlerFunc(func(w http.ResponseWriter, r *http.
Request) {
        w.Header().Set("X-Frame-Options", "DENY")
        w.Header().Set("X-Content-Type-Options", "nosniff")
        next.ServeHTTP(w, r)
    })
}
```

Advanced Case: Capturing Status Codes

```
type responseWriter struct {
    http.ResponseWriter
    status int
}

func (rw *responseWriter) WriteHeader(code int) {
    rw.status = code
    rw.ResponseWriter.WriteHeader(code)
}
```

This wrapper allows middleware to log which status code was returned, or trigger alarms on failures.

Middleware Performance Considerations

Although middleware enriches server behavior, excessive layering can degrade performance. In Go, this overhead is usually minimal compared to interpreted languages, but unnecessary chains still increase allocations and function calls.

Key considerations include:

- Prefer lightweight operations inside middleware (avoid heavy I/O).
- Reuse objects where possible (such as use **`sync.Pool`** for buffers).
- Avoid nesting overly complex middleware trees.
- Apply expensive middleware only to specific route groups.

Frameworks like Chi optimize handler chaining, but developers should still evaluate the cost of each layer.

JSON Requests and Responses with encoding/json

Go embraces JSON handling through its powerful encoding/json package, which provides fast, reliable serialization and deserialization functions. This section examines how Go-based REST APIs parse JSON requests, produce well-structured JSON responses, and manage validation, error handling, and performance considerations. Since Go models JSON through strongly typed structs, developers benefit from early validation, predictable APIs, and safe transformations between client payloads and Go objects.

Go's JSON ecosystem centers around two core functions: **json.Marshal** (convert Go values → JSON) and **json.Unmarshal** (convert JSON → Go values). These functions interact primarily with Go structs, using field tags to customize how data is mapped. A typical JSON-to-struct mapping involves using tags such as:

```
type User struct {
    ID    int    `json:"id"`
    Name  string `json:"name"`
    Email string `json:"email"`
}
```

Struct tags tell the JSON encoder/decoder how to match JSON keys to Go fields. Without them, Go uses field names directly—which may not always align with API conventions. Tags also support options such as omitempty, case transformations, and string value coercion. The following is the JSON Flow in pictorial form in a Go API request.

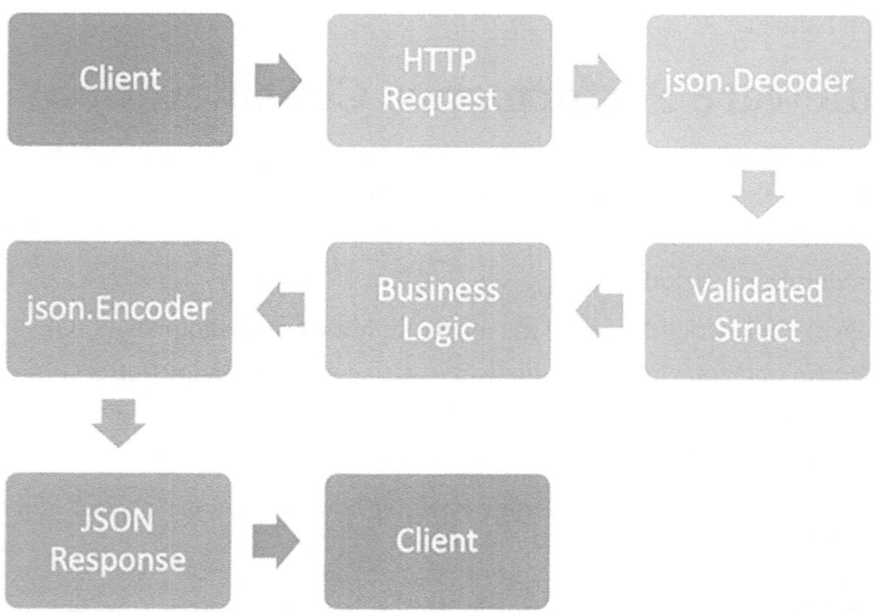

Figure 7.1: *JSON Flow in a Go API Request*

When a client sends data to a Go REST API—typically during **POST**, **PUT**, or **PATCH** operations—the server must read the request body, validate the JSON payload, and convert it into the corresponding Go struct. The **json.Decoder** type is ideal for reading directly from the request body stream, reducing memory usage, and avoiding unnecessary buffering.

Basic Example of Reading JSON:

```
func CreateUserHandler(w http.ResponseWriter, r *http.Request) {
    var input User

    decoder := json.NewDecoder(r.Body)
    if err := decoder.Decode(&input); err != nil {
        http.Error(w, "invalid JSON", http.StatusBadRequest)
        return
    }

    // Use 'input' safely here...
}
```

Using **`json.NewDecoder`** supports incremental parsing, and prevents clients from sending malformed or oversized bodies that crash the server. A production-ready code often includes checks to prevent "infinite JSON objects" or overly large inputs.

For stricter validation:

```
decoder := json.NewDecoder(r.Body)
decoder.DisallowUnknownFields()
```

This prevents clients from sending unexpected JSON fields, improving API predictability.

Although Go's type system prevents many issues, JSON payloads still require domain-level validation. For example, an empty email or a negative age may pass JSON decoding but still be invalid. Validation can be done manually or via libraries such as go-playground/validator.

Example:

```
if input.Email == "" {
    http.Error(w, "email is required", http.StatusBadRequest)
    return
}
```

Well-structured APIs handle incorrect input through a consistent error response format. For example:

```
{
  "error": "validation_error",
  "message": "email is required"
}
```

Maintaining this structure makes debugging easier for clients, and also enables AI-based tools to suggest improvements or detect missing validation rules.

To send JSON responses back to the client, the server uses **`json.Marshal`** or **`json.NewEncoder`**. The best practice is to set the Content-Type header explicitly, and to write JSON through a streaming encoder, which avoids unnecessary allocations.

Basic JSON Response Example:

```
func GetUserHandler(w http.ResponseWriter, r *http.Request) {
    user := User{ID: 1, Name: "Alice", Email: "alice@example.com"}

    w.Header().Set("Content-Type", "application/json")
    json.NewEncoder(w).Encode(user)
}
```

The Encode method automatically appends a newline, and handles serialization errors. However, developers must ensure that the handler does not write headers after writing body content—Go does not allow rewriting headers once output begins.

Struct tags allow extensive control over how JSON fields are handled.

Example:

```
type Product struct {
    ID       int     `json:"id"`
    Name     string  `json:"name"`
    Price    float64 `json:"price,string"`
    Internal string  `json:"-"` // excluded
}
```

Encoding numeric fields as strings is useful when interacting with systems that expect integer IDs or prices as quoted strings.

Go naturally models nested JSON using nested structs.

```
type Order struct {
    ID       int       `json:"id"`
    Items    []Product `json:"items"`
    Total    float64   `json:"total"`
}
```

Decoding or encoding arrays uses the same JSON pipeline, making it easier to work with lists of resources in APIs.

Some REST endpoints may need to return large datasets—potentially thousands of items. To avoid memory spikes, Go supports JSON streaming through encoders that write items incrementally.

Example: Writing a stream of log lines

```
func StreamLogs(w http.ResponseWriter, r *http.Request) {
    w.Header().Set("Content-Type", "application/json")
```

```
        encoder := json.NewEncoder(w)

        w.Write([]byte("[")) // start array

        for i, line := range getLogLines() {
            if i > 0 {
                w.Write([]byte(","))
            }
            encoder.Encode(line)
        }

        w.Write([]byte("]"))
    }
```

This allows servers to send data while still generating it, improving responsiveness.

Some structures require custom JSON behavior. Types implementing the **`json.Marshaler`** and **`json.Unmarshalerinterfaces`** can override the default behavior.

Example: Formatting time fields

```
type JSONTime time.Time

func (t JSONTime) MarshalJSON() ([]byte, error) {
    ts := time.Time(t).Format(time.RFC3339)
    return []byte(`"` + ts + `"`), nil
}
```

This is useful for timestamps, currency formatting, or redacting sensitive data.

Effective APIs avoid sending raw Go errors to the client. Instead, they use structured error responses:

```
type ErrorResponse struct {
    Error   string `json:"error"`
    Message string `json:"message"`
}
```

Returning errors using consistent JSON improves Developer Experience (DX) and enables automated tools—including AI validators—to analyze API behavior. It is a good practice to use Go validators instead of manual validation for the JSON request.

Security Considerations When Handling JSON

JSON handling requires attention to several security best practices:

- **Limiting Request Body Size:**

  ```
  r.Body = http.MaxBytesReader(w, r.Body, 1<<20) // 1 MB limit
  ```

This prevents denial-of-service attacks caused by oversized bodies.

- **Avoiding `interface{}` for Unknown JSON:**

  Using `map[string]any` or `json.RawMessage` is safer than interface{} parsing, which can lead to type confusion.

- **Sanitizing Output:**

  Although Go structs provide inherent cleanliness, developers must remain cautious with user-provided strings to avoid injection vulnerabilities in downstream systems.

AI-Assisted JSON Handling

Modern tooling allows AI to simplify and improve JSON workflows.

AI can:

- Generate example request and response schemas from English descriptions.
- Suggest struct definitions based on OpenAPI specs or sample payloads.
- Auto-detect mismatched JSON tags in large codebases.
- Compare JSON schemas across API versions to identify breaking changes.
- Generate example test cases, including invalid JSON, missing fields, and malformed payloads.
- Optimize large JSON marshalling code, including suggesting streaming approaches.
- Propose refactors for complex marshaling logic.
- Autogenerate documentation for request/response shapes.

These AI-assisted features reduce boilerplate, enforce schema consistency, and increase the reliability of API data models.

Error Handling in Web Servers

Error handling is a central part of building reliable HTTP servers in Go. Unlike languages that use exception-driven control flow, Go emphasizes explicit error propagation and structured responses, which map naturally onto HTTP's status-code-based communication model. A production-grade API must not only detect and classify errors correctly but also express them clearly to clients, log them for observability, and ensure that failures do not cascade across goroutines or requests. This section explores the full spectrum of error handling within Go's net/http ecosystem—from request validation and JSON parsing to handler-level failures, middleware-based error interception, and unified error response patterns. It also examines how Go's standard library, combined with idiomatic design patterns, helps developers create predictable and fault-tolerant web servers, well-suited for real-world deployments.

Errors in web servers originate from diverse sources: malformed input, failed authentication, missing database records, network timeouts, panics in handler functions, and even background goroutine failures. Go encourages designers to categorize errors carefully, and return them in a structured, client-friendly format.

Typical categories include:

- **Client Errors (4xx):** Invalid payloads, missing fields, unsupported HTTP methods.
- **Server Errors (5xx):** Failed queries, unreachable downstream services, unexpected panics.
- **Context-Driven Errors:** Deadlines exceeded, cancellations triggered when clients disconnect.
- **Validation Errors:** Domain-specific constraints violated during request processing.

Within the net/http model, every request is isolated, meaning a failure in one handler must not affect others. This isolation simplifies error handling but also means that developers must explicitly check for issues at every system boundary: reading r.Body, decoding JSON, querying databases, or generating responses. The absence of exceptions forces developers to think in terms of "error propagation paths," resulting in cleaner, more auditable code.

Returning Structural Error Responses

A well-defined API does not simply write error text into the HTTP response body. Instead, it uses structured JSON error envelopes that communicate both high-level error categories and human-readable messages. A common format might include fields such as:

```
type ErrorResponse struct {
    Error   string `json:"error"`
    Message string `json:"message"`
}
```

A typical handler might produce errors like this:

```
func writeError(w http.ResponseWriter, status int, msg string) {
    w.Header().Set("Content-Type", "application/json")
    w.WriteHeader(status)

    resp := ErrorResponse{
        Error:   http.StatusText(status),
        Message: msg,
```

```
        }

        json.NewEncoder(w).Encode(resp)
    }
```

This pattern ensures consistency across the entire server. No matter which handler fails–authentication, database lookup, or payload decoding–the client receives the same structured format, with improved debuggability. It also allows API documentation and automated clients to rely on predictable structures, which enhances interoperability.

Handling JSON Parsing Errors

A significant portion of errors in REST APIs arises from malformed JSON payloads or mismatched data shapes. Go's **json.Decoder** provides detailed error messages, and developers must ensure that these errors are surfaced properly.

```
var input CreateUserRequest
decoder := json.NewDecoder(r.Body)
decoder.DisallowUnknownFields()

if err := decoder.Decode(&input); err != nil {
    writeError(w, http.StatusBadRequest, "invalid JSON: "+err.
Error())
    return
}
```

Several issues must be anticipated:

- Trailing tokens, where clients send extra data beyond the expected payload.
- Type mismatches, such as strings sent where integers are required.
- Unexpected fields, which may indicate version drift or client-side bugs.
- Oversized bodies, solved using **http.MaxBytesReader** to prevent memory exhaustion.

Each issue produces a different failure mode, and Go obliges developers to check for all of them explicitly. The benefit is clarity: validation logic resides in the handler itself, avoiding hidden control flow.

Web servers typically follow layered designs: routers dispatch to handlers, handlers call services, services call repositories, and repositories talk to databases. In these architectures, errors must bubble up cleanly through layers without losing their context. Go supports this through error wrapping:

```
if err := repo.CreateUser(ctx, u); err != nil {
    return fmt.Errorf("create user: %w", err)
}
```

By wrapping underlying errors, developers provide contextual breadcrumbs that help diagnose failures during logging or debugging. At the edges–typically the HTTP handler–these wrapped errors are unraveled into structured responses.

```
if err != nil {
    writeError(w, http.StatusInternalServerError, err.Error())
    return
}
```

In more advanced systems, the wrapped error is not returned directly to the client; instead, a mapping table converts specific domain errors into appropriate HTTP status codes (which includes **`ErrUserExists`** → 409 Conflict, **`ErrNotFound`** → 404 Not Found). This prevents leaking low-level details while preserving enough information on the server side for proper debugging.

Using Middleware for Centralized Error Handling

Middleware is one of the most effective strategies for error handling because it centralizes the interception of errors, logs them consistently, and provides common responses. A middleware wrapper often logs panics, enforces security policies, and even measures request-level performance metrics.

Panic Recovery

To prevent panics from crashing the entire server, developers wrap handlers in a recover block:

```
func RecoverMiddleware(next http.Handler) http.Handler {
    return http.HandlerFunc(func(w http.ResponseWriter, r *http.
Request) {
        defer func() {
            if rec := recover(); rec != nil {
                log.Printf("panic: %v", rec)
                writeError(w, http.StatusInternalServerError,
"internal server error")
            }
        }()
        next.ServeHTTP(w, r)
    })
}
```

This construct transforms unexpected panics–which may include nil pointer dereferences, slice boundary errors, or third-party library failures–into safe, structured HTTP responses. Without this middleware, Go's default behavior is to terminate the request abruptly and print a stack trace to stderr, which is unsafe for production.

Context-Aware Error Handling

HTTP in Go tightly integrates with **context.Context**, enabling handlers to detect client cancellations or timeouts. Many downstream operations—especially database queries, API calls, and file I/O—propagate context errors automatically. Developers must catch and interpret them:

```
user, err := repo.GetUser(ctx, id)
if errors.Is(err, context.DeadlineExceeded) {
    writeError(w, http.StatusGatewayTimeout, "operation timed
out")
    return
}
if errors.Is(err, context.Canceled) {
    // Client disconnected; safe to abort.
    return
}
```

Handling context errors correctly prevents unnecessary computation after clients disconnect and ensures that long-running tasks do not block the system indefinitely.

Logging and Observability in Error Flows

Errors lose their diagnostic value unless logged correctly. Handlers typically log:

- Source of the error
- Request path and method
- Correlation IDs or request IDs
- User identity or authentication metadata
- Contextual information about the operation

Example:

```
log.Printf("failed to create user: %v (path=%s method=%s)",
    err, r.URL.Path, r.Method)
```

In production systems, structured logging formats such as JSON logs allow log aggregators and APM tools to parse error records. This plays a crucial role in debugging distributed systems where HTTP servers interact with queues, upstream APIs, and databases across multiple machines.

AI-Assisted Insights for Error Handling

Modern tooling allows AI models to analyze error patterns from logs, suggest improved status code mappings, and detect inconsistencies in error responses. For example:

- AI can scan handlers for missing error checks, such as ignoring **r.Body.**

`Close()`, forgetting to check Decodeerrors, or failing to return correct status codes.

- AI-based tools can evaluate error envelope consistency, detecting when handlers return mismatched field names or inconsistent metadata.
- AI can auto-generate human-readable explanations of panics captured in logs.
- LLM-enhanced linters can propose refactoring strategies such as consolidating duplicate error-handling branches into middleware.

This form of automated assistance is especially valuable in large codebases where error paths become scattered, and it is difficult to audit them manually.

AI-Assisted Generation of API Endpoints

As AI continues to shape modern software development, tools such as ChatGPT, GitHub Copilot, Amazon Q Developer, and Claude are becoming invaluable in helping developers design and implement API endpoints faster and with fewer errors. While AI does not replace a developer's understanding of HTTP, JSON, or Go's backend design principles, it significantly boosts productivity by generating boilerplate, suggesting patterns, and highlighting potential improvements in API structure and documentation.

This section explores how AI can support the design and implementation of API endpoints in Go, particularly when working with the net/http package or frameworks such as Gin, Echo, or Fiber. We will also look at practical examples of how AI-assisted prompts can accelerate backend development.

Using AI Assistance in Designing API Endpoints

AI tools can assist at several stages of API development:

- **Generating Initial Endpoint Scaffolds:** You can describe the behavior you want–**`GET`**/**`POST`**, JSON input/output, validation rules–and AI can produce the starting code.
- **Suggesting Naming, Structuring, and REST Conventions:** AI can help ensure consistency in naming patterns, URL structures, and resource modeling.
- **Creating Request/Response Struct Definitions:** AI can convert a plain English description of an object into Go structs with proper field tags.
- **Generating Validation or Error-Handling Patterns:** AI can suggest reusable patterns for input validation, status codes, or error responses.
- **Documentation Support:** AI can generate OpenAPI (Swagger) components, inline comments, or README-style endpoint documentation.

Using AI to Generate a Basic CRUD Endpoint

Imagine you ask an AI tool:

"Create a Go **net/http** handler for managing books.

Implement **GET** to fetch a book by **ID** and **POST** to create a new book. Use JSON request/response."

An AI tool might generate something like this:

```
package main

import (
	"encoding/json"
	"log"
	"net/http"
	"strconv"
)

type Book struct {
	ID     int    `json:"id"`
	Title  string `json:"title"`
	Author string `json:"author"`
}

var books = make(map[int]Book)
var nextID = 1

// GET /books/{id}
func getBookHandler(w http.ResponseWriter, r *http.Request) {
	idStr := r.URL.Path[len("/books/"):]
	id, err := strconv.Atoi(idStr)
	if err != nil {
		http.Error(w, "invalid id", http.StatusBadRequest)
		return
	}

	book, ok := books[id]
	if !ok {
		http.NotFound(w, r)
		return
	}

	json.NewEncoder(w).Encode(book)
}
```

```
// POST /books
func createBookHandler(w http.ResponseWriter, r *http.Request) {
	var newBook Book
	if err := json.NewDecoder(r.Body).Decode(&newBook); err !=
nil {
		http.Error(w, "invalid JSON", http.StatusBadRequest)
		return
	}

	newBook.ID = nextID
	nextID++
	books[newBook.ID] = newBook

	w.WriteHeader(http.StatusCreated)
	json.NewEncoder(w).Encode(newBook)
}

func main() {
	http.HandleFunc("/books/", getBookHandler)
	http.HandleFunc("/books", createBookHandler)

	log.Println("Server running on :8080")
	http.ListenAndServe(":8080", nil)
}
```

This is a clean, functional endpoint scaffold that a developer can review, refine, and expand.

AI-Assisted Input Validation

If you tell AI:

"Add JSON validation: ensure 'title' and 'author' aren't empty."

It may respond with:

```
if newBook.Title == "" || newBook.Author == "" {
	http.Error(w, "title and author are required fields", http.
StatusBadRequest)
	return
}
```

AI supports these "micro-tasks" quickly, reducing development friction.

AI-Assisted Error Response Standardization

Suppose you want consistent API errors. You can prompt:

"Create a reusable JSON error response function."

AI might generate:

```
type ErrorResponse struct {
	Error   string `json:"error"`
	Details string `json:"details,omitempty"`
}

func writeJSONError(w http.ResponseWriter, status int, msg
string, details string) {
	w.Header().Set("Content-Type", "application/json")
	w.WriteHeader(status)
	json.NewEncoder(w).Encode(ErrorResponse{
		Error:   msg,
		Details: details,
	})
}
```

You can then plug this into any endpoint.

AI-Assisted Generation of Query/Response Models

AI excels at converting natural language requirements into Go struct definitions.

Example Prompt:

"Create a request struct for a user profile update containing name, email, and age (optional)."

AI Output:

```
type UpdateProfileRequest struct {
	Name  string `json:"name"`
	Email string `json:"email"`
	Age   *int   `json:"age,omitempty"`
}
```

This saves time and enforces consistent JSON field naming.

Using AI for Complete Endpoint Flows

Given a prompt like:

"Build a **`PATCH /books/{id}`** endpoint that updates only the fields provided."

AI could generate a full handler:

```
func updateBookHandler(w http.ResponseWriter, r *http.Request) {
  idStr := r.URL.Path[len("/books/"):]
  id, err := strconv.Atoi(idStr)
  if err != nil {
        writeJSONError(w, http.StatusBadRequest, "invalid id",
err.Error())
        return
  }

  book, exists := books[id]
  if !exists {
        writeJSONError(w, http.StatusNotFound, "book not found", "")
        return
  }

  var patch struct {
        Title  *string `json:"title,omitempty"`
        Author *string `json:"author,omitempty"`
  }

  if err := json.NewDecoder(r.Body).Decode(&patch); err != nil {
        writeJSONError(w, http.StatusBadRequest, "invalid JSON",
err.Error())
        return
  }

  if patch.Title != nil {
        book.Title = *patch.Title
  }
  if patch.Author != nil {
        book.Author = *patch.Author
  }

  books[id] = book
  json.NewEncoder(w).Encode(book)
}
```

This is the kind of boilerplate an AI tool can reliably produce.

Best Practices When Using AI for Endpoint Generation

AI assistance is powerful, but developers must still apply good engineering judgment:

- **Validate AI output.**

Check for:

- ○ Missing error handling;
- ○ Insecure patterns;
- ○ Incorrect status codes; and,
- ○ Inefficient data structures.

- **Apply your architecture for the project.**

  AI may not know your:

  - ○ Repository patterns
  - ○ Domain models
  - ○ Framework preferences (which includes chi versus net/http versus Gin)

- **Keep prompts precise:**

  High-quality prompts lead to high-quality code.

  Examples:

  - ○ "Use chi router and return JSON errors in this format..."
  - ○ "Follow REST conventions and include pagination parameters."
  - ○ "Add middleware for authentication and inject the user ID into the handler."

- **Treat AI as a collaborator, not as a replacement.**

  AI boosts development speed but cannot replace:

  - ○ Architectural decision-making
  - ○ Code reviews
  - ○ Security and performance considerations

Conclusion

In this chapter, we have explored how Go powers modern web development by combining simplicity, performance, and clarity. By walking through the fundamental components of building a web server, you learned how Go's standard library—especially net/http—enables developers to build scalable, maintainable, and production-ready backend services with minimal overhead.

We began by understanding how to set up a basic web server and respond to incoming HTTP requests. You have seen how Go structures handlers, how routing works, and why Go's request–response model makes it straightforward to manage different HTTP methods such as GET, POST, PUT, and DELETE. From there, we moved into designing more advanced routing patterns, organizing handlers cleanly, and implementing method-specific logic that keeps code readable and predictable.

The chapter then introduced middleware patterns in Go, demonstrating how cross-cutting concerns—logging, authentication, rate limiting, error wrapping, CORS, and metrics—can be implemented in simple yet powerful ways. You have also learned how middleware reinforces the separation of concerns while remaining flexible enough to use across small projects or large, modular systems. Then, we have worked with JSON, a core element of API development. By using the encoding/json package, you learned to decode request bodies, marshal structured responses, manage optional or nullable fields, and handle unexpected inputs gracefully. This section emphasized correctness, security, and usability—three pillars of well-designed web APIs.

Error handling was another key component. You have explored strategies to capture, classify, and report errors consistently across an application. The chapter highlighted the importance of returning meaningful HTTP status codes, crafting structured JSON error messages, and designing reusable helper functions to avoid boilerplate. By understanding both the mechanics and the philosophy of error handling, you gained the tools needed to build APIs that are predictable, debug-friendly, and trustworthy.

Finally, we have examined how AI tools can assist in generating, refining, and documenting API endpoints. You saw examples of how AI can scaffold handlers, structure JSON models, suggest validation rules, or even generate full CRUD flows. This section underscored a practical reality: AI does not replace engineering judgment—but it meaningfully accelerates development when used thoughtfully.

In the next chapter, we will look into Concurrent Processing Pipelines. It focuses on the architectural patterns and techniques that power these pipelines. You will learn how to design pipelines that are not only fast and scalable, but also predictable, maintainable, and production-ready.

CHAPTER 8
Concurrent Processing Pipelines

Introduction

The concurrency model of Go enables developers to construct highly efficient data-processing pipelines that scale seamlessly across cores and workloads. This chapter introduces the architectural patterns and techniques that power these pipelines–ranging from goroutine-based parallelism and channel-driven coordination to fan-out/fan-in structures and worker pools. By combining the lightweight concurrency of Go with systematic profiling and AI-assisted insights, readers will learn how to design pipelines that are not only fast and scalable, but also predictable, maintainable, and production-ready.

Structure

In this chapter, we will cover the following topics:

- Designing Data Pipelines in Go
    - Ensuring Backpressure and Flow Control
    - Error Handling Strategies across Stages
    - Pipeline Cancellation with Context
    - Composing Pipelines for Reusability
    - A Fully Composed Example
- Fan-out and Fan-in Concurrency Patterns
    - Understanding Fan-out: Distributing Work across Goroutines
    - Understanding Fan-in: Consolidating Work from Multiple Goroutines
    - Combining Fan-out and Fan-in for Parallel Pipelines
    - Design Considerations and Best Practices

- Worker Pools and Task Scheduling
  - The Core Idea behind Worker Pools
  - Task Scheduling in Worker Pools
  - Using WaitGroups for Worker Pool Coordination
  - Dynamic Worker Pools
  - Integrating Context for Cancellable Pools
- Channel-Based Communication Strategies
- Performance Profiling Using Go **pprof**
  - Understanding What **pprof** Measures
  - Activating **pprof** in a Go Application
  - Using **pprof** to Analyze Concurrent Pipelines
  - Interpreting Flamegraphs
  - Optimizing Pipelines Using **pprof** Insights
- AI-Assisted Optimization of Concurrent Pipelines
  - AI-Assisted Optimization Examples

Designing Data Pipelines in Go

Designing data pipelines in Go requires an understanding of how the data flows through concurrent components and how each stage of the pipeline transforms, filters, enriches, or aggregates information before forwarding it. Go's concurrency primitives–goroutines, channels, and the **select** statements–provide the foundation for constructing pipelines that are both high-performance and highly maintainable. A well-designed pipeline not only increases throughput, but also isolates responsibilities, thereby allowing each stage to be independently tested, tuned, and replaced. This modularity is essential for systems that scale to millions of events, parallel workloads, or real-time streams.

At its core, a Go pipeline mirrors the conceptual model used in production systems such as stream processors, ETL workflows, event-driven architectures, and microservices that process queues. A stage receives input, performs a unit of work, and emits output. The output becomes the input of the next stage, forming a chain of transformations connected by channels. These channels define both the boundary between stages, and the synchronization mechanism for coordinating work across concurrent goroutines. Because Go channels are typed, each stage also has a clearly defined contract regarding the shape and semantics of the data it handles.

A typical pipeline begins with a source stage, which is responsible for ingesting data into the system–whether from files, APIs, message queues, or generated streams. This stage should usually run in its own goroutine to avoid blocking downstream logic. The data then flows into one or more transform stages, where the information is cleaned, parsed, enriched, validated, or split into multiple derived streams. The design of these stages should focus on ensuring that each transformation performs a single well-defined task. This aligns naturally with Go's emphasis on small, composable functions and reduces the cognitive load for readers of the code. Finally, the pipeline ends with a sink stage, responsible for storing the results, emitting metrics, triggering downstream actions, or returning output to the caller.

A minimal pipeline in Go might look like this:

```
func generator(out chan<- int) {
    for i := 1; i <= 5; i++ {
        out <- i
    }
    close(out)
}

func square(in <-chan int, out chan<- int) {
    for n := range in {
        out <- n * n
    }
    close(out)
}

func printer(in <-chan int) {
    for v := range in {
        fmt.Println("Result:", v)
    }
}

func main() {
    gen := make(chan int)
    sq := make(chan int)

    go generator(gen)
    go square(gen, sq)
    printer(sq)
}
```

This simple pipeline illustrates three key principles that scale to production systems:

- Each stage is isolated (generator, square, printer).
- Channels define the flow and prevent over synchronization.
- Termination is explicit, requiring careful closing of channels.

Ensuring Backpressure and Flow Control

Real-world pipelines often involve multiple stages with varying processing speeds. When an upstream stage produces data faster than a downstream stage can consume it, the system requires backpressure to prevent memory bloat or uncontrolled goroutine growth. Go channels handle this naturally: an unbuffered channel forces the sender to block until the receiver is ready, while a buffered channel provides limited elasticity, but still applies inherent pressure.

Choosing the correct channel type for each stage is central to pipeline design:

- Unbuffered channels guarantee synchronous handoff, and are ideal for tightly coupled stages.
- Buffered channels allow bursts of work, and help improve throughput when a small queue is acceptable.
- Large buffers can hide performance issues and should be used cautiously.

Pipeline behavior can be subtly influenced by these choices.

Error Handling Strategies across Stages

A robust pipeline must incorporate an error-handling strategy that preserves correctness without halting the entire system unnecessarily. Go's explicit error model maps cleanly to pipelines: each stage can emit error values alongside data, pass errors through dedicated error channels, or wrap data in structs containing error metadata.

A common pattern is to use a struct type:

```
type Item struct {
    Value int
    Err   error
}
```

With such a wrapper, any stage can signal an issue while still allowing downstream components to decide how to proceed. This approach avoids races between multiple channels and keeps the flow of information unified. In more complex pipelines, separate error channels may be used, especially when errors need aggregation or centralized logging.

Another important consideration is graceful termination when errors occur. When a stage exits early due to an unrecoverable error, it must close its output channels to notify downstream consumers. The design should avoid scenarios where goroutines become stuck waiting indefinitely on a channel that no longer receives data. Proper use of defer close(out) within worker goroutines ensures predictable and safe shutdown behavior.

Pipeline Cancellation with Context

Modern Go applications often require cancellation support for long-running operations. Incorporating **`context.Contextinto`** pipeline design prevents resource leaks, simplifies shutdowns, and integrates naturally with HTTP servers, RPC frameworks, and databases.

A stage that respects context may look like this:

```
func squareWithContext(ctx context.Context, in <-chan int, out
chan<- int) {
    defer close(out)
    for {
        select {
        case <-ctx.Done():
            return
        case n, ok := <-in:
            if !ok { return }
            out <- n * n
        }
    }
}
```

By embedding **`ctx.Done()`** checks in the loop, the stage reacts immediately to cancellations, allowing the entire pipeline to stop cleanly. Designing pipelines with context-awareness is especially important for real-time APIs, distributed workers, or scheduled batch processes that must respond quickly to shutdown signals.

Composing Pipelines for Reusability

Go pipelines are easiest to maintain when each stage is implemented as a parameterized function that accepts channels and returns new channels. This enables pipeline composition, in which stages are combined flexibly based on application needs.

For example:

```
func multiply(factor int) Stage {
    return func(in <-chan int) <-chan int {
        out := make(chan int)
        go func() {
            defer close(out)
            for v := range in {
                out <- v * factor
            }
```

```
        }()
        return out
    }
}
```

Such designs make pipelines easy to extend, replace, or rearrange without modifying internal logic. Complex pipelines–such as ETL workflows, real-time event processors, and analytics pipelines–benefit significantly from this composability, particularly when adding new transformation steps or debugging individual stages.

A Fully Composed Example

A more expressive pipeline showing staged transformations, concurrency, and composition is as follows:

```
func generator(n int) <-chan int {
    out := make(chan int)
    go func() {
        defer close(out)
        for i := 1; i <= n; i++ {
            out <- i
        }
    }()
    return out
}

func filterEven(in <-chan int) <-chan int {
    out := make(chan int)
    go func() {
        defer close(out)
        for v := range in {
            if v%2 == 0 {
                out <- v
            }
        }
    }()
    return out
}

func square(in <-chan int) <-chan int {
    out := make(chan int)
    go func() {
        defer close(out)
        for v := range in {
            out <- v * v
        }
    }()
```

```
    return out
}

func main() {
    p := square(filterEven(generator(10)))
    for v := range p {
        fmt.Println(v)
    }
}
```

This example demonstrates several essential practices:

- Each stage has a single responsibility.
- Stages are composable and chainable.
- The pipeline remains easy to reason about as it grows.

In large systems, this pattern scales into pipelines that handle file ingestion, message streaming, distributed event processing, ML scoring, and more.

Fan-out and Fan-in Concurrency Patterns

Fan-out and Fan-in patterns form the backbone of scalable concurrent architectures in Go. These patterns enable the distribution of work across multiple Goroutines and the consolidation of results back into a unified output stream. By pairing Go's lightweight Goroutines with channel-based communication, developers can create highly parallel processing pipelines that fully exploit multicore CPUs and adapt gracefully to fluctuating workloads. These patterns are particularly valuable in scenarios such as parallel I/O operations, CPU-bound computations, distributed event pipelines, and real-time data processing systems.

Understanding Fan-out: Distributing Work across Goroutines

The fan-out pattern distributes the incoming tasks across multiple worker goroutines that process them in parallel. A single input channel feeds a pool of workers, each responsible for consuming jobs and producing output. Because goroutines are extremely lightweight—often consuming only a few kilobytes of stack space—Go can comfortably launch thousands of workers when required.

Fan-out improves throughput by allowing independent tasks to proceed concurrently instead of serially. For example, a pipeline that processes thousands of URLs, transforms data frames, or applies CPU-intensive transformations benefits significantly from dividing work among multiple workers.

A classic fan-out design looks like this:

```
func worker(id int, jobs <-chan int, results chan<- int) {
    for j := range jobs {
        results <- j * j // Example: square computation
    }
}

func main() {
    jobs := make(chan int, 100)
    results := make(chan int, 100)

    // Fan-out: create 3 workers
    for w := 1; w <= 3; w++ {
        go worker(w, jobs, results)
    }

    // Send jobs
    for i := 1; i <= 10; i++ {
        jobs <- i
    }
    close(jobs)

    // Receive results
    for i := 1; i <= 10; i++ {
        fmt.Println(<-results)
    }
}
```

This pattern demonstrates several important ideas:

- Multiple workers concurrently read from the same input channel, and distribute tasks automatically in a load-balanced fashion.
- Jobs must eventually close to inform workers that no more tasks will arrive.
- Workers continue until the channel is drained, ensuring deterministic completion.

Fan-out allows the system to match computation parallelism to available CPU cores, improving utilization and reducing task latency.

Understanding Fan-in: Consolidating Work from Multiple Goroutines

While fan-out distributes tasks, fan-in addresses the opposite challenge: merging multiple output streams into a single coherent result channel. A fan-in pattern is essential when work is parallelized but must converge before subsequent processing stages.

A fan-in implementation often involves:

1. Launching multiple goroutines, each generating or processing data.
2. Returning results to a shared output channel.
3. Using a **WaitGroup** to ensure that all workers finish before closing the channel.

The following example illustrates fan-in:

```
func generate(nums ...int) <-chan int {
    out := make(chan int)
    go func() {
        for _, n := range nums {
            out <- n
        }
        close(out)
    }()
    return out
}

func squareWorker(in <-chan int) <-chan int {
    out := make(chan int)
    go func() {
        for n := range in {
            out <- n * n
        }
        close(out)
    }()
    return out
}

func fanIn(channels ...<-chan int) <-chan int {
    var wg sync.WaitGroup
    out := make(chan int)

    wg.Add(len(channels))
    for _, ch := range channels {
        go func(c <-chan int) {
            defer wg.Done()
            for v := range c {
                out <- v
            }
        }(ch)
    }
```

```
        go func() {
            wg.Wait()
            close(out)
        }()

        return out
    }
```

Here, the fan-in function merges the results from multiple channels into a single stream. It ensures safety by closing the output channel only after all input channels are exhausted. This avoids deadlocks and ensures consistent termination—a common source of subtle bugs in concurrent designs.

Combining Fan-out and Fan-in for Parallel Pipelines

Real-world systems often rely on the combination of both patterns to create scalable parallel data pipelines. A typical pipeline looks like:

1. **Generator Stage:** It produces tasks.
2. **Fan-out Stage:** It distributes tasks across worker Goroutines.
3. **Worker Stage(s):** It performs CPU or I/O-bound work in parallel.
4. **Fan-in stage:** It merges results into a single output stream.

A Combined Example:

```
    func main() {
        in := generator(1, 2, 3, 4, 5, 6, 7, 8)

        // Fan-out to 4 workers
        worker1 := squareWorker(in)
        worker2 := squareWorker(in)
        worker3 := squareWorker(in)
        worker4 := squareWorker(in)

        // Fan-in results into a single stream
        merged := fanIn(worker1, worker2, worker3, worker4)

        // Consume output
        for v := range merged {
            fmt.Println("Output:", v)
        }
    }
```

This design provides several benefits:

- Parallelism increases throughput as workers process independent tasks concurrently.
- Workers are symmetrical, simplifying reasoning and testing.
- The fan-in stage fully decouples worker lifecycles from consumer logic.

Many production systems—including distributed crawlers, stream processors, ETL pipelines, log processors, and image transformation services—rely on this structure, quite precisely.

Design Considerations and Best Practices

When adopting fan-out and fan-in patterns, several design considerations ensure long-term maintainability:

- Channel closure must be explicit and deterministic to avoid goroutine leaks.
- Worker pool sizes should be tuned to available CPU cores or I/O parallelism.
- Buffered channels can reduce contention, but excessive buffering may hide performance bottlenecks.

Contexts should be integrated for cancellation, allowing pipelines to terminate gracefully under timeouts, service shutdowns, or user cancellation events. Error handling should either flow through separate error channels or structured result objects, allowing downstream logic to react appropriately.

Fan-out/fan-in patterns demonstrate the expressiveness and power of Go's concurrency model. When used correctly, they make it possible to build pipelines that are fast, scalable, and resilient—forming the foundation for more advanced structures such as worker pools, distributed schedulers, and AI-assisted performance tuning covered in subsequent sections.

Worker Pools and Task Scheduling

Worker pools form one of the most essential concurrency constructs in Go, offering a structured method for processing large volumes of tasks with controlled parallelism. While Goroutines are incredibly lightweight, spawning an unbounded number of them is neither sustainable nor desirable in production environments. Worker pools solve this problem by maintaining a fixed—or dynamically controlled—number of workers that pull tasks from a shared queue. This pattern ensures predictable CPU and memory usage while still allowing high throughput and efficient concurrency.

The Core Idea behind Worker Pools

A worker pool operates around three fundamental components:

- **A Task Queue:** It is usually implemented as a channel containing work items.
- **A Fixed Number of Workers:** Goroutines that continuously read from the task queue.
- **An Output or Result Collection Stage:** Either using another channel or updating shared state using synchronization primitives.

By controlling the number of active workers, the application avoids resource exhaustion and allows developers to fine-tune throughput based on machine capacities. CPU-bound workloads may scale linearly up to the number of available CPU cores, while I/O-bound workloads may benefit from a larger number of workers because many goroutines will be idle, waiting for I/O operations.

A minimal worker pool design appears as follows:

```
func worker(id int, tasks <-chan int, results chan<- int) {
    for t := range tasks {
        time.Sleep(time.Millisecond * 100) // Simulate work
        results <- t * 2                   // Process task
    }
}

func main() {
    tasks := make(chan int, 50)
    results := make(chan int, 50)

    // Start a pool of 5 workers
    for w := 1; w <= 5; w++ {
        go worker(w, tasks, results)
    }

    // Submit 20 tasks
    for i := 1; i <= 20; i++ {
        tasks <- i
    }
    close(tasks)

    // Collect results
    for i := 1; i <= 20; i++ {
        fmt.Println(<-results)
    }
}
```

This simple pattern demonstrates predictable concurrency: only five goroutines perform the work regardless of the number of incoming tasks, thus preventing a workload spike from overwhelming system resources.

Task Scheduling in Worker Pools

Task scheduling refers to the strategy used to distribute workloads across workers and determine processing order. While Go's channel semantics provide a built-in form of scheduling–workers pull tasks in FIFO order–many applications require more sophisticated policies.

FIFO Scheduling (Default Channel Behavior)

The simplest form of scheduling is the implicit FIFO ordering of channel sends. Workers read tasks as they are available, thus ensuring that all workers remain busy when there is sufficient demand. This mode is ideal for homogeneous workloads where each task takes roughly the same time.

Work Stealing and Load Balancing

When task complexity varies significantly, FIFO distribution may lead to suboptimal utilization–some workers may remain idle, while others process long-running tasks. A work-stealing approach, although not built into Go's standard library, can be simulated by assigning each worker its own internal queue and letting idle workers pull tasks from others' queues.

Priority Scheduling

Certain applications require more than FIFO behavior. For example, real-time data processing pipelines may prioritize urgent tasks while deferring low-priority ones. This can be implemented using:

- Heap-based priority queues,
- Multiple channels (one per priority), or
- A centralized dispatcher goroutine that sorts tasks before dispatching them.

A priority-aware dispatcher example:

```
type Task struct {
    Priority int
    Payload  int
}

func dispatcher(tasks []Task, workerCh chan<- Task) {
    sort.Slice(tasks, func(i, j int) bool {
```

```
        return tasks[i].Priority > tasks[j].Priority
    })

    for _, t := range tasks {
        workerCh <- t
    }
    close(workerCh)
}
```

This model separates scheduling logic from execution, keeping workers simple and focused on computation.

Rate-Limited Scheduling

Worker pools are often paired with rate limiters when interacting with external APIs or services. The **time.Ticker** combined with a dispatcher allows precise control:

```
ticker := time.NewTicker(100 * time.Millisecond)
for _, job := range jobs {
    <-ticker.C
    taskChan <- job
}
```

This ensures safety when the backend cannot handle bursts.

Using WaitGroups for Worker Pool Coordination

A **sync.WaitGroup** is central to coordinating the lifecycle of worker pools. Workers decrement the counter when finished, allowing the main goroutine to block until all work completes.

```
var wg sync.WaitGroup
wg.Add(numWorkers)

for i := 0; i < numWorkers; i++ {
    go func() {
        defer wg.Done()
        workerLoop()
    }()
}

wg.Wait() // Ensures all workers have exited
```

This pattern ensures graceful shutdown and eliminates race conditions commonly introduced when channels are closed prematurely.

Dynamic Worker Pools

Though fixed pools are easy to implement, dynamic worker pools—where the number of workers scales up or down depending on system load—are more flexible. A dynamic pool monitors:

- Queue depth,
- Worker idle times,
- Task processing latency,
- CPU usage.

When the queue grows, the pool may spawn additional workers (up to a maximum limit). When demand drops, unused workers can exit to free resources. This adaptive concurrency model resembles the worker scaling strategies used by high-performance distributed systems and cloud orchestration platforms.

Integrating Context for Cancellable Pools

Worker pools often operate in long-running services. Integrating **`context.Context`** allows graceful cancellation when:

- A request times out,
- A user cancels the operation,
- The system begins shutdown procedures.

Workers check for context cancellation:

```
func worker(ctx context.Context, tasks <-chan Task) {
    for {
        select {
        case <-ctx.Done():
            return
        case t, ok := <-tasks:
            if !ok {
                return
            }
            process(t)
        }
    }
}
```

This makes the pool responsive to changing runtime conditions and failures.

Channel-Based Communication Strategies

Channels are the backbone of Go's concurrency model, enabling goroutines to communicate safely without sharing memory. Instead of manually coordinating access to the shared data using locks, channels allow developers to pass values directly, creating a more structured and readable approach to concurrent design. In the context of processing pipelines and worker systems, how you use channels often determines whether your program performs efficiently or suffers from bottlenecks, deadlocks, and unpredictable latency. This section explores the most effective communication strategies, when to apply them, and how to design channel flows that scale with increasing workloads.

A fundamental strategy is directional channel usage, where channels are explicitly restricted to either sending or receiving. Instead of allowing a channel to be used in both directions, you declare a parameter or return value as chan<-for sending or <-chan for receiving. This pattern improves code clarity and prevents accidental misuse. For example, when building a data pipeline, each stage typically receives data from an inbound channel and forwards processed data to an outbound one. Using directional channels ensures that no goroutine mistakenly tries to write to a channel meant only for reading, or vice versa. The type system becomes a guidepost, reinforcing the structure of the pipeline. This strategy is especially helpful when pipelines become long or involve multiple contributors, as it locks the architecture into a predictable data flow.

Another core communication strategy is buffered versus unbuffered channels. Unbuffered channels create a strict synchronization point: the sender and receiver must meet at exactly the same time for data to move. This is ideal when you want precise coordination or want to control rate flow—for example, ensuring that producers never outrun consumers. Buffered channels, by contrast, allow temporary queuing of messages. The buffer acts like a small in-memory mailbox where goroutines can drop tasks without waiting for a receiver. Buffered channels shine in fan-out systems, where producers push work faster than any single worker can process it. However, designing with buffers requires careful tuning—too small a buffer, and your pipeline stalls; if too large, you risk hiding the performance issues until memory usage spikes. Go developers often benchmark various buffer sizes to identify the ideal balance between throughput and resource utilization.

A third strategy is channel closing conventions, which determine how pipeline shutdowns and completion signals propagate. Channels do not have a "done" value by default; instead, closing a channel becomes the mechanism for communicating that no more data is coming. Receivers use the two-value receive (value, ok := <-ch) to detect closure and gracefully exit loops. A key rule is that only the sender should close a channel, as it would prevent crashes caused by duplicate close calls. In multi-stage pipelines, closures propagate automatically across downstream stages, allowing each goroutine to finish work cleanly. For bidirectional or feedback-based systems, developers often introduce a separate done or quit channel to signal cancellation without interfering with main data flow. This separation reduces complexity and avoids scenarios where closing the primary channel triggers unintended shutdowns.

Another important communication design pattern involves selecting statements for channel multiplexing. Instead of blocking on one channel at a time, select allows a goroutine to wait on multiple channels simultaneously. This is necessary when coordinating timeouts, merging data streams, or building responsive pipelines that adapt to workload fluctuations. For example, a worker might simultaneously listen for inbound tasks, cancellation signals, and heartbeat updates, responding dynamically depending on which event arrives first. Select blocks can also incorporate defaultcases, enabling non-blocking communication—useful for implementing backpressure or dropping tasks when the system is overloaded. Though powerful, select must be used thoughtfully; too many branches or deeply nested selects can make logic hard to follow. Well-structured systems use select sparingly and document each branch's intent clearly.

Finally, a highly effective communication strategy is fan-in and fan-out coordination through channels, which enables multiple producers to write into a shared output channel or a single producer to distribute tasks to many workers. Fan-in merges results from parallel goroutines, but implementing it correctly requires ensuring that all producers finish, and that the shared output channel is closed safely. Fan-out, meanwhile, involves reading from one input channel and distributing tasks to multiple downstream stages. Both patterns rely heavily on channels to maintain order, avoid data races, and enforce lifecycle boundaries. When designed carefully, these patterns produce highly scalable pipelines that leverage Go's lightweight goroutines effectively.

Across all these strategies, clear channel ownership rules, thoughtful buffering, clean shutdown patterns, and judicious use of select statements form the foundation of robust concurrent architectures. Thus, whether you are designing a simple worker pool or a multi-stage data processing system, channels provide the connective tissue that keeps your goroutines coordinated, predictable, and performant.

Performance Profiling Using Go pprof

When building concurrent processing pipelines, it is often easy to assume that adding more goroutines or channels automatically results in a faster execution. In reality, concurrent systems can introduce their own performance challenges: excessive context switching, hidden blocking operations, misconfigured buffers, unexpected memory allocations, and uneven worker utilization. Without the right diagnostic tools, these problems remain invisible until the program slows down under real workloads.

Go provides one of the most powerful built-in profiling tools in modern programming languages: **pprof**. The **pprof** suite allows developers to analyze CPU usage, memory allocations, goroutine states, block profiling, mutex contention, and execution traces—all essential for understanding the behavior of concurrent pipelines. This section explores how to activate, collect, and interpret **pprof** data, and how to apply the insights to optimize pipeline throughput, reduce latency, and eliminate bottlenecks.

Understanding What pprof Measures

The **pprof** toolkit generates snapshots of a running Go program and visualizes how resources are being consumed. For concurrent pipelines, certain profiles are especially valuable:

CPU Profile

This identifies which functions consume the most CPU time. For data pipelines, CPU profiles can reveal:

- Expensive transformations or data parsing functions.
- JSON or encoding operations that dominate runtime.
- Hot loops in worker Goroutines.
- Goroutine creation costs when workers are not reused.

CPU profiling is particularly important when performance degrades as input volume increases.

Goroutine Profile

This shows what all the active goroutines are doing at the time of sampling. It helps detect:

- Goroutines blocked on channel sends or receives.
- Deadlocks caused by mismatched buffer sizes.
- Workers waiting idly due to slow producers.
- Fan-in stages that cannot catch up.

Seeing thousands of goroutines stuck on <-chan receive is an immediate sign of pipeline backpressure.

Block Profile

This profile reveals where goroutines are waiting on synchronization primitives:

- Channel send and receive waits.

- Mutex lock contention.
- Misconfigured worker pools.
- Long pauses caused by unbuffered channels.

Block profiling is especially useful because channel operations that appear harmless in code can behave very differently under load.

Memory and Heap Profiles

These measure allocations and garbage collection behavior. Concurrent pipelines frequently cause:

- Hidden allocations inside loops.
- Large temporary buffers in parsing functions.
- Excessive copying of messages or work units.
- Heap pressure leading to long GC pauses.

Memory optimization can unlock significant throughput improvements.

Trace Profile

Execution tracing records everything the runtime does: goroutine creation, channel operations, syscalls, and scheduler decisions. It is invaluable when diagnosing:

- Pipeline stalls
- Intermittent delays
- Competition between goroutines
- Priority misbehavior of the runtime scheduler

While the trace can be overwhelming, it is the most precise way to spot concurrency bottlenecks.

Activating pprof in a Go Application

Profiling requires importing and starting the **`net/http/pprof`** package. A minimal setup is:

```
import (
    _ "net/http/pprof"
    "net/http"
)

func main() {
    go func() {
```

```
        http.ListenAndServe("localhost:6060", nil)
    }()
    runPipeline()
}
```

Running your program now exposes profiling endpoints such as:

```
/debug/pprof/
/debug/pprof/profile
/debug/pprof/goroutine
/debug/pprof/heap
```

Once the server is running, you can collect a CPU profile:

```
go tool pprof http://localhost:6060/debug/pprof/profile
```

Or, view goroutine states:

```
go tool pprof http://localhost:6060/debug/pprof/goroutine
```

You can view profiles as text or generate visual flamegraphs using:

```
web
```

This opens an interactive UI showing exactly which functions are consuming the most of the time.

Using pprof to Analyze Concurrent Pipelines

Profiling concurrent systems is less about raw CPU usage and more about identifying waiting, blocking, and imbalanced workloads. The most common patterns and how **pprof** helps uncover them is elucidated in the following section.

Detecting Channel Bottlenecks

A pipeline using unbuffered channels may work fine during development but collapse under real traffic. Using the goroutine profile, you might find:

```
goroutine 200 [chan send]:
```

This indicates a producer is waiting for a consumer to read from the channel. If hundreds of goroutines display the same state, the pipeline is experiencing severe backpressure. The fix may be to:

- Add a buffer to the channel.
- Increase worker pool size.
- Reduce input batch size.
- Introduce load-shedding.

pprof makes the bottleneck obvious rather than guesswork.

Finding Uneven Worker Utilization

In fan-out systems, some workers may be overloaded while others remain idle. CPU profiles reveal this:

- One worker shows high CPU usage.
- Others barely register.

This often results from:

- A hash-based distribution that has skewed keys.
- Long tasks that dominate worker time.
- Tasks with varying complexity.

Solutions include randomized task assignment, job batching, or measuring queue depth per worker.

Diagnosing Deadlocks and Starvation

Goroutine profiles commonly reveal subtle deadlocks:

```
goroutine 88 [select]:
goroutine 102 [chan receive]:
goroutine 103 [chan send]:
```

If the pipeline has a cycle—such as workers waiting on each other—`pprof` highlights the blocked goroutines instantly.

Identifying Memory Spikes in Pipeline Stages

Heap profiles show which stages allocate most aggressively. For example, JSON serialization inside a pipeline may produce:

```
120MB in encoding/json.(*encodeState).marshal
```

Switching to a reusable buffer pool (sync.Pool), or using a more efficient codec significantly reduces allocations.

Tracing Scheduler Behavior

The Go scheduler's interactions with goroutines sometimes cause unpredictable delays. Trace events such as:

- Stop-the-World GC pauses (STW)
- `Goroutine Park`
- `Goroutine Ready`
- `Proc Steal`

They reveal precisely when and why the runtime paused your pipeline. These insights guide decisions like:

- Using fewer but longer-lived workers.
- Reducing goroutine churn.
- Increasing GOMAXPROCS for CPU-bound pipelines.

Interpreting Flamegraphs

Flamegraphs stack functions from bottom (root) to top (leaf). Wide boxes indicate high time spent in that function. For concurrent pipelines, flamegraphs help identify:

- Hot stages
- Inefficient data transformations
- Expensive system calls
- Serialization bottlenecks
- Excessive logging inside workers

Flamegraphs make performance intuitive, not theoretical.

Optimizing Pipelines Using pprof Insights

Profiling without applying fixes is only half of the process. Typical optimizations based on `pprof` data include:

- **Reducing Blocking:**
  - Add buffering.
  - Increase worker count.
  - Rebalance task distribution.
  - Remove sequential bottlenecks in the pipeline.
- **Reducing Allocations:**
  - Reuse buffers.
  - Pre-allocate slices when possible.
  - Minimize copying of messages.
- **Improving Parallelism:**
  - Convert long-running stages into sub-pipelines.
  - Use batch processing for small tasks.

- **Eliminating Unnecessary Goroutines:**
  - Too many goroutines lead to scheduler thrashing.
  - `pprof` helps identify when a pipeline needs fewer, well-coordinated workers instead of thousands of lightweight tasks.
- **Tuning the Runtime:**
  - Adjust GOMAXPROCS.
  - Enable GC pacing in large pipelines.
  - Control memory growth through streaming.

AI-Assisted Optimization of Concurrent Pipelines

Designing high-performance concurrent pipelines in Go requires more than writing goroutines and connecting them with channels. The real challenge begins when the pipeline is subjected to real-world workloads, unpredictable input patterns, CPU-heavy tasks, bursty network responses, or uneven load distribution. Traditionally, optimizing such systems requires careful analysis of logs, flamegraphs, traces, and manual reasoning about pipeline behavior. However, modern AI tools significantly reduce the friction of this process by assisting in diagnostics, pattern recognition, architectural decision-making, and performance tuning.

AI-based systems such as ChatGPT, GitHub Copilot, and Amazon Q Developer provide sophisticated insights by interpreting runtime data, reading code excerpts, and analyzing bottlenecks that are difficult to spot manually. While AI does not replace human understanding of concurrency principles, it acts as an accelerator—offering suggestions, code transformations, architectural alternatives, and automated refactoring paths to improve throughput and resource usage. This section explores how AI augments the optimization workflow, with four real-world examples demonstrating practical improvements.

AI-assisted optimization goes beyond simple code completion. It can:

- **Interpret Profiling Output:**

  Given a `pprof` flamegraph or goroutine dump, AI can infer:
  - The stage causing backpressure.
  - Channels which are under-buffered.
  - Overloaded workers.
  - Memory-heavy stages requiring buffer reuse.

  This turns raw runtime data into actionable insights within seconds.

- **Suggest Architectural Modifications:**

  AI can recommend:

  - When to use buffered and unbuffered channels.
  - When to switch from fan-out to worker pools.
  - How to batch tasks to reduce overhead.
  - How to convert blocking stages into asynchronous or parallel operations.

- **Provide Code-Level Micro-Optimizations**

  AI helps to identify:

  - Unnecessary allocations
  - Non-streaming I/O in tight loops
  - Race conditions
  - Contention hotspots

- **Validate Concurrency Safety**

  Models trained on large datasets recognize common concurrency mistakes and can warn about:

  - Missing channel closes.
  - Misordered defer calls.
  - Goroutine leaks.
  - Incorrect use of sync primitives.

- **Explain Complex Pipeline Behavior**

  When the pipeline behaves unexpectedly—stalls, fluctuating throughput, excessive memory spikes—AI can articulate the root cause using natural language.

AI-Assisted Optimization Examples

The following examples demonstrate how AI can assist in diagnosing and optimizing concurrent pipelines:

Example 1: AI Suggests Buffer Sizes for Channels

Consider a pipeline where a producer sends messages to multiple transformation goroutines:

```
jobs := make(chan Job)
results := make(chan Result)
```

```
go producer(jobs)
for i := 0; i < 5; i++ {
    go worker(jobs, results)
}
go collector(results)
```

During load testing, CPU usage is low and throughput is poor. Goroutine profiling reveals:

```
150 goroutines [chan send]:
    producer -> jobs
```

This means the producer is blocked because workers cannot read fast enough.

AI-assisted insight:

By feeding the goroutine stack dump into an AI tool, it identifies the pattern:

"Your workers are taking longer to process each job than the producer needs to generate them. This causes the producer to block on sending to an unbuffered channel. Consider adding a buffer size proportional to expected burst size or worker throughput."

Suggested ix:

```
jobs := make(chan Job, 200)    // AI-suggested buffer
results := make(chan Result, 100)
```

Buffering allows the producer to continue generating tasks during bursts, smoothing pipeline flow. The pipeline throughput increases immediately under load.

Example 2: AI Recommends Converting a Fan-out Stage to a Worker Pool

A pipeline uses naive fan-out to distribute tasks:

```
for _, item := range items {
    go func(v Data) {
        out <- process(v)
    }(item)
}
```

The Issue:

Launching thousands of goroutines causes high allocation overhead, excessive scheduling, and ultimately a throughput regression.

Developers upload a snippet of code and profiling results to an AI model, which recognizes a common anti-pattern:

"This code creates one goroutine per item. For large item sets, this causes goroutine churn and GC pressure. Replace this with a worker pool and fixed concurrency level."

AI-proposed refactor:

```
func processPipeline(items []Data) []Result {
    in := make(chan Data)
    out := make(chan Result)

    // AI suggests optimal worker count based on CPU cores
    workerCount := runtime.NumCPU() * 2

    for i := 0; i < workerCount; i++ {
        go func() {
            for v := range in {
                out <- process(v)
            }
        }()
    }

    go func() {
        for _, item := range items {
            in <- item
        }
        close(in)
    }()

    var results []Result
    for range items {
        results = append(results, <-out)
    }

    return results
}
```

The Result:

Stable workers reuse stack memory, reduce scheduling overhead, and work at CPU-efficient levels. Latency becomes predictable and memory use drops.

Example 3: AI Helps Eliminate a Subtle Deadlock

A pipeline with fan-in behavior shows occasional hangs under load. The code looks harmless:

```
func merge(cs ...<-chan int) <-chan int {
    out := make(chan int)
    var wg sync.WaitGroup

    for _, c := range cs {
        wg.Add(1)
        go func(ch <-chan int) {
```

```
            defer wg.Done()
            for v := range ch {
                out <- v
            }
        }(c)
    }

    go func() {
        wg.Wait()
        close(out)
    }()

    return out
}
```

Under a high load, the program deadlocks. A **pprof** goroutine dump shows:

```
goroutine blocked on send to out
```

AI analysis identifies the root cause:

"The out channel is unbuffered, so workers block while trying to send values. Because the main goroutine reading from out also spawns workers, it may not drain out fast enough. Consider adding a buffer or increasing the consumer's read rate."

Fix:

```
out := make(chan int, 1000)
```

Or, redesign the fan-in stage to ensure that the consumer is not starved.

The deadlock disappears instantly.

Example 4: AI Optimizes a CPU-Bound Stage with Batch Processing

A pipeline looks like this:

```
read -> transform -> encode -> write
```

Each stage is independent and runs in parallel. The transform stage performs CPU-heavy hashing:

```
func transform(in <-chan Record, out chan<- Transformed) {
    for r := range in {
        out <- heavyHash(r)
    }
}
```

Using **pprof**, developers discover **heavyHash** dominates CPU time. They send the flamegraph and code to an AI tool.

AI Recommendation:

"Transform each item individually causes repeated hashing overhead. Batch records and hash them in groups to utilize vectorized operations and reduce function call overhead."

Optimized Version:

```
func transform(in <-chan Record, out chan<- Transformed) {
    batch := make([]Record, 0, 100)

    for r := range in {
        batch = append(batch, r)
        if len(batch) == 100 {
            for _, b := range batch {
                out <- heavyHash(b)
            }
            batch = batch[:0]
        }
    }

    for _, b := range batch {
        out <- heavyHash(b)
    }
}
```

The performance improvement:

- 20–30% fewer allocations.
- Higher CPU utilization.
- Reduced runtime due to amortized hashing cost.

AI transformed micro-optimizations into a practical and measurable speedup.

Conclusion

This chapter has explored one of Go's most powerful capabilities–building high-performance, concurrent processing pipelines. It began by laying out the foundational principles of pipeline design, emphasizing the importance of structuring data flow into discrete, composable stages connected by channels. Readers saw how these stages naturally align with goroutines, enabling efficient parallel execution and non-blocking communication.

We have also examined the fan-out and fan-in patterns, demonstrating how Go can distribute work across multiple workers and aggregate results back into a unified stream. By analyzing the strengths and trade-offs of each approach, the chapter highlighted how these patterns enhance throughput and responsiveness, especially under heavy load. This naturally led into a discussion on worker pools and task scheduling, where controlled concurrency becomes essential. Instead of spawning unbounded goroutines, worker pools ensure predictable resource usage and stable performance—an important characteristic for production-grade systems.

A deep dive into channel-based communication strategies revealed how buffering, channel directionality, and graceful closing influence pipeline reliability. We furthermore, explored how channels can coordinate flow control, prevent goroutine leaks, and maintain backpressure, all of which are vital for building systems that behave consistently under real-world conditions.

Performance profiling using Go's **`pprof`** tooling offered the analytical perspective necessary to understand pipeline bottlenecks. Readers learned how CPU profiles, heap traces, and goroutine dumps can illuminate hidden inefficiencies. Finally, AI-assisted optimization showcased a modern layer of refinement, where tools such as ChatGPT or Amazon Q Developer analyze profiling output, suggest architectural improvements, detect concurrency hazards, and even generate optimized code. Concrete examples demonstrate how AI can detect deadlocks, right-size buffer capacities, recommend batching, or propose worker-pool refactoring.

Together, these insights equip engineers with the knowledge needed to design, debug, and optimize sophisticated concurrent pipelines. By combining Go's concurrency primitives with systematic profiling and AI-guided recommendations, developers can construct pipelines that scale gracefully, maintain high throughput, and remain robust in the face of complex workloads.

In the next chapter, we will explore how to work intelligently with AI systems such as ChatGPT, GitHub Copilot, and Amazon CodeWhisperer, focusing on practical techniques for crafting effective prompts, guiding AI-generated code, and integrating these tools into professional Go workflows.

CHAPTER 9
Integrating AI Tools in Go Development

Introduction

As AI-powered developer tools become more capable and accessible, they are rapidly transforming the way Go applications are designed, written, and maintained. Rather than replacing human expertise, these tools amplify it–helping developers generate code more quickly, uncover subtle bugs, refactor complex logic, and optimize performance-critical paths with unprecedented efficiency. This chapter explores how to work intelligently with AI systems such as ChatGPT, GitHub Copilot, and Amazon CodeWhisperer, focusing on practical techniques for crafting effective prompts, guiding AI-generated code, and integrating these tools into professional Go workflows. By understanding both their strengths and their boundaries, developers can use AI not just as an assistant, but also as a force multiplier for high-quality, scalable software.

Structure

In this chapter, we will cover the following topics:

- Writing Effective Prompts for ChatGPT, Copilot, CodeWhisperer
  - Understanding the Prompting Philosophy in Software Development
  - Prompting Techniques for ChatGPT
  - Writing Effective Prompts for GitHub Copilot
  - Prompting Effectively with Amazon CodeWhisperer (Amazon Q Developer)
  - Prompt Structuring Patterns for Maximum Effectiveness
  - Avoiding Anti-Patterns in Prompting
  - Examples of Effective Prompting across Tools

- Generating Go Code Using AI Tools
    - AI as a Scaffolding Engine
    - AI-Generated Examples for Common Go Components
    - Integrating AI into Iterative Coding Workflows
    - Generating Code for Performance-Critical Workloads
    - Quality Assurance for AI-Generated Go Code
- Debugging and Refactoring Go Code with AI Assistance
    - AI-Assisted Debugging Workflows
    - Leveraging AI for Static and Runtime Code Analysis
    - AI-Assisted Refactoring for Cleaner, Idiomatic Go
    - Refactoring with AI as a Pair Programmer
    - Using AI to Learn from the Codebase
- Optimizing Concurrent and Performance-Critical Code
    - Designing with Concurrency in Mind
    - Reducing Contention and Bottlenecks
    - Minimizing Allocations and Memory Pressure
    - Choosing the Right Concurrency Pattern
    - Removing Goroutine Leaks and Ensuring Clean Shutdown
    - Measuring, Profiling, and Validating Improvements
    - AI-Guided Performance Refactoring Examples
- Ethical Considerations and Limitations of AI-Generated Code
    - Ownership, Licensing, and Attribution
    - Hallucinations and Incorrect Code
    - Security and Privacy Risks
    - Ethical Use in Production Systems
    - Bias, Safety, and Ethical Implications in Prompting
    - Limitations of AI in Go Development
    - Guidelines for Responsible Use

Writing Effective Prompts for ChatGPT, Copilot, CodeWhisperer

As AI-assisted development becomes a foundational part of modern software engineering, the effectiveness of these tools depends significantly on the clarity, structure, and completeness of the prompts provided to them. While ChatGPT, GitHub Copilot, and Amazon CodeWhisperer differ in their architectures and integration environments, they share a common requirement: they need high-quality instructions to produce high-quality Go code. Effective prompting is both an art and a technique—one that transforms AI tools from simple autocomplete engines into intelligent collaborators capable of generating production-grade functions, debugging complex concurrency issues, designing APIs, or offering alternative implementations. This section explores strategies for crafting prompts that yield accurate, maintainable, and context-aware Go code.

Understanding the Prompting Philosophy in Software Development

AI models are pattern recognizers trained on vast repositories of code, documentation, and problem-solving examples. They do not read minds; instead, they infer intent from the textual signals given to them. Therefore, precise specifications yield precise results. In the context of Go development, effective prompts communicate four key components:

- **The Task:** What needs to be built, fixed, explained, or improved.
- **The Context:** Existing code, architecture constraints, Go version used, database layers, or concurrency considerations.
- **The Constraints:** Performance requirements, coding style, idioms, preferred libraries, or error-handling approaches.
- **The Expected Format:** Code-only output, explanation plus code, step-by-step logic, or alternative solutions.

Without these elements, AI tools often produce generic or suboptimal code. When they are included, the model can operate closer to the developer's expectations and project conventions.

Prompting Techniques for ChatGPT

Among the AI coding assistants, ChatGPT offers the most flexible conversational interface. Developers can explain nuanced requirements, iterate on ideas, and request refinements based on evolving design decisions. Effective ChatGPT prompting includes the following strategies:

- **Provide Explicit Requirements**

  Instead of writing a vague prompt such as:

  "Write a Go function to process orders."

A more effective prompt is:

"Write a Go function **`ProcessOrders`** that takes a slice of Order structs, validates required fields, logs invalid entries, and inserts valid records into a PostgreSQL database using the **`database/sql`** package. Use **`context.Context`** for cancellation and return descriptive errors."

This level of specificity causes ChatGPT to produce a code that aligns with real-world expectations.

- **Include Existing Code or Constraints**

  Prompts become significantly more accurate when the model understands the developer's environment:

  - Provide the struct definitions being used.
  - Specify expected behavior under concurrency.
  - Include the part of the codebase where integration occurs.

  Example:

  "Here is my **`UserRepository`** interface and current implementation. Modify it so all methods accept a **`context.Context`** and use prepared statements for performance. Avoid external ORMs."

  This leads the model towards a code that is compatible with the larger system.

- **Ask for Alternatives or Trade-off Discussions**

  ChatGPT can compare patterns–something conventional IDE tools cannot do. Developers can prompt:

  "Provide two approaches for implementing a worker pool in Go: one using buffered channels and one using a task queue with goroutine pooling. Compare their performance characteristics under high contention."

  Such prompts not only generate code but also reinforce architectural thinking.

- **Request Step-by-Step Reasoning When Needed**

  For complex pipelines, cryptic bugs, or concurrency issues, prompts should encourage explicit reasoning:

  "Explain step-by-step why the following goroutine pattern causes a race condition and provide a corrected version using a **`sync.WaitGroup`** and a mutex."

  This results in explanations aligned with Go's memory model and concurrency semantics.

Writing Effective Prompts for GitHub Copilot

GitHub Copilot functions primarily as an inline completion engine. It responds best to **context-heavy code comments, function signatures, and partially written blocks**, rather than long narrative prompts.

Use Intent-Rich Comments

Copilot is extremely responsive to structured comments:

```
// FetchUser loads a user from PostgreSQL by ID.
// Requirements:
// - Use context.Context
// - Return sql.ErrNoRows when the user is not found
// - Use prepared statements
// - Map fields into the User struct
```

After writing this comment and the function signature, Copilot will often generate the body automatically, and correctly.

Provide Surrounding Context

Copilot relies heavily on adjacent code. If the developer writes idiomatic, consistent Go code, Copilot mirrors that style. Conversely, if the surrounding code is inconsistent, the model may mimic undesirable patterns.

Preferred prompts:

- Provide struct definitions in the same file.
- Keep naming conventions uniform.
- Adopt clear error-handling patterns.

This allows Copilot to infer the logical continuation.

Guide Copilot with Example Patterns

Copilot learns from the project's internal patterns. Writing one well-crafted example of a database query or goroutine pattern influences subsequent suggestions. For instance, after defining one standardized error wrapper, Copilot uses it consistently across new functions.

This makes prompting not only a short-term interaction but also a strategy for shaping the stylistic and architectural consistency of the codebase.

Prompting Effectively with Amazon CodeWhisperer (Amazon Q Developer)

As of the latest updates, CodeWhisperer is integrated into *Amazon Q Developer*, providing completions, security scans, and cloud-aware suggestions. Since it is integrated deeply with AWS services, effective prompts should:

- **Specify Cloud Context Explicitly**

  Example:

  "Generate a Go Lambda function that reads from DynamoDB using AWS SDK v2, supports context cancellation, and returns structured errors."

  This prompts the model to use AWS-native idioms.

- Provide Task-Level Descriptions in Comments

  Like Copilot, CodeWhisperer responds well to concise, structured comments:

  ```
  // CreateItemHandler inserts an item into DynamoDB.
  // Validate input fields.
  // Use PutItem API from AWS SDK v2.
  // Return JSON responses and log errors with context.
  ```

- Use Intent-Specific Requests for Security and Performance

  Since Amazon Q prioritizes security scanning:

  "Generate a secure connection configuration for RDS PostgreSQL using IAM authentication. Avoid embedding credentials."

  Such instructions guide the model to follow AWS best practices.

Prompt Structuring Patterns for Maximum Effectiveness

Effective prompts often follow repeatable templates. Three reliable structures are explained in detail in the following subsection.

The "Task + Context + Constraints + Format" Template

Template:

- ***Task:*** What should be built or solved?
- ***Context:*** What code, environment, or architecture is involved?

- ***Constraints*:** Performance, concurrency, libraries, error-handling style.
- ***Format*:** Code-only, explanation first, refactored version, alternatives, and so on.

Example Prompt:

"Refactor the following Go handler to use context-aware database operations. Keep the function signature unchanged. Use parameterized queries. Return structured JSON errors. Provide code only."

The "Explain + Generate + Improve" Loop

1. Ask for an explanation of a concept or problem.
2. Ask for the code generation.
3. Ask for improvement based on constraints.

This iterative prompting mirrors a senior engineer's review cycle and produces highly refined output.

The Diagnostic Prompt Pattern for Debugging

When debugging:

"Here is the error and the code. Explain the root cause, propose a fix, and provide an optimized alternative implementation."

This leads AI to not only fix bugs, but improve the underlying logic.

Avoiding Anti-Patterns in Prompting

Some prompts decrease accuracy and should be avoided:

- Prompts lacking specificity ("Write some Go code for caching.")
- Prompts mixing unrelated tasks ("Build a worker pool and also write documentation for my API routes.")
- Prompts without constraints ("Make this faster." Faster, *how*?)

A good prompt always removes ambiguity.

Examples of Effective Prompting across Tools

Let us understand effective prompting with real use-cases and examples.

Prompt Sent to ChatGPT

"Write a concurrency-safe in-memory cache in Go using `sync.RWMutex` with expiration support, configurable cleanup intervals, and context-aware operations. Provide a complete implementation with comments."

ChatGPT will produce a multi-file equivalent answer with full explanation.

Prompt Sent to Copilot (as Code Comments)

```
// NewCache creates a concurrency-safe cache with expiration.
// Use RWMutex.
// Launch a background goroutine to clean expired entries every
interval.
```

Copilot will complete the constructor and goroutine logic.

Prompt Sent to Amazon Q

```
// Implement a Go-based cache layer for an AWS Lambda function.
// Ensure thread safety, avoid global state, and integrate with
DynamoDB fallback.
```

Amazon Q will incorporate the AWS SDK idioms automatically.

Generating Go Code Using AI Tools

As AI-assisted development becomes mainstream, Go developers increasingly rely on tools such as ChatGPT, GitHub Copilot, and Amazon CodeWhisperer to scaffold projects, produce boilerplate, and explore language features with an unprecedented speed. These tools do not replace the need for understanding Go's idioms and design principles, but they do significantly expand a developer's ability to experiment, iterate, and build production-ready components faster. Generating a Go code with AI can streamline repetitive tasks while allowing developers to maintain focus on architectural decisions, performance considerations, and correctness guarantees–areas where human insight remains essential.

AI tools excel at producing templates, patterns, and illustrative examples that align with Go's ecosystem, including creating REST handlers, data models, concurrency scaffolding, or database layers. When used strategically, an AI-generated code can serve as high-quality starting points that developers refine and adapt to their applications. However, using these tools effectively requires more than simply prompting; it demands context-rich instructions, iterative refinement, and validation to ensure that the generated code aligns with Go's best practices.

This section examines how developers can leverage AI tools to produce a Go code responsibly and efficiently, focusing on code generation workflows, example-driven prompting, and quality assurance practices.

AI as a Scaffolding Engine

One of the most practical uses of AI tools is automatic scaffolding–generating the foundational structure of Go applications. This includes boilerplate for APIs, background workers, CLI tools, or concurrency pipelines. Traditionally, generating scaffolding manually or through fixed templates required a significant setup. AI removes many of these constraints by producing project structures based on descriptive prompts.

For example, a developer designing a new microservice might ask an AI tool:

"Generate a Go project layout for a REST API using clean architecture, including handler, service, and repository layers."

An AI tool such as ChatGPT can produce a folder hierarchy, interface definitions, and initial files aligning with domain-driven or layered design principles. Copilot can further assist by generating file contents as developers' type inside an IDE. CodeWhisperer enhances this process with AWS-specific integrations–for example, scaffolding Lambda handlers, DynamoDB access layers, or Amazon SQS consumers.

The key pattern is a **human-led architecture plus AI-generated boilerplate**. Developers define their architecture, while AI accelerates implementation by generating consistent code blocks, comments, and interface stubs.

AI-Generated Examples for Common Go Components

AI tools perform exceptionally well when asked to produce idiomatic examples of common components in Go. Unlike older code-generation templates, AI can customize the output to a project's conventions, dependencies, or its complexity level.

Example 1: HTTP Handlers

A strong prompt such as:

"Write an idiomatic Go HTTP handler that validates JSON input, returns structured errors, and integrates with `context.Context`."

...can yield a fully formed example:

```
func (h *UserHandler) CreateUser(w http.ResponseWriter, r *http.
Request) {
```

```
        ctx := r.Context()
        var req CreateUserRequest

        if err := json.NewDecoder(r.Body).Decode(&req); err != nil {
            http.Error(w, "invalid JSON body", http.StatusBadRequest)
            return
        }

        user, err := h.service.CreateUser(ctx, req)
        if err != nil {
            http.Error(w, err.Error(), http.StatusInternalServer-
    Error)
            return
        }

        w.Header().Set("Content-Type", "application/json")
        json.NewEncoder(w).Encode(user)
    }
```

Such examples serve as **starting points**, which developers tune for middleware frameworks, error-mapping utilities, or logging systems, which are already present in their project.

Example 2: Database Access Layer

Asking for:

"Generate a PostgreSQL repository in Go using **`database/sql`** with context support and prepared statements."

...produces repository methods that ensure connection reuse, error handling, and efficient scanning.

Example 3: Concurrency Patterns

AI tools can produce structures for worker pools, semaphore-limited goroutines, or fan-out/fan-in pipelines–helpful when developers need consistent patterns without memorizing detailed syntax.

Integrating AI into Iterative Coding Workflows

AI code generation works best through **iterative refinement**, not single-shot results. Developers should adopt a feedback loop:

1. **Describe the goal:** Specify features, constraints, performance expectations, and context.
2. **Generate an initial version:** Allow the AI to produce a baseline implementation.

3. **Review and critique output:** Look for inefficiencies, missing edge cases, or anti-patterns.
4. **Request improvements.**

   Give targeted feedback such as:

   - "Refactor this to use `sync.Pool`."
   - "Fix potential race conditions."
   - "Improve error wrapping and context propagation."
5. **Integrate into real code.**

   Apply static analysis tools (go vet, and golangci-lint), run tests, and adjust, based on the project conventions.

AI tools can now integrate directly into IDEs, making this cycle faster. Copilot provides inline suggestions as developers' type. ChatGPT can analyze files or multi-file structures, explaining behavior or generating improved variants. CodeWhisperer performs security scanning as a part of its generation flow, identifying risky patterns such as unsanitized SQL queries.

Generating Code for Performance-Critical Workloads

AI tools can also assist in generating high-performance or concurrency-sensitive Go code—although this must always be combined with careful review. For instance, developers can ask for:

"Write an optimized worker pool handling 10,000 tasks with bounded concurrency and context cancellation."

Or,

"Generate a memory-efficient buffer management strategy for high-throughput I/O."

AI-generated snippets provide frameworks that developers refine using profiling tools such as `pprof`, trace, and race detectors. AI suggestions may serve as stepping stones to help navigate Go's performance ecosystem, particularly when dealing with atomic operations, channel buffering decisions, goroutine limits, or lock-free algorithms.

For example, an AI tool might propose alternatives to minimize allocations, such as using `sync.Pool`, preallocating slices, or avoiding unnecessary goroutine creation under heavy load.

Quality Assurance for AI-Generated Go Code

Since AI-generated code varies in quality, developers must apply validation techniques to ensure correctness:

- **Static Analysis:** Tools such as go vet, staticcheck, gosec.
- **Benchmarking:** Verifying AI-generated optimizations using real data.
- **Unit Tests:** Asking AI to *also* generate tests for its own code improves coverage.
- **Race Detection:** Especially pivotal for concurrency-heavy examples.
- **Consistency with Project Structure:** Reviewing naming conventions, dependency choices, and interface compatibility.

AI should be treated as a junior developer—fast, helpful, and creative, but requiring review and oversight.

Developers may also ask AI to **audit its own output**:

"Review the following Go code for concurrency issues and suggest improvements."

This enables a layered approach where AI assists both in creation, and verification.

Debugging and Refactoring Go Code with AI Assistance

Debugging and refactoring are the integral parts of the Go development lifecycle—activities that traditionally demanded meticulous attention to detail, domain knowledge, and extensive tooling. With the rise of AI-driven development assistants, these workflows have evolved significantly. Tools such as ChatGPT, GitHub Copilot, and Amazon CodeWhisperer, now offer contextual reasoning, pattern recognition, and code-aware insights that can diagnose issues, propose improvements, and guide developers toward a cleaner, safer, and more idiomatic Go code. Rather than replacing Go's debugging tools or linters, AI complements them by interpreting outputs, explaining errors in depth, and recommending targeted fixes.

AI assistance allows developers to analyze complex codebases more rapidly, especially when dealing with concurrency issues, subtle race conditions, memory mismanagement, or architectural inconsistencies. It can interpret stack traces, identify suspicious function interactions, highlight missing edge cases, or provide optimized variants of problematic code segments. For refactoring tasks, AI can simplify unwieldy functions, reorganize modules, standardize naming conventions, or convert ad-hoc logic into reusable patterns. This combination of automated insight and human oversight dramatically accelerates the maintenance phase of Go projects.

This section explores how developers can use AI tools to debug Go programs, interpret runtime information, refactor codebases, and enforce idiomatic coding practices—while preserving the reliability and predictability that Go is known for.

AI-Assisted Debugging Workflows

When debugging Go applications, developers often rely on logs, stack traces, and error messages that are generated at runtime. AI tools enhance these workflows by interpreting this information and mapping it to the larger context of the application. For example, a developer can paste a lengthy panic trace into ChatGPT or Copilot Chat and ask:

"Explain what caused this panic and suggest a fix."

AI tools can parse the stack trace, identify the deepest cause, and walk through the call sequence to explain why the error occurred. They can highlight common culprits—nil pointer dereferences, misuse of slices or maps, data races, improper channel operations, or failing to handle an error returned by **`database/sql`**.

Consider a typical Go panic trace:

```
panic: runtime error: invalid memory address or nil pointer
dereference
goroutine 42 [running]:
app/service.(*OrderService).Process(0x0, ...)
    service/order.go:74 +0x45
app/handler.(*OrderHandler).Handle(...)
    handler/order.go:58
net/http.HandlerFunc.ServeHTTP(...)
```

An AI tool can break this down:

- The receiver for **`OrderService`** is nil (0x0).
- The call site indicates the handler created or retrieved a nil service.
- The likely root cause is improper initialization or a missing dependency.

The AI may then offer multiple corrective strategies—constructor injection, nil checks, or improved test coverage.

Beyond interpreting traces, AI can reason about concurrency. By showing code that behaves non-deterministically or deadlocks under load, developers can ask:

"Why does this goroutine block? Explain potential deadlocks."

AI can identify incorrect channel direction, unbuffered channels used under load, forgotten defer cancel() calls, or misuse of sync primitives. These explanations augment Go's built-in race detector (go test -race) by translating the raw findings into actionable insights.

Leveraging AI for Static and Runtime Code Analysis

AI interfaces increasingly integrate with static analysis outputs from tools such as **`go vet`**, **`staticcheck`**, or **`gosec`**. Instead of manually deciphering dozens of warnings, a developer can paste the output into ChatGPT and ask:

"Group these findings by category and recommend how to fix them."

AI tools excel at clustering issues into themes such as:

- Unchecked errors
- Inefficient memory usage
- Misuse of contexts
- Vulnerable SQL queries
- Incorrect synchronization

They can also suggest refactoring strategies or provide idiomatic alternatives based on standard library usage or popular Go patterns.

Runtime logs—especially those from distributed systems—can also be fed into AI queries. For example:

"Analyze these logs and determine why request latency spikes after 5 minutes."

AI might identify:

- Goroutines accumulating due to unbounded worker creation.
- Database connections leaking due to forgotten **`rows.Close()`**.
- Backpressure issues from slow consumers in a pipeline.

This form of automated log triage helps developers narrow down root causes before diving into deeper profiling.

AI-Assisted Refactoring for Cleaner, Idiomatic Go

Refactoring is often more time-consuming than writing a new code. AI tools expedite this by proposing structural improvements, rewriting segments to follow idiomatic Go style, and converting verbose or repetitive logic into clean abstractions.

Simplifying Complex Functions

Developers can paste a long function and ask:

"Refactor this into smaller helper functions following Go best practices."

AI will typically extract logical sections into separate functions, improve naming, streamline error handling, and remove duplicated branches. It can also enforce consistent patterns such as early returns, value semantics, or structured logging.

Improving Module Structure and Project Organization

AI tools can analyze a folder structure and suggest more modular designs. For example:

- Moving domain logic to /internal.
- Creating service, repository, and handler layers.
- Renaming packages to avoid stutter.
- Introducing interfaces only where needed.

This helps maintain large Go codebases that grow organically.

Transforming ad-hoc Code into Reusable Patterns

AI can convert:

- Repeated SQL queries into repository methods.
- Repeated HTTP boilerplate into middleware.
- Scattered goroutine spawning into a managed worker pool.
- Manual JSON parsing into structured types.

Because AI recognizes abstract patterns, it can generalize and formalize the code more quickly than a manual inspection.

Recommending Performance-Oriented Refactors

By asking:

"Optimize this function for high concurrency."

AI might propose:

- Preallocating slices.
- Using sync.Pool for expensive buffers.
- Eliminating unnecessary locking.
- Replacing channels with atomic operations.
- Avoiding goroutine leaks via context cancellation.

Such suggestions help developers reason about the performance before running profiling tools.

Refactoring with AI as a Pair Programmer

Integrating AI tools directly into the IDE creates a pair-programmer experience. Copilot, CodeWhisperer, and ChatGPT-based extensions can:

- Suggest refactored variants in real time.
- Highlight code smells.
- Explain anti-patterns immediately after writing them.
- Offer corrections before compilation.

For example, if a developer writes a loop that appends to a nil slice inefficiently, Copilot might suggest:

```
items := make([]Item, 0, len(rows))
```

Similarly, if a function returns a naked panic, AI tools might suggest returning wrapped errors instead.

Developers should actively review these suggestions, and accept or reject them based on the context. The goal is not a blind automation, but rather an intelligent collaboration.

Using AI to Learn from the Codebase

AI can act as a codebase tutor–explaining architecture, dependencies, and flows. Developers often encounter complex legacy systems or multi-module repositories; asking AI questions such as:

"Explain how requests flow through this handler-service-repository stack."

Or,

"Describe potential race conditions in this file."

It provides an insight that would otherwise require hours of manual reading.

This is particularly useful while onboarding new engineers or handing off large projects. AI provides a comprehension layer that reduces cognitive fatigue, making debugging and refactoring more manageable.

Optimizing Concurrent and Performance-Critical Code

Optimizing performance-critical Go code requires a deliberate blend of architectural decisions, efficient memory usage, concurrency discipline, and deep observability. As Go applications scale–handling thousands of simultaneous requests, ingesting streaming data, or orchestrating distributed systems–the cost of suboptimal synchronization, excessive allocations, or mismanaged goroutines becomes increasingly visible. Go provides the tools to write high-performance systems–goroutines, channels, atomic operations, escape analysis, and profiling utilities–but it is the developer's ability to apply these tools judiciously that ultimately determines its performance. AI-powered optimization tools add a modern layer to this workflow by analyzing code patterns, suggesting micro-optimizations, and identifying the concurrency traps that manual inspection might overlook.

This section examines the core considerations for writing and optimizing concurrent Go programs, clarifies the trade-offs between concurrency strategies, and demonstrates how AI tools can assist in discovering inefficiencies, redesigning pipelines, and validating performance improvements.

Designing with Concurrency in Mind

The most effective optimizations begin before any code is executed. Concurrency should not be sprinkled into an existing code as an afterthought–poorly structured parallelism can degrade performance, rather than improving it. Instead, developers are benefitted from thinking in terms of *data flow*, *work decomposition*, and *contention boundaries*.

Go enables concurrency at extremely low cost using goroutines, but these lightweight threads only perform well when work is decomposed into sufficiently granular, independent tasks. A common mistake is spawning goroutines for trivial workloads, which introduces scheduling overhead greater than sequential execution. Conversely, too much work in a single goroutine can create bottlenecks that limit throughput.

Key design questions include:

- Are tasks independent enough to benefit from concurrency?
- Is the workload CPU-bound, I/O-bound, or memory-bound?
- Where will goroutines contend for shared state?
- Are channels an appropriate communication mechanism, or would locks/atomics be more efficient?

AI tools can analyze code and highlight weak concurrency patterns–for example, pointing out that a goroutine is created inside a tight loop without proper throttling, or that a shared map is being accessed without synchronization.

Reducing Contention and Bottlenecks

One of the largest performance killers in Go concurrency is *contention*. When multiple goroutines fight over the same resource—locks, channels, memory access—the program behaves less like a parallel system and more like a serialized one.

- **Using `sync.Mutex` and `sync.RWMutex` Effectively**

  A mutex should be applied sparingly. Over-locking a critical section severely limits parallelism. Go's **`sync.RWMutex`** allows multiple readers and one writer, making it valuable for read-heavy operations. Developers must measure read/write ratios and choose locks accordingly.

  Poor practice:

  ```
  mu.Lock()
  value := shared[key]
  mu.Unlock()
  ```

  Better practice (if reads dominate):

  ```
  mu.RLock()
  value := shared[key]
  mu.RUnlock()
  ```

AI tools can spot locking patterns that introduce unnecessary contention, and suggest reducing the granularity of locks or applying sharding techniques.

- Avoiding Channel Congestion

  Channels are powerful but can easily become bottlenecks if:

  - The channel buffer is too small.
  - A consumer is slower than a producer.
  - Multiple producers overwhelm a single funnel.

Profiling can reveal where goroutines block, and AI can interpret this as:

"Your pipeline is backpressured because the consumer cannot keep up. Add buffering or scale out the worker pool."

Minimizing Allocations and Memory Pressure

Memory allocation patterns heavily influence Go's concurrency performance. Frequent allocations slow down the program and increase garbage collector activity.

Preallocate slices:

Instead of:

```
var results []Item
for i := 0; i < n; i++ {
    results = append(results, compute(i))
}
```

Use:

```
results := make([]Item, 0, n)
```

Reuse Buffers:

`sync.Pool` provides temporary object storage to avoid repeated allocations:

```
var bufPool = sync.Pool{New: func() interface{} {
    return make([]byte, 1024)
}}
```

AI tools can analyze code and annotate suggestions such as:

- "Use **`sync.Pool`** here to avoid allocating large buffers repeatedly."
- "Slice is reallocated on each iteration; preallocate using make."
- "Escape analysis indicates this variable escapes to the heap; switch to stack allocation if possible."

Such memory-aware insights are invaluable for performance-critical sections of a codebase.

Choosing the Right Concurrency Pattern

Go supports several concurrency patterns, each suitable for different workloads:

- **Worker Pools**: This is optimal for CPU-bound workloads, controlling parallelism via a fixed number of worker goroutines.
- **Fan-out/Fan-in**: It is ideal for distributing heterogeneous tasks and recombining results.
- **Pipeline Architectures**: This is useful for staged transformations where each step can run concurrently.
- **Stateful goroutines ("actors")**: Reduce lock contention by giving each goroutine an exclusive ownership of state, communicating via channels.

AI tools, given a code snippet, can evaluate whether the chosen pattern matches the problem. For example:

"This loop spawns one goroutine per item but has no back-pressure. Convert this to a worker pool for better control."

Or:

"Your stage architecture has a bottleneck in the middle step. Consider parallelizing this stage."

Removing Goroutine Leaks and Ensuring Clean Shutdown

Goroutine leaks occur when goroutines block forever, often due to:

- Channels never closed.
- select statements missing default cases.
- Context cancellations not respected.
- Improper fan-in logic.

Example of a leak:

```
func worker(ch <-chan int) {
    for {
        val := <-ch // blocks forever if ch not closed
        fmt.Println(val)
    }
}
```

AI tools can inspect such code and warn:

"Goroutine leak: this worker blocks if the channel is never closed. Add a second return path or use ok pattern."

Corrected version:

```
func worker(ch <-chan int) {
    for val := range ch {
        fmt.Println(val)
    }
}
```

AI-assisted reviews are exceptionally good at catching leaks because they can check for missing cancellation logic across multiple files–something developers often overlook.

Measuring, Profiling, and Validating Improvements

Optimization without measurement is guesswork. Go's profiler (`pprof`) and tracing tools reveal where CPU time, memory usage, and blocking occurs. AI assistance becomes particularly powerful when interpreting profiling outputs.

Example Workflow

1. Developer captures a CPU profile:

   ```
   go tool pprof cpu.out
   ```

2. They export the graph or text and paste it into ChatGPT.
3. AI identifies:
    i. Heavy allocations.
    ii. Excessive locking.
    iii. Long GC pauses.
    iv. Goroutines blocked on channels.
4. AI suggests targeted refactors.

For example, after seeing a profile where a map lock dominates 38% of the runtime, AI may suggest:

- Sharded maps.
- Reducing lock width.
- Introducing atomic updates.
- Caching memoized results.

This automated interpretation shortens the iteration cycle dramatically.

AI-Guided Performance Refactoring Examples

Example 1: Reducing Channel Bottlenecks

Input from Developer:

```
jobs := make(chan int)
results := make(chan int)

go func() {
    for i := 0; i < 10000; i++ {
        jobs <- i
    }
}()
```

AI Suggestion:

- Add buffering to jobs to avoid blocking.
- Use a worker pool to prevent goroutine explosion.

Example 2: Avoiding Excessive Goroutine Creation

```
for _, item := range items {
    go process(item)
}
```

AI Recommendation:

"Unbounded goroutine creation may overwhelm the scheduler. Use a fixed-size worker pool."

Example 3: Fixing Lock Contention

```
mu.Lock()
for _, v := range items {
    total += v
}
mu.Unlock()
```

AI determines from the preceding code that the lock spans too large a section, and suggests computing locally, then locking briefly:

```
local := 0
for _, v := range items {
    local += v
}

mu.Lock()
total += local
mu.Unlock()
```

Example 4: Improving Memory Efficiency

AI spots that a buffer is being allocated in every iteration:

```
buf := make([]byte, 1024)
```

Therefore, it recommends using `sync.Pool`.

Ethical Considerations and Limitations of AI-Generated Code

As AI tools continue to integrate deeply into Go development, they bring tremendous efficiency gains, but also new ethical responsibilities. While these tools can accelerate coding, debugging, and optimization, developers must remain vigilant about how an AI-generated code is produced, validated, deployed, and maintained. Ethical use means understanding not only *what* AI tools can do, but also *what they should not do*, and where human judgment is mandatory. This section examines the key ethical concerns and practical limitations of an AI-generated code, and provides guidance for using AI responsibly in real-world Go applications.

Ownership, Licensing, and Attribution

One of the central ethical questions surrounding AI-generated code is: *Who owns the output*? Different AI tools have different terms of service, and developers must comply with licensing, attribution, and Intellectual Property (IP) requirements.

Risk of Unintended License Contamination

Early AI systems were known to generate code snippets that closely resembled copyrighted material. Although modern systems have mitigated this risk, developers must still be mindful:

- Never paste proprietary or internal company code into public AI systems unless explicitly allowed.
- Ensure that the generated code does not inadvertently mimic GPL or other restrictive licenses.
- When in doubt, run the AI output through the existing company policies on open-source compliance.

Code Provenance and Traceability

AI systems cannot always explain the exact origin of generated logic. To avoid compliance risks:

- Treat all AI-generated codes as requiring code review.
- Maintain commit history that documents the contributions of AI.
- Use internal/private AI models for a code that must remain confidential.

Developers remain accountable for the code that enters production–regardless of whether they wrote it manually, or generated it through AI.

Hallucinations and Incorrect Code

AI systems occasionally generate a code that is syntactically correct but logically wrong, subtly flawed, or based on outdated assumptions. These "hallucinations" can be dangerous when developing performance-critical or security-sensitive Go systems.

AI-generated code may:

- Ignore edge cases.
- Misuse concurrency primitives (for example, race-prone channel usage).
- Provide unsafe defaults.
- Introduce data races or deadlocks in goroutine orchestration.
- Produce insecure patterns, especially around crypto, auth, or validation.

Outdated API Usage

AI systems may generate code using:

- Old Go versions (for example, deprecated **`io/ioutil`**).
- Outdated versions of libraries/frameworks.
- Obsolete patterns for gRPC, HTTP, ORMs, and so on.

One should, therefore, always cross-check the AI-generated code against documentation or go doc.

Overconfidence Bias

AI tools often present incorrect solutions with high confidence. Developers must resist the temptation to trust the output blindly.

Always review the AI-generated code as if it came from a junior engineer, not an authoritative expert.

Security and Privacy Risks

Developers may accidentally expose:

- API keys
- Access tokens
- Proprietary framework code
- Confidential algorithms or architecture designs

To avoid this:

- Mask or sanitize any sensitive data before sending prompts.
- Use self-hosted/local AI models for confidential development.
- Follow the policies of the organization for data retention and security.

Security Anti-Patterns

AI may generate insecure code such as:

- Hardcoded credentials.
- Weak password hashing.
- Unsafe concurrency (leading to data races in critical systems).
- Inadequate input validation.
- Vulnerable file handling or network code.

Security audits remain mandatory, regardless of AI's involvement.

Ethical Use in Production Systems

Teams should document:

- Where AI-generated code was used?
- Why it was used?
- How it was reviewed and validated?
- Who approved it?

This maintains accountability and allows future engineers to understand the reasoning behind certain design decisions.

Avoiding Over-Automation

Developers may be tempted to outsource complex logic or architectural decisions to AI. But AI lacks:

- Context about system constraints.
- Deep domain expertise.
- Accountability for long-term maintainability.
- Ability to anticipate real-world failure modes.

AI should never replace system design, only augment it.

Bias, Safety, and Ethical Implications in Prompting

AI tools may inadvertently produce code or logic that:

- Assumes non-inclusive defaults.
- Favors certain algorithms, frameworks, or patterns without justification.
- Embeds cultural or data-driven biases in business logic.

Developers must ensure ethical, fair, and inclusive system behavior.

Overreliance and Skill Degradation

As AI takes on more routine tasks, engineers may risk losing proficiency in:

- Systems thinking
- Algorithmic reasoning
- Concurrency problem-solving
- Debugging complex goroutine behaviors

Use AI to enhance learning–not replace critical thinking.

Limitations of AI in Go Development

AI may propose optimizations that look correct but:

- Cause higher memory usage under load.
- Increase lock contention.
- Introduce unnecessary goroutines.
- Misuse sync primitives (for example, excessive mutexes).

Profiling tools such as pprof still outperform AI for real performance tuning.

Difficulty with Large Codebases

AI struggles with:

- Deeply interconnected Go modules.
- Multi-service microservice architectures.
- Projects with heavy interfaces, generics, or custom types.
- Concurrency-heavy systems with nuanced goroutine lifecycles.

In such contexts, human architectural judgment is critical.

AI Cannot Replace Domain Expertise

AI can generate code, but it cannot:

- Understand business requirements.
- Analyze trade-offs between competing solutions.
- Predict long-term maintenance costs.
- Guarantee correctness under all conditions.

Developers remain fully responsible for system reliability.

Guidelines for Responsible Use

Here are practical guidelines for ethically integrating AI into a Go workflow:

- Treat AI as a collaborator, not an authority.
- Always review the generated code, especially in concurrency-heavy or performance-critical systems.
- Avoid sharing private, sensitive, or regulated data in prompts.
- Document AI involvement in production code.
- Verify licensing and compliance.

- Perform security and performance audits, even if the code "looks correct."
- Use AI to learn, not to replace engineering fundamentals.

Thus, by following these guidelines, teams can enjoy the benefits of AI while minimizing ethical and technical risks.

Conclusion

In this chapter, we have explored how modern AI tools such as ChatGPT, GitHub Copilot, and Amazon CodeWhisperer can meaningfully enhance Go development workflows. We began by establishing how to craft effective prompts–structured, contextual, and iterative–to guide AI systems toward producing more accurate, relevant, and efficient output. Through practical examples, we saw how developers can turn vague requests into precise instructions that help AI generate better code, explain complex concepts, or offer targeted recommendations for Go-specific tasks. This section emphasized that prompt engineering is not about tricking AI, but about communicating with clarity and intention.

We then examined how AI tools can support core development activities, including generating Go code, accelerating prototyping, assisting with debugging, and improving code readability through guided refactoring. These tools can identify subtle issues, suggest alternative approaches, and help developers validate assumptions–especially in areas such as concurrency, memory management, and API design. We also explored how AI complements traditional optimization techniques by offering insights into goroutine design, channel usage, and bottleneck analysis. Hence, rather than replacing established Go practices, AI enhances them by providing fast feedback, multiple solution paths, and deeper contextual understanding.

Finally, we addressed the ethical and practical limitations of AI-generated code. This chapter underscored the importance of code review, security awareness, and responsible data handling when integrating AI into production workflows. We highlighted risks such as hallucinations, outdated API suggestions, licensing ambiguities, and the potential for overreliance on AI. Developers remain accountable for the correctness, safety, and maintainability of the systems they build. By understanding both the potential and the boundaries of AI tools, Go developers can harness them effectively–boosting productivity while maintaining high engineering standards.

In the next chapter, we will dive into taking the Go applications from development to production. We will focus on building production grade services and AI-assisted deployment automation.

CHAPTER 10
Deploying Production-Grade Go Microservices

Introduction

In this chapter, we shall focus on taking Go applications from development to production by building robust, scalable, and maintainable microservices. Readers will learn how to design production-grade services, containerize them using Docker, implement automated CI/CD pipelines, and monitor application performance effectively. The chapter also explores performance tuning, AI-assisted deployment automation, and forward-looking trends, equipping developers with practical strategies and modern tools to ensure their Go microservices run efficiently and reliably in real-world production environments.

Structure

In this chapter, we will cover the following topics:

- Designing Production-Grade Go Microservices
    - Principles of Microservice Architecture in Go
    - Defining Clear Service Boundaries and Responsibilities
    - Communication Strategies: REST, gRPC, and Event-Driven Designs
    - Resilience and Reliability Patterns
    - Observability as a First-Class Concern
    - Security and Configuration Management
    - How AI Influences Microservice Design

- Containerization Using Docker
  - Why Docker Works So Well with Go
  - Building a Go Service for Docker Deployment
  - Writing an Efficient Dockerfile
  - Container Security Best Practices
  - Observability and Logs inside Containers
  - Container-Oriented Configuration Management
  - Testing and Validating Dockerized Go Services
  - Deploying Dockerized Go Services
  - How AI Enhances Dockerization Workflows
- CI/CD Pipelines for Go Applications
  - Understanding the CI/CD Lifecycle for Go
  - Setting up a CI Pipeline for Go
  - Building Go Binaries and Docker Images in CI
  - Deploying Go Applications with CD
  - Example CI/CD Pipeline Using GitHub Actions
  - Adding Security, Compliance, and Observability to the Pipeline
  - AI-Assisted CI/CD Pipeline Generation and Optimization
- Monitoring, Logging, and Error Reporting
  - Why Observability Matters in Go Microservices
  - Monitoring Go Microservices
  - Logging in Go Microservices
  - Error Reporting and Alerting
  - Distributed Tracing in Go Microservices
- Performance Tuning and Resource Optimization
  - Understanding Go's Performance Model
  - Profiling, Benchmarking, and Evidence-Based Optimization
  - Tuning Concurrency and Scheduler Behavior
  - Memory Optimization and Allocation Control
  - Network and I/O Optimization
  - Garbage Collector (GC) Tuning
  - Runtime and Deployment Optimization

Designing Production-Grade Go Microservices

Designing production-grade Go microservices involves far more than exposing a few HTTP endpoints or packaging handlers into a container. A service becomes "production-grade", only when it demonstrates resilience under failure; stability under version changes; predictability under load; and, clarity in both its code structure and operational behavior. Go is uniquely well-positioned for this environment: Its minimal runtime footprint, static compilation model, fast startup time, strong concurrency primitives, and predictable memory behavior makes it an ideal foundation for modern distributed systems. This section explores the architectural foundations of robust microservices, focusing on service boundaries, communication strategies, resilience models, observability structures, and the patterns that allow teams to evolve systems safely.

Principles of Microservice Architecture in Go

Microservices architecture is centered on decomposition–splitting a system into independently deployable units that map to specific business capabilities. In Go, these boundaries translate naturally into cohesive packages, well-defined modules, and clearly separated layers. A production-grade microservice must take ownership of a single domain concern, manage its own data model, and expose a contract (HTTP, gRPC, events) that remains stable over time. Anything that violates this cohesion–

shared models, hidden dependencies, or "god services" dictating logic across domains–degrades the system.

Go's design philosophy encourages architectural discipline. Go prioritizes composition over inheritance hierarchies or intricate type relationships. This makes it easier to isolate business logic behind interfaces and create adapters for I/O boundaries (databases, caches, and authentication providers). With interfaces placed at module boundaries rather than sprinkled through code, developers gain the ability to swap implementations, build mock services for tests, and evolve internal components without breaking consumers.

A production-grade Go microservice should be organized around three core layers:

- **Transport Layer:** HTTP, gRPC, WebSockets, message listeners.
- **Service/Domain Layer:** Business rules, invariants, workflows.
- **Persistence Layer:** Repositories, data access patterns, cache interaction.

This separation is not merely stylistic; it is operationally critical. A microservice that exposes transport concerns directly within its domain logic becomes brittle, difficult to test, and nearly impossible to evolve across versions.

Defining Clear Service Boundaries and Responsibilities

Service boundaries define both the autonomy and the accountability of a microservice. A production-grade Go microservice should:

- Own its domain logic entirely.
- Own its data schema (or its slice of a shared schema in transitional systems).
- Enforce invariants internally without relying on upstream services.
- Communicate through well-defined APIs.
- Fail gracefully when dependencies become unavailable.

Boundary decisions often determine the long-term health of the system. Poorly designed boundaries create service entanglement, making even small changes require cross-team coordination. Well-drawn boundaries allow teams to iterate independently, deploy continuously, and test predictably.

Go's interfaces become pivotal here: by modeling repositories, dispatchers, or external clients using small, focused interfaces, services remain decoupled from specific implementations. This also aligns well with the dependency injection patterns in Go, which emphasize explicit construction rather than an implicit resolution. As a result, each microservice becomes a self-contained system with clear dependency graphs and predictable behavior.

Communication Strategies: REST, gRPC, and Event-Driven Designs

Communication is at the heart of microservices, and Go supports multiple styles with equal strength.

REST with `net/http`

Go's **`net/http`** package remains one of the most robust and battle-tested HTTP servers in production environments. Its simplicity encourages clear handler design, while its middleware patterns allow extension without overwhelming abstraction. REST is often chosen for:

- Public APIs.
- Systems requiring human readability.
- Interoperability with heterogeneous services.
- Internal APIs where latency is less critical.

As Go's JSON ecosystem continues to evolve—particularly with the introduction of the new json API and structured logging—building REST APIs in Go has become more expressive and safer.

gRPC with Protocol Buffers

For high-performance internal communication, gRPC is often the preferred choice. Its advantages include:

- Strong typing and schema enforcement.
- Bidirectional streaming.
- Very low latency and small message sizes.
- Automatic generation of Go client and server code.

Go's gRPC implementation is exceptionally mature and integrates cleanly with middleware, interceptors, load balancers, and observability frameworks like OpenTelemetry.

Event-Driven Messaging

Event-driven systems—powered by Kafka, NATS, Google Pub/Sub, AWS SNS/SQS, or Redis Streams—provide asynchronous workflow orchestration. Go's concurrency model makes it ideal for high-throughput consumers:

- Long-lived goroutines

- Worker pools
- Select-based fan-out/fan-in patterns
- Backpressure control

Building resilient consumers often requires the geatures Go excel at—combining channels, contexts, and retry logic.

Choosing the right communication style involves evaluating latency requirements, operational complexity, failure handling strategies, and versioning constraints.

Resilience and Reliability Patterns

The difference between a prototype, and a production microservice is how it behaves under failure. Go makes it straightforward to embed resilience patterns directly into the service logic.

Timeouts and Deadlines

context.Context provides built-in cancellation and timeout propagation across goroutines, HTTP requests, database queries, and gRPC calls. A production microservice propagates context consistently, ensuring slow dependencies do not degrade the entire service.

Retries and Backoff

Retry loops must be implemented carefully to avoid amplifying load during partial outages. Techniques often used in Go microservices include:

- Exponential backoff
- Jitter
- Circuit breakers
- Budgeted retries controlled by context deadlines

Circuit Breakers

Using libraries such as `sony/gobreaker`, developers wrap remote calls to prevent cascading failures. Circuits open when error thresholds exceed limits, allowing services to degrade gracefully.

Bulkheading and Isolation

Worker pools, buffered channels, and goroutine limits prevent individual endpoints from monopolizing resources. This pattern is essential in systems with unpredictable load profiles.

A production-grade microservice assumes failure is guaranteed and prepares for it architecturally.

Observability as a First-Class Concern

A production microservice must be observable, not just functional. Observability is achieved by collecting:

- **Logs** (structured, query-friendly JSON)
- **Metrics** (latency, throughput, error rates)
- **Traces** (end-to-end request paths)

Go integrates naturally with OpenTelemetry, Prometheus, Grafana, and vendor-specific platforms. Developers typically expose:

- /metrics for Prometheus
- Tracing exporters (OTLP)
- Structured logs using zerolog, slog, or logrus

Good observability enables high-confidence deployments, rapid debugging, and performance tuning without any guesswork.

Security and Configuration Management

Production-grade services require secure defaults. Go supports secure microservices with:

- TLS everywhere (HTTP or gRPC).
- OAuth2, JWT, or mTLS authentication.
- Sanitized structured logs.
- Dependency scanning using tools like `gosec` and `govulncheck`.

Configuration should be externalized through environment variables, config maps, or secret stores like Vault or AWS Secrets Manager. Go's static binaries simplify this: containers remain immutable, configuration remains dynamic.

How AI Influences Microservice Design

AI tools increasingly contribute to architectural decisions. During service design, AI can help:

- Generate initial service blueprints.
- Draft interface boundaries.
- Suggest domain-driven decomposition.

- Propose gRPC schemas and OpenAPI designs.
- Review communication patterns and point out anti-patterns.
- Suggest resilience strategies based on described workloads.

However, AI assistance must remain a guide—never a substitute for architectural judgment. Human oversight ensures that decisions align with business constraints, reliability expectations, and long-term maintenance.

Containerization Using Docker

Containerization is one of the foundational pillars of deploying production-grade Go microservices. Docker offers a uniform, replicable, and secure environment for services to operate, regardless of variations in the host system. When integrated with Go's statically built binaries and tiny runtime footprint. Docker facilitates exceptionally lightweight, high-performance microservice deployments. This section explores how to containerize Go applications effectively, optimize images for production, implement multi-stage builds, and follow best practices for security, performance, and operational reliability.

Why Docker Works So Well with Go

Unlike languages that require heavy runtimes or virtual machines, Go compiles to a single static binary. This allows microservices to run in extremely small container images—sometimes as small as 5–10 MB. The absence of external dependencies simplifies distribution, reduces attack surfaces, accelerates startup times, and makes containers easier to orchestrate across cloud environments.

Some of the core advantages of combining Go with Docker include:

- **Minimal Base Images:** Alpine or distroless images produce small, secure containers.
- **Fast Startup:** Essential for autoscaling, serverless workloads, and rolling updates.
- **Predictable Memory Usage:** Reduces throttling and container restarts.
- **Static Linking:** Fewer moving parts, fewer runtime surprises.
- **Platform-Specific Builds:** Cross-compilation enables building images for ARM, x86, or cloud-specific architectures.

In production environments where reliability, speed, and resource efficiency matter, Go + Docker becomes a natural pairing.

Building a Go Service for Docker Deployment

Before writing a Dockerfile, a microservice must be structured in a way that supports containerization. This includes:

- A well-defined entry point (main package).
- Externalized configuration via environment variables.
- Graceful shutdown via **context.Context** and signal handling.
- Dependency injection for storage, messaging, and service adapters.
- Logging directed to **stdout/stderr** (crucial for containerized observability).

A simple **main** function prepared for containerization may look like:

```
func main() {
    ctx, stop := signal.NotifyContext(context.Background(),
syscall.SIGTERM, syscall.SIGINT)
    defer stop()

    addr := os.Getenv("HTTP_ADDR")
    if addr == "" {
        addr = ":8080"
    }

    srv := &http.Server{
        Addr:    addr,
        Handler: setupRouter(),
    }

    go func() {
        if err := srv.ListenAndServe(); err != nil && err !=
http.ErrServerClosed {
            log.Fatalf("server failed: %v", err)
        }
    }()
    log.Println("server running on", addr)

    <-ctx.Done()
    shutdownCtx, cancel := context.WithTimeout(context.Back-
ground(), 5*time.Second)
    defer cancel()
    _ = srv.Shutdown(shutdownCtx)
}
```

Such a structure ensures that the service reacts predictably when the container receives termination signals during rolling deployments.

Writing an Efficient Dockerfile

A naive Dockerfile can produce unnecessarily large images and expose security risks. A production-grade Dockerfile for Go typically uses a **multi-stage build**, where one stage compiles the application, and another runs the final minimal binary.

Example: Multi-Stage Dockerfile

```
# Stage 1: Build
FROM golang:1.23 AS builder

WORKDIR /app

# Better caching
COPY go.mod go.sum ./
RUN go mod download

COPY . .

RUN CGO_ENABLED=0 GOOS=linux GOARCH=amd64 go build -o service ./
cmd/service

# Stage 2: Run
FROM gcr.io/distroless/base-debian12

COPY --from=builder /app/service /service

EXPOSE 8080

ENTRYPOINT ["/service"]
```

Key Production Considerations:

- **Multi-stage builds** dramatically reduce image size.
- **Distroless or scratch images** minimize attack surface and reduce runtime footprint.
- **Static binaries (`CGO_ENABLED=0`)** enable running in scratch/distroless containers.
- **Explicit `ENTRYPOINT`** ensures predictable startup.
- **ENV variables** configure ports, credentials, or feature flags without rebuilding the image.

In organizations that undergo security audits, using minimal base images reduces CVE exposure and simplifies vulnerability scanning.

Container Security Best Practices

Production-ready microservices must treat containers as security boundaries. Essential security practices include:

- **Use Minimal Images:** The smaller the image, the fewer dependencies can be exploited. Distroless and scratch images drastically reduce surface area.
- **Run as Non-Root:** A microservice should not require root privileges.

  ```
  USER nonroot:nonroot
  ```
- **Read-Only File Systems:** Immutable container filesystems prevent certain classes of attacks.
- **Externalize Secrets:** Credentials must never be baked into images. Kubernetes secrets, Vault, or AWS Secrets Manager are standard choices.
- **Image Scanning:** CI pipelines must integrate tools such as Trivy, Grype, or Docker Scout to detect vulnerabilities.

Together, these practices elevate the safety profile of Go microservices operating in large-scale deployments.

Observability and Logs inside Containers

Containers should log exclusively to standard output and error. This allows Kubernetes, ECS, Docker Compose, or any orchestrator to aggregate logs automatically.

In practice:

```
log.Println("starting background job...")
log.Printf("error fetching user: %v", err)
```

Avoid writing logs to local files, as containers are ephemeral and files disappear when containers are replaced.

Instrumentation layers—OpenTelemetry metrics exporters, trace exporters, Prometheus /metrics endpoints—must also operate independently of the filesystem.

Container-Oriented Configuration Management

Go microservices should use environment variables as their primary configuration interface. Containers do not assume details about the runtime environment; configuration is injected at deploy time.

Typical configuration values include:

- Database DSNs
- Caches (Redis, Memcached)
- External API URLs
- Feature flags
- Timeouts
- Log verbosity

The Go standard library makes environment variable loading straightforward:

```
dbURL := os.Getenv("DATABASE_URL")
if dbURL == "" {
    log.Fatal("missing DATABASE_URL")
}
```

This decouples the service from deployment environments such as Docker Compose, Kubernetes, Nomad, or serverless platforms.

Testing and Validating Dockerized Go Services

A critical aspect of containerization is verifying that the container behaves as expected after each and every change. Typical validation workflows include:

Local Testing via Docker Compose

Spin up containers for databases, message queues, and your Go service.

Smoke Tests

Run a small suite of automated health checks in CI:

```
docker run --rm myservice:latest /service --version
docker run --rm -p 8080:8080 myservice:latest curl localhost
:8080/health
```

Integration Tests

Combine Go's testing framework with ephemeral Docker containers using tools like Testcontainers-Go.

Thus, by developing services "container-first," teams ensure consistency between development and production environments.

Deploying Dockerized Go Services

Once a service is containerized, it becomes a building block for larger platforms. Common deployment targets include:

- Kubernetes (EKS, GKE, AKS, K3s, Minikube)
- AWS ECS or Fargate
- Google Cloud Run
- Nomad
- Docker Swarm
- Edge devices (ARM-based images)

Go's cross-compilation and small binaries allow teams to produce multiple architecture-specific images:

```
GOOS=linux GOARCH=arm64 go build
```

Combined with Docker's **`--platform` flag**, deployment pipelines can push multi-platform images to registries, ensuring compatibility across diverse environments.

How AI Enhances Dockerization Workflows

AI tools can assist in containerization by:

- Generating initial Dockerfiles based on project structure.
- Suggesting multi-stage optimization strategies.
- Detecting inefficient commands or caching problems.
- Auditing Dockerfiles for security risks.
- Proposing Kubernetes YAML configurations.
- Explaining CI/CD errors when Docker builds fail.

A well-crafted prompt—"Optimize this Dockerfile for production, and explain potential security vulnerabilities"—can save hours of manual tuning.

CI/CD Pipelines for Go Applications

Continuous Integration and Continuous Deployment (CI/CD) pipelines are becoming a key part of modern software delivery. Go's simplicity, speed, and static binaries make it a great choice for automated processes. A well-designed CI/CD pipeline ensures that every change—whether a minor refactor or a major feature—is rigorously tested, compiled, scanned, packaged, and deployed with minimal friction. This reliability lowers the chance of human error, speeds up release cycles, and keeps ensuring that deployments are the same across all environments in production. This section explores how to design robust CI/CD workflows for Go microservices, covering essential pipeline stages, tooling options, security checks, automated deployments, and AI-assisted enhancements.

Understanding the CI/CD Lifecycle for Go

A complete CI/CD pipeline for a Go microservice typically includes the following stages:

1. **Code Linting and Static Analysis:**

   Tools like `golangci-lint`, `staticcheck`, and `gosec` ensure code quality and security.

2. **Dependency and Vulnerability Scanning:**

   Modern pipelines integrate security scanning tools such as GitHub Dependabot, Trivy, or Snyk.

3. **Running Automated Tests:**

   Go test with coverage, benchmarks, and race detection ensures reliability.

4. **Building Binaries and Docker Images:**

   Go's fast builds and single-binary outputs make this stage efficient.

5. **Artifact Storage:**

   Storing binaries or container images in registries like Amazon ECR, GitHub Packages, or Google Artifact Registry.

6. **Staging Deployment:**

   Running the service in staging with integration tests or contract tests.

7. **Production Deployment:**

   This may use Kubernetes, AWS ECS/Fargate, Google Cloud Run, Nomad, or Docker Swarm.

8. **Post-Deployment Checks:**

   Health checks, metrics validation, smoke testing, and automated rollbacks.

A pipeline is not just a sequence of automation steps—it is a repeatable and a safe path from a Git commit to a running, production-grade Go service.

Setting up a CI Pipeline for Go

A typical job includes running:

```
golangci-lint run
staticcheck ./...
gosec ./...
```

These tools catch style violations, race conditions, insecure code patterns, unused variables, mutating global state, and more.

Running Tests with Coverage

Go supports fast and reliable testing:

```
go test ./... -v -race -coverprofile=coverage.out
```

- **`-race`** detects data races (critical for concurrency-heavy Go apps).
- **`-coverprofile`** generates a coverage report that CI systems visualize.

CI systems like GitHub Actions or GitLab CI can enforce minimum coverage thresholds.

Building Go Binaries and Docker Images in CI

Go's static binaries make the build stage incredibly simple.

Building Multi-Platform Binaries

A typical CI step looks like:

```
GOOS=linux GOARCH=amd64 go build -o app .
GOOS=linux GOARCH=arm64 go build -o app .
```

This is especially important when deploying to Kubernetes on ARM or multi-architecture serverless platforms.

Docker Image Builds

A minimal Dockerfile for Go might use multi-stage builds:

```
FROM golang:1.23 AS builder
WORKDIR /app
COPY . .
RUN go build -o server .

FROM alpine:latest
WORKDIR /root/
COPY --from=builder /app/server .
CMD ["./server"]
```

CI systems can then build and push to registries:

```
docker build -t registry/app:latest .
docker push registry/app:latest
```

Deploying Go Applications with CD

Continuous Deployment expands the automation from building artifacts to actually deploying them.

Common CD Targets for Go Services:

- Kubernetes with Helm, Kustomize, or raw manifests.
- AWS ECS or Fargate using task definitions.
- Google Cloud Run for serverless container hosting.
- Docker Compose for small-scale environments.
- Nomad or Fly.io for global deployment.

A CD pipeline typically performs:

1. Config validation (for example, Helm lint, kubeval).
2. Apply deployment to staging.
3. Run integration tests or smoke tests.
4. Promote to production on success.

Promotion can be manual (Continuous Delivery), or fully automated (Continuous Deployment).

Example CI/CD Pipeline Using GitHub Actions

A simplified, but realistic workflow is as follows:

```
name: Go CI/CD Pipeline

on:
  push:
    branches: [ "main" ]

jobs:
  build-test:
    runs-on: ubuntu-latest
    steps:
      - uses: actions/checkout@v4

      - name: Setup Go
```

```
        uses: actions/setup-go@v4
        with:
          go-version: "1.23"

      - name: Install linters
        run: |
          curl -sSfL https://raw.githubusercontent.com/golangci/
golangci-lint/master/install.sh | sh
          go install honnef.co/go/tools/cmd/staticcheck@latest
          go install github.com/securego/gosec/v2/cmd/gosec@
latest

      - name: Run linters
        run: golangci-lint run

      - name: Run tests
        run: go test ./... -race -coverprofile=coverage.out

      - name: Build Docker image
        run: |
          docker build -t ghcr.io/myorg/myapp:${{ github.sha }} .
          echo "${{ secrets.GITHUB_TOKEN }}" | docker login ghcr.
io -u USERNAME --password-stdin
          docker push ghcr.io/myorg/myapp:${{ github.sha }}

  deploy:
    needs: build-test
    runs-on: ubuntu-latest
    steps:
      - name: Deploy to Kubernetes
        run: |
          helm upgrade --install myapp ./deploy \
            --set image.tag=${{ github.sha }}
```

This pipeline:

- Validates code quality.
- Runs tests with race detection.
- Builds and pushes a Docker image.
- Deploys using Helm.

Adding Security, Compliance, and Observability to the Pipeline

Modern pipelines for Go microservices also integrate:

- **Security Scanning**
  - Trivy for container and dependency vulnerabilities.
  - Snyk for code, images, IaC.
  - **gosec** for Go-specific security linting.
- **SBOM Generation**

  Software Bill of Materials (SBOM) is increasingly a requirement:

  ```
  syft packages dir:.
  grype sbom:sbom.json
  ```
- **Observability Pipelines**

  CI/CD can automatically:

  - Validate that logging fields follow standards.
  - Ensure that OpenTelemetry instrumentation exists.
  - Check dashboards and alerts are updated before deployment.

AI-Assisted CI/CD Pipeline Generation and Optimization

Modern AI tools significantly speed up CI/CD development:

- **AI Use Cases**
  - Generate pipeline YAML files for GitHub Actions, GitLab CI, Jenkins, or Argo Workflows.
  - Review pipeline logs and identify slow, flaky steps.
  - Suggest better caching strategies for dependencies and Docker layers.
  - Recommend security scans or compliance controls.
  - Autogenerate Helm templates, Kubernetes manifests, or rollout strategies.

For example, the following prompt can produce improved caching, parallel steps, and security checks automatically.

"Optimize this CI workflow to reduce build time and add Trivy container scanning."

Monitoring, Logging, and Error Reporting

Building a production-grade Go microservice involves much more than writing an efficient code and containerizing it. Once your service is deployed, its real-world reliability depends heavily on your ability to observe its behavior–both at a macro (system-wide) level, and a micro (request-by-request) level. Monitoring, logging, and error reporting forms the observability triad, helping teams detect issues early, debug efficiently, measure performance, and deliver a resilient experience to the end users. This section explains how to design a robust observability strategy tailored to Go microservices, covering metrics instrumentation, structured logging, distributed tracing, and automated error reporting workflows.

Why Observability Matters in Go Microservices

Go excels in performance, concurrency, and scalability–ideal traits for production services. However, these same traits create unique challenges:

- High concurrency makes race conditions or goroutine leaks harder to see.
- Highly distributed microservices require correlation across multiple systems.
- Stateless services rely more on external systems (databases, queues, caches), so visibility is essential.

Observability provides answers to the following crucial questions:

- **Is the service healthy?**
- **Why did latency spike?**
- **Which request failed?**
- **Where is the bottleneck?**
- **Who is affected?**
- **How can we reproduce the issue?**

By designing observability early, developers avoid blind spots and reduce the "it works on my machine" problem.

Monitoring Go Microservices

Monitoring provides **numeric,** and **time-series insights** into system performance and health. It helps teams detect trends, set alerts, and diagnose bottlenecks.

Key Metrics to Measure

Common categories include:

- **Application Metrics**
  - Request count
  - Error count
  - Request latency (p95, p99)
  - Queue/wait times

  - Goroutine count
  - Garbage collection duration
  - Memory usage
  - CPU usage
- **Business Metrics**
  - Orders processed per minute
  - Signup failures
  - User conversion rates
- **Infrastructure Metrics**
  - Pod restarts (Kubernetes)
  - Disk I/O
  - Network throughput

Integrating Prometheus in Go

Prometheus is the de facto standard for metrics in Go apps.

1. **Install the Prometheus client:**

```
go get github.com/prometheus/client_golang/prometheus
```

2. **Create metrics:**

```
var requestDuration = prometheus.NewHistogramVec(
    prometheus.HistogramOpts{
        Name: "http_request_duration_seconds",
        Help: "Request latency distributions",
    },
    []string{"method", "endpoint"},
)

func init() {
    prometheus.MustRegister(requestDuration)
}
```

3. **Record metrics:**

```
start := time.Now()
handler(w, r)
duration := time.Since(start).Seconds()

requestDuration.WithLabelValues(r.Method, r.URL.Path).Observe
(duration)
```

4. **Expose metrics at `/metrics` to be scraped by Prometheus.**

Dashboards with Grafana

Grafana visualizes:

- Latency heatmaps
- Error spikes
- Resource usage
- Custom Service Level Indicators (SLIs)

Teams typically create:

- SLO dashboards (with error budgets)
- Deployment dashboards
- Infrastructure dashboards

These guide the operational decisions during key incidents.

Logging in Go Microservices

Logging provides context-rich insights into what your application is doing. Unlike metrics (numeric), logs are event-based, descriptive, and detailed.

Principles of Good Logging

The following are the principles:

- Use structured logs.
- JSON is standard in modern microservices.
- Log only what is useful.
- Avoid noise and sensitive data.
- Prefer semantic fields over raw text.

Example: `"user_id"`: “1234” instead of “User 1234”.

Use log levels effectively:

- **`INFO`:** Expected behavior.
- **`WARN`:** Unusual, but not failing.
- **`ERROR`:** Something went wrong.
- **`FATAL`:** Application cannot continue.

Using Structured Logging Libraries

Popular libraries:

- **`zerolog`**
- **`zap`** (Uber)
- **`logrus`** (classic, but slower)
- **`slog`** (Go 1.21 official structured logger)

Example using slog:

```
logger := slog.Default()

logger.Info("request received",
    "method", r.Method,
    "path", r.URL.Path,
    "user_agent", r.UserAgent(),
)
```

Error logging example:

```
if err != nil {
    logger.Error("failed to process payment",
        "error", err.Error(),
        "user_id", uid,
    )
}
```

Centralized Log Aggregation

In production, logs must be aggregated:

Common tools:

- Elasticsearch + Kibana (ELK stack)
- Loki + Grafana
- AWS CloudWatch Logs
- Google Cloud Logging

Benefits:

- Query logs across all services.
- Correlate logs with metrics/traces.
- Search by request ID or user ID.
- Build alerts on error patterns.

Error Reporting and Alerting

Error reporting closes the loop between monitoring and incident response. It centralizes exceptions, stack traces, and contextual metadata.

Automated Error Reporting Tools

Popular tools include:

- Sentry
- Honeycomb
- Datadog APM
- Rollbar
- New Relic

These tools gather:

- Stack traces.
- Request metadata.
- Host/container information.
- User information (if included).
- Repeat occurrence frequency.

Integrating Sentry with Go

Install:

```
go get github.com/getsentry/sentry-go
```

Initialize:

```
sentry.Init(sentry.ClientOptions{
    Dsn: os.Getenv("SENTRY_DSN"),
    Environment: "production",
    Release: "v1.0.0",
})
```

Capture errors:

```
if err != nil {
    sentry.CaptureException(err)
}
```

This ensures:

- Critical errors are recorded.

- Alerts can be triggered.
- Developers get immediate insights.

Error Correlation with Request IDs

Add a unique request ID for each HTTP request:

```
id := uuid.NewString()
ctx := context.WithValue(r.Context(), "request_id", id)
```

Log it and attach it to every error:

```
logger.Error("database timeout", "request_id", id)
```

This enables searching related logs, traces, and metrics–pivotal for debugging distributed systems.

Distributed Tracing in Go Microservices

Although monitoring and logging provide valuable insights, tracing shows the entire path of a request across multiple services.

Using OpenTelemetry with Go

OpenTelemetry (OTEL) has become the standard for distributed tracing.

Install:

```
go get go.opentelemetry.io/otel
```

Instrumentation example:

```
ctx, span := tracer.Start(r.Context(), "processOrder")
defer span.End()

err := processOrder(ctx)
if err != nil {
    span.RecordError(err)
}
```

Traces are exported to:

- Jaeger
- Tempo
- Honeycomb
- Datadog
- AWS X-Ray

Benefits of Distributed Tracing:

- Identify slow components.
- Visualize call graphs across microservices.
- Detects bottlenecks (database latency, API delays, and queue backlogs).
- Understand concurrency behavior.
- Improve debugging during incidents.

Performance Tuning and Resource Optimization

Designing a production-grade Go microservice requires more than a clean code and reliable APIs; it demands rigorous attention to performance tuning and resource optimization. Even well-written Go programs can experience performance degradation under real-world workloads due to excessive allocations, inefficient concurrency patterns, suboptimal network usage, or poor memory locality. At scale, these inefficiencies manifest as increased tail latencies, higher CPU usage, and unnecessary infrastructure costs. This section explores the major dimensions of performance optimization–CPU profiling, memory tuning, concurrency design, network efficiency, garbage collection control, and resource-aware deployments–while providing practical, field-tested techniques that production teams use to keep Go microservices fast, scalable, and cost-effective.

Understanding Go's Performance Model

To optimize Go services effectively, developers must understand the properties that make Go unique:

Go is Concurrent by Design

The Go scheduler multiplexes goroutines over OS threads. Performance is deeply influenced by:

- Number of runnable goroutines
- Scheduler fairness
- Channel contention
- Mutex lock contention
- System call boundaries

Garbage Collection (GC) is Low Latency but Not Free

Go's garbage collector is optimized for services:

- 0.2–0.5% pause time
- Concurrent mark-and-sweep
- Tunable with GOGC

But, unnecessary allocations drastically increase GC work. Tuning memory allocation is one of the most impactful performance levers.

Go Favors Locality

Go performs best when:

- Data structures minimize heap usage.
- Memory access patterns are predictable.
- Structs are compact.
- Slices and maps grow infrequently.

Understanding these factors allows developers to make targeted optimizations, rather than blanket micro-tuning.

Profiling, Benchmarking, and Evidence-Based Optimization

Performance optimization must be **evidence-driven**, and not intuitive. What feels slow to a developer is often not what impacts latency.

Benchmarking with go `test -bench`

Benchmarks provide controlled performance measurement:

```
func BenchmarkHasher(b *testing.B) {
    for i := 0; i < b.N; i++ {
        Hash([]byte("hello"))
    }
}
```

Analyze allocations:

```
go test -bench=. -benchmem
```

Output reveals:

- `ns/op`
- `bytes/op`
- `allocs/op`

Reducing allocations is often the quickest way to increase performance.

CPU Profiling with pprof

```
go tool pprof -http=:8081 cpu.prof
```

CPU profiling identifies:

- Hot paths
- Unnecessary computations
- Inefficient loops
- Hashing/crypto costs
- JSON marshalling overhead
- Reflection-heavy code

When a small number of functions dominate CPU, focus optimization there.

Memory Profiling

Memory profiles expose:

- Unexpected heap usage
- Excessive allocations
- Overgrown buffers or maps
- Retained objects preventing GC

An excessive escape-to-heap behavior signals structural issues.

Tuning Concurrency and Scheduler Behavior

Concurrency is one of the greatest strengths of Go—but also one of its biggest sources of inefficiency if used incorrectly.

Avoid Goroutine Explosion

Launching goroutines unboundedly:

```
for _, job := range jobs {
    go process(job)
}
```

leads to:

- Massive scheduling overhead.
- Memory pressure.
- Increased GC cycles.
- Starvation.

Solution: Worker pools with backpressure.

Reduce Channel Contention

Hot channels become bottlenecks when many goroutines compete for the same send/ receive path.

Common fixes:

- Use sharded channels.
- Use buffered channels.
- Prefer lock-free designs (atomic operations).
- Replace channel signaling with wait groups when appropriate.

Use Context Deadlines to Trigger Early Abort

Example:

```
ctx, cancel := context.WithTimeout(context.Background(),
200*time.Millisecond)
defer cancel()
```

Timeouts prevent goroutines from piling up during upstream slowdowns.

Avoid Oversynchronization

Using mutexes everywhere leads to lock contention.

Improvement Techniques:

- Reduce critical section size.
- Use RWMutex when reads dominate.
- Use atomic operations for counters.
- Avoid shared state entirely using message passing.

Memory Optimization and Allocation Control

Memory inefficiency is a silent performance killer.

Minimize Escape to Heap

Code patterns like:

```
return &localStruct
```

force the compiler to escape memory to the heap. When possible, restructure the code so that objects remain on the stack.

Reuse Buffers to Reduce GC Pressure

Example using **sync.Pool**:

```
var bufPool = sync.Pool{
    New: func() interface{} { return make([]byte, 0, 4096) },
}

func handle() {
    buf := bufPool.Get().([]byte)
    defer bufPool.Put(buf[:0])
}
```

Effective for:

- JSON serialization
- Network buffers
- Compression
- Image processing

Optimize Slice Growth

Avoid repeated reallocation:

Not Preferred:

```
var items []string
for i := 0; i < 100000; i++ {
    items = append(items, "x")
}
```

Better:

```
items := make([]string, 0, 100000)
```

Reduce Struct Size and Improve Locality

Moving hot fields to the front of the struct improves memory locality.

Packing booleans together reduces padding.

Network and I/O Optimization

Microservices often spend more time in I/O than computation.

Use Connection Pools and KeepAlives

HTTP clients must be reused:

```
var client = &http.Client{
    Transport: &http.Transport{
        MaxIdleConns:       100,
        IdleConnTimeout:    90 * time.Second,
        DisableCompression: false,
    },
}
```

Avoid creating new **`http.Client`** per request.

Optimize JSON Marshalling

encoding/json is powerful, but slow due to reflection.

Faster Options:

- **`jsoniter`**
- **`go-json`**
- **`easyjson`** (code generation)

For highly loaded services, switching JSON libraries can reduce latency by 30–60%.

Use gRPC for High-Throughput Communication

Compared to JSON-over-HTTP:

- Smaller payloads
- HTTP/2 multiplexing
- Automatic code generation
- Bidirectional streaming

Avoid Unbounded I/O Reads

Always set limits:

```
r.Body = http.MaxBytesReader(w, r.Body, 1<<20)
```

It protects against memory exhaustion attacks.

Garbage Collector (GC) Tuning

Go's GC is fast, but GC-heavy workloads can introduce latency.

Tune via GOGC

GOGC=50 reduces memory usage but increases GC frequency.

GOGC=200 uses more memory but reduces GC overhead.

For services with:

- Abundant RAM → increase GOGC.
- Memory constraints → reduce GOGC.

Reduce Heap Growth

If your heap grows steadily:

- Identify memory leaks.
- Reuse buffers.
- Limit caching.
- Ensure that goroutines exit.

Control Allocation Rates

Tools like **`alloc_space`** and **`alloc_objects`** profiles show hotspots.

A function allocating heavily often needs:

- In-place mutation instead of copying.
- Avoidance of map growth.
- Avoidance of interface conversions.

Runtime and Deployment Optimization

Go binaries are lightweight, but deployment strategy affects performance dramatically.

Tune CPU and Memory Limits in Kubernetes

Setting limits too low causes throttling.

Better Approach:

- Set **requests** near the average.

- Set **limits** only slightly above requests.

This prevents:

- CPU starvation
- OOM kills
- GC spikes due to tight memory

Multi-Stage Builds Reduce Image Size

```
FROM golang:1.23 AS build
RUN CGO_ENABLED=0 go build -o app .

FROM alpine:latest
COPY --from=build /app /app
ENTRYPOINT ["/app"]
```

Small Images:

- Pull faster.
- Start faster.
- Reduce attack surface.

Pin Go Version and Enable Build Optimizations

Build with optimizations:

```
go build -ldflags="-s -w"
```

Strips symbol information for smaller binaries.

Enable HTTP/2 and TLS Optimizations

Enable:

- connection reuse
- TLS session resumption
- ALPN

It improves latency for high-throughput APIs.

AI-Assisted Performance Tuning Techniques

AI tools significantly accelerate optimization by identifying issues developers often miss.

AI-Assisted Technique 1: Generate pprof Analysis Summaries

Example prompt:

"Explain the CPU profile output below and identify the top three optimization opportunities."

AI summarizes flame graphs and hotspots.

AI-Assisted Technique 2: Recommend More Efficient Concurrency Patterns

Given code using many goroutines, ChatGPT or CodeWhisperer can suggest:

- Worker pools
- Channel buffering
- Atomic counters instead of mutexes

AI-Assisted Technique 3: Detect Allocations and Suggest Refactoring

Input:

"Here is my benchmark result. How can I reduce allocations?"

AI Highlights:

- Unnecessary copies.
- Converting slices to pointers.
- Unnecessary interface conversions.

AI-Assisted Technique 4: Generate Optimized JSON Serialization Code

Ask:

"Rewrite this struct to reduce JSON serialization overhead."

AI proposes:

- Tags
- Field renaming
- Using **`easyjson`**
- Avoiding **`omitempty`** for hot paths

AI-Assisted Deployment Automation

Modern software development increasingly relies on automation to ensure consistency, reduction of errors, and acceleration of delivery. Deployment of Go microservices is no exception—manual deployment is error-prone, difficult to scale, and hard to maintain across multiple environments. AI-assisted deployment automation leverages machine learning models, large language models, and specialized tooling to streamline deployment workflows. By integrating AI, teams can auto-generate deployment scripts, optimize CI/CD pipelines, predict potential deployment failures, and even receive suggestions for resource configuration, all while maintaining reproducibility and observability.

Automating Deployment Script Generation

One of the most time-consuming aspects of deploying Go microservices is writing and maintaining deployment scripts for different environments–development, staging, and production. AI tools can generate these scripts based on high-level instructions. For example, a developer can provide a prompt to a tool like ChatGPT or GitHub.

Copilot:

"Generate a Kubernetes deployment manifest for a Go microservice named user-service using 3 replicas, 512Mi memory, 0.5 CPU, and exposing port 8080."

The AI generates YAML manifests with the appropriate Deployment, Service, and ConfigMap objects. Similarly, it can create Terraform templates or Helm charts that manage infrastructure provisioning alongside the microservice deployment. These AI-generated artifacts are not only faster to create, but can also follow the best practices for security, resource limits, and horizontal scaling.

Example of an AI-generated Kubernetes deployment snippet:

```
apiVersion: apps/v1
kind: Deployment
metadata:
  name: user-service
spec:
  replicas: 3
  selector:
    matchLabels:
      app: user-service
  template:
    metadata:
      labels:
        app: user-service
    spec:
      containers:
        - name: user-service
          image: myrepo/user-service:latest
          ports:
            - containerPort: 8080
          resources:
```

```
            requests:
              memory: "512Mi"
              cpu: "500m"
            limits:
              memory: "1Gi"
              cpu: "1"
```

AI can even annotate the file with explanations for each configuration, helping less-experienced engineers understand deployment choices.

AI in CI/CD Pipeline Automation

Continuous Integration and Continuous Deployment (CI/CD) pipelines involve complex steps–building, testing, containerizing, and deploying services. AI tools can assist in generating pipeline scripts for platforms like GitHub Actions, GitLab CI, or Jenkins.

Instead of manually writing YAML, developers can instruct AI:

"Generate a GitHub Actions workflow for building, testing, and deploying a Go microservice to Kubernetes when a PR is merged to the main branch."

The AI produces a complete workflow including caching Go modules, running unit tests, building a Docker image, pushing it to a container registry, and applying Kubernetes manifests. It can also suggest optimizations such as parallelizing independent steps, adding retries for flakiness, or enabling conditional deployments based on branch or tag.

Example of an AI-assisted GitHub Actions snippet:

```
name: CI/CD Pipeline

on:
  push:
    branches:
      - main

jobs:
  build-test-deploy:
    runs-on: ubuntu-latest
    steps:
      - uses: actions/checkout@v3
      - name: Set up Go
        uses: actions/setup-go@v4
        with:
          go-version: 1.23
      - name: Cache Go modules
        uses: actions/cache@v3
```

```
          with:
            path: |
              ~/.cache/go-build
              ~/go/pkg/mod
            key: ${{ runner.os }}-go-${{ hashFiles('**/go.sum') }}
        - name: Build
          run: go build -v ./...
        - name: Test
          run: go test -v ./...
        - name: Build Docker image
          run: docker build -t myrepo/user-service:latest .
        - name: Push to Registry
          run: docker push myrepo/user-service:latest
        - name: Deploy to Kubernetes
          run: kubectl apply -f k8s/deployment.yaml
```

AI assistance ensures that all dependencies, caching strategies, and deployment steps are correctly aligned, reducing the risk of human errors in the pipeline.

Predictive Deployment and Rollback Suggestions

AI can analyze historical deployment logs to predict potential failures, or suggest safer deployment strategies. For instance:

- **Blue/Green or Canary Deployments**: AI can recommend gradual rollout percentages based on prior service performance.
- **Resource Adjustments**: Suggest increasing CPU or memory limits for pods with high failure rates.
- **Rollback Triggers**: Automatically detect anomalies post-deployment, like increased error rates or latency spikes, and recommend rollback procedures.

This predictive capability allows teams to avoid common deployment pitfalls and maintain service reliability even in high-traffic environments.

Optimizing Infrastructure Resources with AI

Deploying microservices efficiently also involves resource optimization. AI tools can:

- Analyze historical CPU and memory usage of Go services.
- Recommend autoscaling thresholds.
- Optimize pod placement for load balancing.
- Suggest horizontal or vertical scaling to minimize cloud costs while maintaining performance.

For example, by providing historical metrics to an AI tool, it can generate a recommendation:

"Scale user-service pods from 3 to 5 during peak hours and reduce replicas to 2 at night. Increase memory limit from 512Mi to 768Mi for pods handling batch jobs."

By automating these recommendations, AI helps teams maintain performance without manual monitoring and adjustments.

AI-Assisted Deployment Monitoring

AI is also valuable after deployment. It can analyze logs, metrics, and traces to detect anomalies and provide actionable recommendations. Examples include:

- Suggesting index improvements for database queries used by the microservice.
- Highlighting memory leaks in specific endpoints.
- Recommending Go code changes to reduce response latency in high-load scenarios.

Therefore, by combining pre-deployment automation with post-deployment intelligence, AI ensures end-to-end operational efficiency.

Future Trends in Go and AI-Assisted Development

Developing Go applications with AI-assisted tools promises to redefine how developers build, deploy, and maintain applications. Go has always been celebrated for its simplicity, performance, and concurrency model, which makes it an ideal language for cloud-native, microservices, and high-performance applications. Looking ahead, several emerging trends indicate how Go and AI-assisted development will continue to influence software engineering practices.

AI-Driven Code Generation and Optimization

AI-assisted coding tools, such as ChatGPT, Copilot, and Amazon Q, are already helping developers generate boilerplate code, suggest optimizations, and refactor existing codebases. In the future, these tools are expected to evolve beyond simple suggestions into fully autonomous development assistants capable of:

- Generating production-ready microservices architectures.
- Optimizing concurrent and parallel workloads automatically.
- Providing real-time performance and security recommendations during development.

- Translating high-level system designs into fully implemented Go modules.

This pattern will allow the developers to concentrate on creating resilient system designs and addressing intricate problems instead of engaging in repeated coding activities.

Integration of AI in DevOps and CI/CD Pipelines

The DevOps landscape is increasingly incorporating AI for intelligent automation of build, test, and deployment pipelines. For Go applications, this means:

- AI-assisted CI/CD pipelines that can predict potential deployment failures.
- Automated resource tuning for containers and microservices based on historical usage data.
- Dynamic adjustment of scaling strategies for cloud-native Go services.
- Intelligent rollback and anomaly detection mechanisms for safer production deployments.

This integration of AI will make continuous delivery faster, more reliable, and cost-efficient, particularly in large-scale distributed systems where manual oversight is challenging.

Smarter Observability and Debugging

Observability for Go applications is likely to become more proactive with AI-enhanced monitoring systems. Future trends include:

- AI-driven anomaly detection in logs, metrics, and traces.
- Predictive alerts that anticipate failures before they impact users.
- Automated root cause analysis and guided debugging suggestions.
- Context-aware performance tuning recommendations for high-load Go services.

These advancements will significantly reduce the Mean Time to Detect (MTTD) and Mean Time to Resolve (MTTR) issues in production environments, improving system reliability and developer productivity.

AI-Enhanced Collaboration and Knowledge Sharing

Another emerging trend is the use of AI to facilitate collaboration among Go developers:

- Intelligent documentation generators that summarize code and system designs.
- AI-driven code review assistants providing suggestions for style, security, and performance.
- Shared AI models for team-wide best practices and reusable code patterns.
- Language-agnostic AI tools that bridge Go with other systems in polyglot environments.

This trend will accelerate onboarding, knowledge transfer, and team productivity, especially for large-scale enterprise projects with complex architectures.

Ethical and Responsible AI in Development

As AI becomes more involved in generating and deploying the Go code, ethical considerations will play an increasing role. Future developments will emphasize:

- Ensuring that AI-generated code is secure, unbiased, and reliable.
- Transparent auditing of AI-driven decisions in deployment or refactoring.
- Balancing AI assistance with human oversight to prevent over-reliance.
- Promoting reproducibility and accountability in production systems.

By integrating human discernment with AI functionalities, development teams can retain oversight while utilizing AI for enhanced efficiency and innovation.

Conclusion

In this chapter, we explored the comprehensive process of building, deploying, and maintaining production-ready Go microservices. We began by understanding how to design microservices that are modular, scalable, and maintainable. Key principles such as service decomposition, API design, and inter-service communication were discussed, laying a strong foundation for building reliable cloud-native applications.

Next, we delved into containerization using Docker, learning how to package Go applications with all their dependencies to ensure consistent execution across environments. We examined Dockerfile best practices, multi-stage builds, and image optimization strategies that minimize deployment overhead while improving startup performance. This knowledge is crucial for creating reproducible builds and seamless deployment pipelines.

The chapter then covered CI/CD pipelines, highlighting the importance of automated build, test, and deployment workflows. We explored how Go projects can leverage CI/CD tools to validate code, run unit and integration tests, and safely deploy updates to production. Automation not only speeds up development cycles but also reduces human error and ensures high-quality releases.

Monitoring, logging, and error reporting were emphasized as essential components of production readiness. We discussed implementing structured logging, capturing metrics, and using error reporting tools to detect, diagnose, and resolve issues effectively. Combined with performance tuning and resource optimization, these practices ensure that Go microservices run efficiently under heavy load, making optimal use of system resources and maintaining low latency.

Finally, we explored AI-assisted deployment automation, where AI tools can generate deployment scripts, suggest resource configurations, and optimize CI/CD workflows for Go applications. The chapter concluded with a look at future trends in Go and AI-assisted development, highlighting how AI is increasingly shaping the software development lifecycle–from code generation and optimization to deployment and observability–while emphasizing ethical and responsible use.

Thus, by integrating the concepts from this chapter, developers are equipped to design, deploy, monitor, and optimize Go microservices effectively, leveraging both traditional best practices, and AI-assisted enhancements to achieve scalable, maintainable, and high-performance systems in production environments. The chapter has also demonstrated how AI-assisted tooling can streamline deployment workflows. The impact in reducing operational complexity, and improving system reliability, enables the readers to manage Go services confidently in real-world production environments.

Looking ahead, the convergence of Go's simplicity with AI-assisted software engineering is poised to further transform how systems are built and operated. Emerging trends such as autonomous CI/CD pipelines, AI-driven performance tuning, intelligent observability, and self-healing infrastructure will continue to reduce manual intervention while increasing system reliability. Hence, as Go evolves alongside cloud-native and AI-powered platforms, developers who combine strong architectural foundations with intelligent automation will be best positioned to build the next generation of scalable, maintainable, and resilient distributed systems.

Index

D

P

R

S